Dalits' Encounter With Christianity

A Case Study of Mahars in Maharashtra

Dalits' Encounter With Christianity

A Case Study of Mahars in Maharashtra

S.M. Michael SVD

Tercentenary Publication

ISHVANI KENDRA, PUNE

2010

Dalits' Encounter With Christianity: A Case Study of Mahars in Maharashtra – Jointly published by the Rev. Dr. Ashish Amos of the Indian Society for Promoting Christian Knowledge (ISPCK), Post Box 1585, 1654 Madarsa Road, Kashmere Gate, Delhi-110006 for Ishvani Kendra, Post Box 3003, Pune-411014.

© Ishvani Kendra, 2010

ISBN : 978-81-8465-074-7

Cover Credit : Ronald D'Silva SVD

Laser typeset by
ISPCK, Post Box 1585, 1654, Madarsa Road, Kashmere Gate, Delhi-110006.
Tel: 23866322/23
e-mail: *ashish@ispck.org.in* • *ella@ispck.org.in*
website: *www.ispck.org.in*

Contents

Acknowledgements

Religious conversion is a complex issue in India. It is linked with political and hegemonic powers. All the same, religious conversions have been taking place all throughout Indian history. To understand this complex issue we require more studies. Though Christianity can be traced since 52 A.D., it is struggling to get its place in India. There are several efforts and theoretical models to inculturate Christianity in the Indian soil. This also requires much reflection and study. Fr. L. Stanislaus SVD, the then Director of Ishvani Kendra had requested me to do a field study on the above areas of religious conversion and inculturation. Knowing the importance of this research, I accepted the invitation and this research was carried out between January 2006 to April 2008 in Mumbai. Two of my past students, namely Ms. Shusila Yadav and Ms. Anita Kamble, from the Department of Sociology, University of Mumbai assisted me in this project by fieldwork. I thank them for their research assistance. I also thank the librarian Ms. Christa Fernando of the Institute of Indian Culture for her library assistance in this research. I am also grateful to Dr. Joy Thomas SVD, the present Director of Ishvani Kendra for publishing this research work.

Fr. S. M. Michael SVD (Ph.D.)
Professor in Cultural Anthropology
Department of Sociology
University of Mumbai
December 2008

Foreword

Inculturation is an accepted policy of evangelization by the Church, especially since Vatican II. Cultural enfleshment of the Gospel is one of the thrusts of Vatican II documents like *Lumen Gentium* (23) and *Ad Gentes* (12, 22). The encyclical of Paul VI, *Evangelii Nuntiandi* (20, 63) and teaching of John Paul II of happy memory (AAS 74, 615-616) have all stressed the absolute necessity of evangelizing the whole people and cultures in their totality, fully respecting the cultural autonomy of different peoples (GS 22, 59). Especially in the theological and missiological field, the process of inculturation of the Indian Church and conversion are greatly debated. And these are all very important fields of concern. We require field data to understand these complex processes.

The growing identification of nationalism with Hinduism and Indian culture is another cause of great concern, especially now when this nationalism is turning itself into a political movement of great force and getting itself organized at grassroots level. In the resultant atmosphere Christianity in India is accused of and increasingly attacked as foreign and anti-national.

The present study, **"Dalits' Encounter with Christianity: A Case Study of Mahars in Maharashtra"** by Dr. S. M. Michael SVD, a renowned anthropologist from the University of Bombay, attempts to throw some light on the above concerns of the Church in India. Since India is a pluralistic country, we require field information from diverse angles.

This research concentrates on the religious conversion and inculturation from a Dalit perspective. Since Dalits, tribals and other backward castes form the major portion of the Indian Christian population, such a research is very vital for the Indian

Church. It concentrates on the Dalit encounter with Christianity in order to understand the Dalit conversion process, a comparative study of Buddhists and Christian Mahars in Maharashtra.

I am happy to place on record some of the important objectives this research has undertaken like identifying the most important religious ideas, myths, symbols, ritual practices and socio-cultural traits characteristic of the Mahars. This research looks into the levels of alienation of the Christian Mahars from the triple roots of their historical identity, namely, cultural, social and religious.

Valuable insights have been gathered by direct observation of the cultural, social, and religious life of Mahars through lived-in experience for a sufficient length of time, as well as through interviews and questionnaires. All important existing documents and literature on the Mahars were studied, as the Bibliography suggests, which were used as the theoretical basis of the project. This study provides useful insights into the complex process of religious conversion and inculturation in India. It also throws light on the areas where training for inculturation of the Church personnel should be imparted.

Ishvani Kendra is grateful to Missio, Aachen, Germany for consenting to support this project by providing the financial aid required for the completion of the project. This indeed is a valuable contribution to evangelizing efforts in India, and has certainly emerged as a model study of considerable missiological significance. Similar research works among the various castes, tribes and other ethnic communities are urgent to understand the complex process of religious conversion and the method of inculturation in India. It is hoped that this study sets a trend towards this field oriented research in the process of evangelization in the country and beyond.

Dr. Joy Thomas SVD,
Director, Ishvani Kendra

1
Introduction

For the last several decades the Indian Church is actively involved in the process of Inculturation of its Church. Immediately after Vatican II, there were several vigorous attempts in the form of research seminars, publications, and practical workshops towards inculturation of the Church in India. But this enthusiasm seems to be weakening day by day.

Since this is an important area of the life of the Church in India, we need more scientific research in this field to understand the present predicaments and challenges in the field of inculturation in the Indian Church.

Importance of Scientific Research on Inculturation

When we pay attention to the area of Inculturation in India, we find several reasons for the lack of interest in the field of Inculturation. The Indian Church is made up of a large number of tribals, dalits and people from non-Brahmanic castes.[1] But the earlier attempts of inculturation have been mainly from the upper caste (Sanskritic) perspective. This approach to inculturation was a result of the understanding of India mainly from the Indological perspective. This is a direct follow up from the colonial

---

[1] According to 2001 Census there are 24 million Christians in India, a small minority community comprising only 2.3% of the total population. John Webster says that between 10 and 15% of all Dalits in India are Christians. Between two thirds and three quarters of all Christians in India are Dalits, i.e. 60% of all Christians as Dalits (see Gail Omvedt, "The Doubly Marginalized", *Seminar.* No. 602 – October 2009:71).

understanding of India from the Indological and the Oriental perspectives. Today, anthropological field researches have shown that the field reality of India is very different from the text oriented Indological and Orientalist approaches.

Moreover, there is a power shift in the self understanding of the cultural reality of India. For the last three thousand years, the Brahmins and other upper castes have been defining the identity of the culture of India. With the coming of democracy and each individual having a vote to elect their representatives, the power is slowly shifting to middle, lower, dalit castes and tribals. All this affect the very self-understanding of the culture and identity of India.

Hence, any attempt towards inculturation in India must take into account the field reality of India and the changing self perceptions of the different segments of the Indian population. This requires a scientific research.

Research Proposal on Inculturation: A Case of Mahars
Having this in mind, we undertook a research project on Inculturation in India in order to gather scientific data to help the Indian Church.

Since the non-Brahmanic castes, Dalits and Tribals from over 80 percent of the Indian Christians,[2] we need to understand inculturation from their perspectives. For this reason, we wanted to investigate the cultural responses of Mahar community in Maharashtra to the identity of Indianness in contemporary India. Mahar is a very influential Dalit community in Maharashtra. Dr.

---

[2] John Webster says that between 10 and 15% of all Dalits in India are Christians. Between two thirds and three quarters of all Christians in India are Dalits, i.e. 60% of all Christians as Dalits (see Gail Omvedt, "The Doubly Marginalized", *Seminar.* No. 602 – October 2009:71). According to Hrangkhuma and Ponraj about 25 per cent of the total Christian population in India is Tribal Christians (see Hrangkhuma, F. "Christianity among the Tribes of India: An Overview", *Christ among the Tribals.* Eds. F. Hrangkhuma and Joy Thomas, FOIM X, Bangalore: SAIACS Press, 2007:15; Ponraj, S.D. *Tribal Challenge and the Church's Response*, Madhupur: Mission Educational Books, 1996:62, 159).

Ambedkar came from this community. He has revolutionized and conscientized the Dalits and other marginalized population of India to dream for a new India. His impact on the formation of the Indian Constitution is immense. Today, the Dalit community, and more specially the Mahars are politically very active. In order to understand the complexity of the process of Inculturation in India, it will be very interesting to study the Mahar's perception on Indian cultural identity.

Though originally, i.e. during the Pre-British India, all Mahars were under the broad category of Hindu. A large number of them have been converted to Christianity and Buddhism. Some have retained their traditional Hindu identity. Thus, there are three sub-groups of Mahars. One group is Buddhist, another is Christian and the third is Hindu. It will be useful to study how and where these three groups of the same community share a common culture, where they differ, how they respond to westernization and globalization. Their respective self perception and their cultural similarities and differences will help us to understand their cultural adaptation as Christians, Buddhists and Hindus. We may be able to study their self perception of cultural continuity or alienation from each other and their attempts to belong to the wider community of their neighbourhood.

This investigation will help us to understand the cultural processes active among these communities for self identity and acceptance in the large community of their neighbourhood. This information will be very useful for the study on Inculturation in the Indian Church.

In addition, the emerging culture in India is greatly influenced by globalization, mass media and internet, and they are providing opportunities as well as challenges to traditional Indian cultures and values. Growing secularization and materialism are silently undermining the values and principles of traditional Indian culture. As a result, there is Hindu revivalism as well as secularization of Indian cultures. As far as the upper caste oriented, the so-called "Sanskritization process" and Hindutva strategies are undermining cultural identities of many ethnic groups and tribal communities. As a result there is also an assertive Dalit and Tribal consciousness in today's India. The Inculturation process in India must take the above realities also into its consideration.

The wider cultural heritage in the country as a whole is also fast changing. Hence, there is a tension between tradition, modernity and globalization at the same time. The Church in India must develop a deeper understanding of the contemporary cultural forces at work in order to offer a service that is effective, relevant and meaningful.

This research hopes to deal with the various problems related to culture in India as well as its challenges to Inculturation today.

Methodology

The present study is based on in-depth case studies and observational field research conducted among the Mahars of Mumbai city. The research involved free flowing informal interview sessions with Mahars in concrete social settings such as Samaj Viharas, Christian (Both Catholic and Other denominations) Churches, Mahar Hindu temples. The questions and interviews concentrated on the following aspects of Mahars life:

a. What do Mahars mean by themselves being a Buddhist, Christian and Hindu;

b. How did they become aware of being a Buddhist, Christian and Hindu;

c. What is the nature of the emerging cultural identity among them as a result of their self identification as Buddhist, Christian and Hindu Mahars?

The present research is based on empirical study; it will focus on impact of conversion on Buddhist (Mahar), Christian Mahar and Hindu Mahar. It is a comparative study of all these three communities; comparison is made on Socio-economic, Political and Cultural aspects. We tried to find the similarities and differences in almost all aspect of their life. We tried to analyze how they resemble with each other in social, economic, political and cultural front.

The basis of our study is long in-dept interviews and observations. We prepared an interview schedule and asked questions, however as an interview schedule restricts the responses; we tried to have an informal talk with the respondents. We tried to observe their life-style, food-habits, dressing pattern. We tried to take their views on various issues like how they celebrate various festivals, and we got very interesting responses. We also tried to take their narratives and took down their quotations. We asked them how conversion has changed their life, what they feel about conversion. We took 50 interviews from each Mahar, Buddhist, and Christian Mahars. And we did a comparative study of all these three communities. We made comparisons between their social life, cultural life, political life, and economic life.

The main part of our study is actually in-depth observation of their life-style and behavior pattern. We tried to observe every aspect of their life

The area that we selected for this study is urban area. We have used both primary and secondary data for our study. We carried on our study in Mumbai, the capital of Maharashtra. It is a city of West Central India on coastal Mumbai Island and adjacent Salsette Island. It is India's main port and commercial center. Mumbai, the most populous city of India and the world, has an estimated population of about 13 million as per Census 2001. It is the industrial and business centre of India. Throughout the nineteenth and twentieth century the city was known as Bombay, but now officially spelled Mumbai, reflecting the way it is pronounced in the Marathi language, has often served as a bellwether for India as a whole. From a colonial seaport and enter port, Bombay transformed itself into a factory town, producing first cotton cloth and later more sophisticated goods such as pharmaceuticals. India's railroads and air transport system, daily newspaper and Dalit poetry had their beginnings in Bombay. (Session 60:Bombay/Mumbai: Issues of space, status and power.)

According to 1991 census total Indian population was 836 million, out of which 130 millions scheduled castes, 60 million Scheduled Ttribes and 424 millions Other Backward Castes. The Buddhists were 0.76 percent of total population; Scheduled Castes were 15 percent. Total population of Buddhists was 6.3 million. There are 25 states and Union territories where Buddhists are less than 1 percent and 16 districts have not a single Buddhist. Maharashtra has 6.39 percent Buddhists. Then only the North East (excluding Assam and Nagaland) has an average of about 5 percent of traditional Buddhist population, Himachal 1.24 percent-perhaps due to Dalai Lama, top most is Sikkim with 27.18 percent. There is no mention of Buddhist population in Laddhak. The state of Bihar, Rajasthan, Andhra, Tamil Nadu, Karnataka, Hariyana, Uttar Pradesh, Gujarat, Kerala, Orrisa, Punjab, Nagaland and Assam has negligible population of Buddhists.

Concentrating only on Mahars in Maharashtra, we find that Mahars are 6.45 percent of the State. There are 4.64 percent non-Mahar Scheduled Castes in Maharashtra. Among the total population of the State, 6.39 percent have registered as Buddhist in the total population of the State. **(Dr. K. Jamanadas - Some self-introspection on future of Buddhism)**

Importance and Significance of Such a Study

Such research is very important because the worlds of Dalit Christians suffered from a double marginality. On the one hand, the traditional focus on caste Hinduism within the Brahmanical or Sanskritic framework tends to marginalize Dalits. Dalit religion is constituted negatively; it is characterized by what it *lacks* in terms of the dominant framework. On the other hand, Dalit Christians are also marginalized both in actuality as well as in the scholarship, which has until recently focused much more on the sphere of caste Christianity.

This research centres the worlds of Dalit Christians in comparison with other religious Dalits. Working its way from the periphery to the nucleus, the volume queries some of the received wisdoms regarding faith and its practice by those deemed to be on the edges of the social world. It begins from the idea that Christianity as practiced on Dalit terrain looks significantly different from what one might perceive among the higher echelons of the social order. At the periphery of the faith, as it were, Christian concepts and beliefs are incorporated but reinterpreted in radical ways and even liberating ways. For Dalits, religious conversion especially in the 19th century was often perceived as one of the ways of escaping from caste oppression. However, it is a moot point as to whether such expectations were fulfilled. As said above, around 65 to 70 percent of Indian Christians are of Dalit roots and around 15 to 20 percent are tribals. Despite such large numbers, however, the number of works bringing out the distinctiveness of Dalit and tribal Christianity are few.

In recent literature, some authors have begun to highlight the use of the drum and accompanying songs as modes of expression of Dalit liberation and divinity. At one point of time, the breaking of the drum by the Dalit was considered a necessary preliminary to his entry into the Christian church. However, the drum remains at the heart of the Dalit religious world and the beating of the drum a symbol of resistance to the social and ritual boundaries of caste. The accompanying songs often bring out the caste exploitation experienced by the Dalits and their struggle for release from suffering. The songs are rendered to the beat of the same drums that were traditionally employed by the Dalits during religious rituals or to summon village meetings. An erstwhile instrument of forced service and pollution is now transformed into one of liberation.

Today, moreover, the worlds of Dalit and tribal Christians are challenged and interrogated by the simultaneous enactment of a variety of different processes. The Tribal and Dalit churches, which are basically communities of people, are crucially influenced by forces outside. There has been a change in the thinking in the Church. The post-Vatican II discourses in India on Indianization, Indigenization, adaptation, inculturation and tribalization are the result of the dialectics between continuity and change, tradition and modernity. Interestingly, the changes in the externals within the Church have taken place at a comparatively much faster pace than those in inner beliefs and structures, which have remained relatively rigid and orthodox. However, even within the framework of the Indian theology and liturgy, there has always been an assertion for subaltern theologies and liturgical expressions. Dalit and liberation theology encapsulate some of these efforts. In the process, some doctrinal issues and practices have been seriously questioned and contested. The church's centralized attempt to 'indigenize' itself in the aftermath of Vatican II has often backfired because Dalits and tribals chafe against forms and processes of indigenization that seem to draw more from Sanskritic or Brahmanical Hinduism than from their own culturally familiar worlds.

Many tribal and Dalit communities are reasserting their traditional cultural identities and there is ferment in these societies between different groups. For instance, the case of the Õrâons brings out the ways in which tribal society is driven by tensions between Christians, non-Christian Sarnas and those seeking to 'Hinduize' the tribes. Conversion to Christianity among the Õrâon led to the distinction between the Christian Õrâons and those adhering to the traditional religion, the Sarna Õrâons. For a long period, Sarnas looked on the converts with suspicion because of their betrayal of the parental community. Sarnas even demanded in the 1960s that Christians should not be considered Scheduled Tribes. Under missionary influence, the converts also had to cut themselves off from all aspects of the old religion and culture. Nowadays, there are further complications because of the presence of elements seeking to convert the tribes to Hinduism. Fundamentalist Hindu religious and political forces such as the Hindu Dharm Sansad, the Vanvasi Nawjagran Yuwa Sangh and the Rashtriya Swayamsevak Sangh are seeking, on the one hand, to hinduize the tribals and, on the other, to de-recognize the tribal identity of Christians and Sarnas who refuse the 'Hindu' label. Politicians, especially from the Bharatiya Janata Party, have on occasion justified violence against Christian tribes and the movements ('home-comings') being organized for conversion to

Hinduism. Such battles over conversion and attacks against Christians in different parts of the country have been critical concerns for Indian Christians in recent times.

The focus of the present work will be on the Dalit communities in relation to their traditions and new developments, including new experiments in ritual and theologies. While attention will be paid to historical trajectories of mission and conversion in the volume, the important shift in our perspective will be the attempt to turn the lens on the contemporary and always changing face of Dalit Christianity, the different inflections in practice and the shifts under the influence of political movements, identity assertion, cultural revivalism and attempts at the systematization of paths of indigenization.

This research has three parts. The first part deals with the question of "Who are Dalits? and "How they came to attain this position. It also concentrates on the "Dalits Encounter with Christianity". The second part of this research studies a Dalit community in Maharashtra, namely, the Hindu, Christian and Buddhist Mahars. The last section draws some conclusions with regard to Sociology of Conversion in India and some practical suggestions for the Incultration Process in the Indian Church.

Part 1 :

Dalits' Encounter with Christianity

2

Importance of Understanding Dalits in Contemporary India

Introduction

Increased intellectual activism has marked Dalit-Bahujan cultural life at both the national and the regional levels in recent years. An interesting feature of this development is that the growth is well outside the formal educational sites that are supposed to be the normal locations for such a flourish (Guru and Geetha, 1997). This new trend of Dalit intellectual activism need to be understood sociologically.

The Dalit intellectual, social and cultural activism in contemporary India, thus, represents a very interesting scenario in which an urgent need is felt to make sense of Dalit reality at an abstract theoretical level. These intellectual efforts also show that Dalit theory might acquire a critical mass in the future.

All the same, it is well known that there is an intellectual critique and challenge on the very term 'Dalit' especially from the post-modernist and post-strualist scholars. Some intellectuals and activists are of the view that the term 'Dalit' is hostile to the ex-untouchables of today and this term has no ontological abilities and hermeneutic capacities of its own to help the ex-untouchables in their total emancipation. Thus, on the one hand, the category Dalit faces violent rejection both by the Dalits and the non-Dalits.

There are two sets of arguments that have been put forward by the scholars while responding to this theoretical construct of the category Dalit. For example, Prof. Romila Thapar says that there is a notion of 'out of date history', and in this notion of history, certain categories lose their significance, e.g., the Arya-Anarya category. By the same logic, one can also argue that the categories like Shudra, adi-dhmma, etc., have also become part of the 'out of date history'. She, however, maintains that Dalit is a specific category and there is a political necessity to hold on to it. Satyanarayana, another scholar, says that it is important to look at the category Dalit as a construction achieved through recruiting and restoring the hidden culture and textual history of Dalits. Without understanding this cultural and historical rootedness of the category Dalit, it is not possible to understand the complex and pluralistic culture of India (Guru and Geeta, 1997).

Thus, it is true, that the subject of "Dalit" is under continuous scrutiny and critical examination. However, many scholars and activists see that the category Dalit has a promising start and also the better future and thus are not ready to give up the claims to this category that easily (see Guru and Geeta, 1997:18-19). However, we need to be open to theoretical argument in favour of the redefinition of Dalit and the possibility of more rigorous argument. For this there is an urgent need for knowledge on Dalit communities.

Untouchables by Various Names

To be an Untouchable in the Indian caste system is to be very low in and partially excluded from, an elaborately hierarchical social order. Untouchables are persons of a discrete set of low castes, excluded on account of their extreme collective impurity from particular relations with higher beings (both human and divine). They make up about 16 percent of the Indian population and number about 138 million. They have been called by various names, such as 'Untouchables', 'Harijans' (a glorified term, coined by Narasimha Mehta and adopted and popularized by Mahatma Gandhi), 'Exterior Castes' (used by J. H. Hutton), 'Depressed Classes' (by British officials), 'Outcastes,' 'Pariahs' (commonly, but undoubtedly derived from the Tamil word para or parai, the drum, see Deliege, 1997). In more ancient times the terms

'Mlechha,' 'Chandala' (used by Manu), also Panchama (the fifth class), Avarna (i.e. outside the four varnas), Nishada, Paulkasa, Antyaja, Atishudra etc., were used.

The term 'Scheduled Castes' appeared for the first time in April 1935, when the British Government issued the Government of India (Scheduled Caste) Order 1936, specifying certain castes, races and tribes as Scheduled Castes. Prior to that these population groups were generally known as 'Depressed Classes.' The term 'Dalit', first used in journalistic writings as far back as 1931 to connote the untouchables, did not gain currency until the early 70s with the Dalit Panther Movement in Maharashtra. As now used, it implies a condition of being underprivileged and deprived of basic rights and refers to people who are suppressed on account of their lowly birth.

The Origins of Caste and Untouchability
The origins of caste and of untouchability lie deep in India's ancient past and the evidence of those origins provided by the archaeological and literary sources now available is, at best, circumstantial. Consequently, scholars have been forced to engage in considerable speculation in their efforts to reconstruct the past history of untouchability. What we now have are not hard and clear facts but a variety of competing theories, all of which have proved difficult to substantiate in a convincing manner.

The dominant view traces the origins of caste and Untouchability to the Aryans themselves and to their ways of relating to the peoples of India with whom they came into contact. The Aryans, a set of related and highly self-conscious tribes sharing a common language and religion, began their invasions of India from the northwest around 1500 B.C. For centuries they remained in seemingly constant conflict with the indigenous peoples, whom the miscegenation, between a member of a high caste and that of a low caste or an outcaste. The children of such an unequal pair become untouchables, and the greater the social gap between the two parents, the lower the status of their children. The consequences are also more severe if the mother is of the superior caste. Thus the offspring of a Brahmin father and a Shudra mother is called Nishada; the child becomes a fisherman. The offspring of a Shudra father and a Brahmin mother is called Chandala; he is the most degraded of all mortals. To Manu a degraded occupation is not the cause of untouchability, rather untouchability condemns a person to a low and impure occupation. In later times racial mixture was added as a factor of impurity. In the period after Manu increasing numbers of the members of the lower castes belonged to different races and cultures. The practice of untouchability was intensified and applied to more groups in the years following 200 A.D., while Candala became a label not simply for a tribe but for all whom the Aryans considered to be at the very bottom of society.

What has been described thus far relates to North India. The literature from South India suggests that the people whom the Aryans conquered were Dravidians, who subsequently moved south subjugating the indigenous people. It was only later, when Aryan influences spread to the South that the *Varna* system and untouchability came into being there.

H. Hutton, eminent anthropologist and author of the best book on caste, *Caste in India* (1963), locates the origins of caste in the taboos and divisions of labour in the pre-Aryan tribes of India as well as in their efforts at self-preservation in the face of invasion. In his opinion untouchability is the consequence of ritual impurity. He says: "The origin of the position of the exterior castes is partly racial, partly religious, and partly a matter of social custom. There can be little doubt but the idea of untouchability originates in taboo" (Hutton, 1963:207).

Von Fuerer-Haimendorf, another eminent anthropologist believes that untouchability is an urban development and is the result of an unclean and ritually impure occupation (see the Foreword in *Children of Hari*, Fuchs 1950). Once untouchability had developed in urban or semi-urban settlements, its gradual spread to the villages was inevitable for it is everywhere the towns which set the standard.

Dr. Ambedkar's thesis on the origin of untouchability, as expounded in his book, *The Untouchables* (1948) is an altogether novel one. The distinction between the Hindus and the untouchables in its original form, before the advent of untouchability, was the distinction between Tribesmen and Broken Men from alien tribes. It is the Broken Men who subsequently came to be treated as untouchable. There are two roots from which untouchability has sprung: a) Contempt and hatred for the Broken Men, as for Buddhism by the Brahmins. b) Continuation of beef-eating by the Broken Men after it had been given up by the others.

Dr. Ambedkar tries to explain what he means by Broken Men. He proposes an ingenious hypothesis: When primitive society began to settle down and to cultivate, certain tribes remained nomadic and warlike. They began to attack the settled tribes as the latter were wealthier. In addition, they had grain which the nomads wanted but did not possess. The settled men needed defenders as they had lost their warlike spirit. They employed 'broken men' - defeated nomads, and stray individuals who needed protection and shelter. These became mercenaries of the settlers, but were not allowed to stay within the settlement. They were kept at a distance, as they belonged to a different tribe. They were treated with disrespect, as 'broken men' and as mercenaries. Dr. Ambedkar provided supporting evidence for such a process from Ireland and Wales. The difference was that in those countries the outsiders were after nine generations absorbed into the settled community. This did not happen in India, for the Hindus had contempt for the broken men who were Buddhists and beef-eaters.

At first sight this theory may seem rather far-fetched. However, agreeing with the views of Dr. Ambedkar, Dr. Stephen Fuchs says: "It is a well-known fact that the nomadic animal breeders of Inner Asia, for example, enjoyed nothing more than raiding and fighting. When a tribe was defeated and routed, the survivors often used to be sold into slavery by their conquerors. Those who managed to escape had to seek the protection of another tribe. Being powerless they had often to content themselves with menial jobs, tending horses and cattle, making and repairing saddles and other leather-work, such as tongs and bridles, making and cleaning weapons, etc. As these animal breeding nomads generally despised menial and manual work, this contempt was also extended to those who had to perform it" (Fuchs, 1981:13). There was thus a deep social cleavage between the masters and their servant class. Dr. Ambedkar believes that the root cause of untouchability lies in a pronounced cultural or racial difference of contempt and hatred coupled with a close economic dependence of the inferior society on the superior one.

Dr. Stephen Fuchs proposes a new theory regarding the Origin of Untouchability (1981:15ff.). According to him the above proposed theories as well as various others presented by a number of indologists seem to suffer from one great defect: they do not penetrate deeply enough into the past of the dominant Indian peoples. They restrict themselves unduly to happenings in India. It is true that the caste system and untouchability developed after the arrival of the Aryans and, most probably, of the Dravidians in India, that caste system, as it has grown in India, is unique and not found elsewhere in the world, and that nowhere in the world are untouchables found in such vast numbers - 138 millions! Yet, the roots must be sought in an age when both population groups lived on the steppes of Inner Asia. Here the animal breeding societies developed a pronounced hierarchical structure. These animal breeders gave up cultivation completely and regarded manual work of any kind as unworthy of a shepherd and a warrior. They also developed a social structure of their own: an extended joint family system with a patriarch at its head in whom all power was vested.

According to Dr. Stephen Fuchs, there is sufficient evidence to prove that the Aryans as well as the Dravidians on their arrival in India still belonged to such an animal breeding culture. They must have brought along also their aversion to manual work and to foreign people. The Aryans, on their slow advance through northern India, and the Dravidians wandering down along the west coast into South India, encountered on their way a multitude of earlier settlers who either submitted passively to their conquest or were defeated in fierce battles. As conquerors they managed to impose many of their cultural values and prejudices on the subject peoples of India. Adding to their inherited attitude to manual work and racial purity a new dimension, namely that of ritual purity, they gradually developed this unique Hindu caste system which is intimately connected ideologically with the concept of untouchability.

None of the above explanations for the origin of untouchability are conclusively proved facts. As so often happens with human institutions, no single cause can explain untouchability. It is deeply rooted in Indian history, in the agrarian social order that dominated the Indian economy until the advent of the British, and which remains today India's largest economic sector. Though the relation of India's rural Untouchables to this social order has shifted in subtle ways in the past two centuries, there remain pervasive continuities, especially of meaning and of cultural construction, with this deeply rooted past.

Early Images of Indian Untouchability during Colonial Rule

a. Abbe Dubois

Perhaps the earliest and simplest Western image of Untouchability is embodied in the term "outcaste." In this view, to be an Untouchable is to be beyond the reach of Hindu culture and society, to be almost cultureless. The stress in the outcaste image is on the Brahmins possessing culture and the Untouchables lacking it. Thus the Abbe Dubois, a remarkable French missionary with first-hand knowledge of village India between 1792 and 1823, contrasts the Untouchable "Pariahs" with those higher-caste Hindus on whom the system has had its beneficent moral effect: "We can picture what would become of the Hindus if they were not kept within the bounds of duty by the rules and penalties of caste, by looking at the position of the Pariahs, or outcastes of India, who, checked by no moral restraints, abandon themselves to their natural propensities" (1959:29). The word "pariah" which derives from the Tamil name of an Untouchable caste has accordingly moved into the English language as a synonym for the socially ostracised and the morally depraved (see Deliege, 1997).

The Untouchables described by Dubois accept their status and believe in the legitimacy of the system so that there is no thought of equality in their mind: "The idea that he (untouchable) was born to be in subjection to the other castes is so ingrained in his mind that it never occurs to the Pariah to think that his fate is anything but irrevocable. Nothing will ever persuade him that men are all made of the same clay" (Dubois, 1959:50, quoted in Moffatt, 1979:7).

The early outcaste image, as it is articulated by Dubois, implies a major disjunction between the higher "caste Hindus" and the lowermost Untouchables, or outcastes. The very terms express the disjunction. The main body of the Hindu population "has caste," and is regulated by its social and cultural conventions, while the Untouchables are outside the system.

b. Dr. Frances Buchanan

Another Western observer of the same period, who surveyed newly acquired territories in Mysore for the British in 1799, describes the Untouchable Madiga as follows: "(The Madiga) are divided into small tribes of ten or twelve houses, and intermarry with the daughters of these houses only, in order to be certain of the purity of their race; of which they seem to be as fond, as those castes that are esteemed infinitely superior in rank" (Buchanan 1807:640 quoted in Moffatt, 1979:8).

These two views of Untouchables and caste, the outcaste image and the simple consensus image, dominated Western thinking through the British period. This approach considered that, "To be an Untouchable is not to be excluded from the culture of caste, but it is to possess this culture in a thinner and less convincing form" (Moffat, 1979:8).

Contemporary Anthropological and Sociological Perspectives

In recent years social anthropologists and ethnographers of South Asia have been preoccupied with the subject of hierarchy in the

Hindu social system. Definitions of the caste system have been advanced in which the authors have sought to isolate the code which differentiates Hindus into exclusive social groups and ranks them in a hierarchical relationship with one another. Two authors in particular, F.G. Bailey and Louis Dumont, have writ-ten on this subject and other social anthropologists have aligned themselves with the theories of either (Dumont 1957, 1960, 1966, 1970, Dumont and Pocock, 1957; Bailey, 1959, 1963).

a.   *System of Ranking Related to Productive Resources*

For Bailey, 'caste is a system of ranks which is related to differential control over the productive resources' (1957:266). Each person in the caste system performs economic, political, and ritual roles and except for certain anomalies, there is a `high degree of coincidence between politico-economic rank and the ritual ranking of caste (Bailey, 1957:266). The anomalies are mainly apparent at the uppermost and lowermost ranks of the ritual system. A Brahman of scant economic means does not fall to a low ritual rank nor can a wealthy Untouchable attain high ritual rank. For caste groups between these two extremes 'their ritual rank tends to follow their economic rank in the village community' (Bailey, 1957:266-7).

b.   *Ritual Purity as the Basis of Hierarchy*

Dumont, however, has criticised Bailey's interpretation of the caste system. For Dumont ritual purity, not differential control over productive resources is the code of the caste hierarchy. "Perhaps as early as the eighth century before Christ tradition has distinguished absolutely between hierarchical status and power" (1966:56). According to Dumont, the hierarchical caste system is founded on two basic ideological principles: first, the opposition between ritual purity and pollution, which defines the hierarchical relationship between the pure Brahmans and the polluted Untouchables, and secondly the absolute separation of religious status, personified by the Brahmans, from politico-economic power, which is ideally concentrated in the hands of Kshatriya kings (see Burghart, 1996:35-42).

In spite of their differences of opinion Bailey and Dumont share an underlying assumption in their analyses of Hindu social relations. They assume the caste hierarchy was the exclusive and exhaustive order of social relations in the traditional Hindu social system. Their differences of opinion relate mainly to the nature of the code of that hierarchy. Bailey's theory of closed social stratification and Dumont's theory of hierarchy are seen to be applicable to the traditional Hindu social system (see Bailey, 1963).

Dumont's Structuralist Approach

Dumont (1966) postulated that caste is the most fundamental and most specifically Hindu institution of Hindu society. He calls his approach 'structuralist,' for the oppositional structure of pure/impure governs the operation of the caste system. These principles are found universally within India, but they are also unique to India. According to Dumont, caste represents the institutionalization of hierarchical values. In his holistic conception of caste, hierarchy is expressed in an Indian cultural code of relative purity and impurity, in a continuously graded status order whose extremes are the Brahmin at the top - the most pure of men - and the Untouchables at the bottom - the least pure of men. Brahmin and Untouchables are conceptually opposed in a number of ways that contribute to their archetypal purity and impurity, according to Dumont. The Brahmin lives in the centre of the village, and is a "god on earth," while the Untouchable lives outside the village and is apparently excluded from religious life. The murder of a Brahmin is as heinous a crime as the murder of a cow, while the Untouchable is the scavenger and the eater of dead cows. The Brahmin purifies himself in order to approach the gods, and thus mediates between man and god. The Untouchable makes personal purity possible by removing the strongest sources of organic impurity, and mediates between man and the maleficent "demons."

For Dumont, however, this opposition of Brahmin and Untouchable is also a complementarily - the completion of a "whole" by two equally necessary but unequally ranked parts. "The impurity of the Untouchable is conceptually inseparable from the purity of the Brahmin." Since "the execution of impure tasks by some is necessary to the maintenance of purity for others...society is a totality made up of two un-equal but complementary parts" (Dumont 1970:92, 93).

The universe of caste is structured by dharma in the sense of the ever-present order of the universe. Here dharma is an absolute concept; all sentient beings including gods are subject to its laws. In the classic Brahmanical formulation the social universe is taken to be a manifestation in time and space of the ever-present Brahma. From the cosmic body of Brahma at the dawn of time issued forth the four main castes (strictly speaking, *Varna*), each endowed with a particular quality necessary to enact the sacrifices necessary to sustain the universe. The first-born were the Brahmans who emerged from the mouth of Brahma. They were possessed of the power of speech and were entitled to effectuate a sacrifice by means of their knowledge of ritual formulae. Next born were the warriors who emerged from the arms of Brahma. They were endowed with the martial qualities necessary to protect the universal order. It was their task to offer the oblation at the sacrifice. Third-born were the *Vaishya*, or herders and tillers (in some regions of India said to be mer-chants) who emerged from the thighs of Brahma. They produced the material wealth of the universe and charged with providing the oblation for the sacrifice. Last born were the servants who sprang from the feet of Brahma. It was their duty to serve the other three castes outside the sacrifical arena.

The four castes were ranked, both in their order of birth and the excellence of their sacrificial function. The Brahmans were the first born and they performed the most excellent function at the sacrifice. Virtue in this system, however, is not defined in terms of emulating the functions of the higher castes; rather it lies in the performance of one's own caste's duties; it is more virtuous for the Cobbler to tan his polluting hides and to beat the drum at the village temple than to imitate the superior ways of the Brahman scholar. In this way - by each caste observing its particular duties - the universe survives as a whole.

Separation pervades the entire caste system. Servants cannot enter the sacrifical arena, for they lack the sacred thread of the upper three castes. The most notorious separation is that of untouchability. The members of the four main castes, which constitute the mouth, arms, thighs and feet of Brahma, do not accept water which has been handled by those castes which are outside Brahma's auspicious body.

Each person is said to have a certain amount of spiritual energy, or *samskara*, which he has accumulated by performing acts of self-sacrifice in previous lives. Unequal birth and unequal achievement in any particular lifetime are attributed to an unequal accumulation of spiritual energy. This energy also deter-mines one's entitlement to follow a particular path of personal salvation. Untouchable castes are not admitted because the bodies and minds of such persons are considered to be impure, dull or otherwise unfit for initiation. Had such persons more spiritual energy, they would have been born into a higher station in life and would have been fit receptacles of religious knowledge (see Fuller and Spencer, 1996:35-42).

Critics of Dumont's Approach

Dumont's understanding of Indian society seems to be situated at the confluence of sociology and indology. His position has been severely criticised by several anthropologists and sociologists like Gerald Berreman (1971), Kathleen Gough (1973) and Joan Mencher (1974). It is a common criticism of Dumont that his use of Brahmanical sources in understanding Hindu society commits him to a Brahmanical view of society and that Untouchables may conceive of society differently (Freeman, 1979; see also Barnett, 1976; Burghart, 1983; Lynch, 1977). In the last two decades or so, many anthropological writings have been devoted to the cultural traditions of low caste groups; and they have emphasized the differences between the socio-religious ideology of upper castes and lower castes, especially Untouchables, who have traditionally been kept outside the *Varna* hierarchy (see Juergensmeyer, 1982; Burghart, 1983:281; Khare, 1984; Appadurai, 1986; Deliege, 1992). Had Dumont seen the Hindu society from 'below' – 'the bottom up' view - his picture would have been different.

Untouchables having a Distinctive Culture of their Own

In her approach, Kathleen Gough points out that cultural differences between the high and low castes are due to political and economic variables generated by the upper castes. For example: Gough has analysed the Untouchable Pallans of South India. Unlike most modern ethnographers of Indian Untouchables, she is emphatically on the side of the low castes and against what she sees as the hierarchical, etiquette-bound high castes. If some of the early observers on caste and Untouchability like Dubois viewed the "nature" of the Untouchables as uncivilized and degraded, Gough reverses the evaluation, and sets up tacit oppositions between the inhibiting "culture" of the Brahmins and the freer "nature" of the Untouchables. She discerns in the Pallans (Untouchables) a looser, more psychologically healthy, approach to life. In their relation to sexuality and aggression, for example, the Pallans are said to be less restricted than the Brahmins: "The expression of aggression toward elders and peers (among the Pallans) is not strictly inhibited (as it is among the Brahmins) ...Similarly, the lower castes do not favour ascetic control of sexuality in marital relationships. ...The ascetic control of sexuality for its own sake does not increase a man's spiritual strength" (Gough 1956:847; see also Moffatt, 1979:9-10).

The cultural dimension of Gough's approach is "certain moral values deriving from the Sanskrit religious tradition, of which (the Brahmins) are the main carriers" (1956:826). Since the Pallans are among the lowest castes, farthest spatially and socially from the Brahmins, they are of all castes in the village the most free of the restraints of this Sanskritic culture.

Most of Gough's cultural typifications of the low castes are framed in opposition to negatively loaded Brahmanic traits: "The low castes place much less emphasis than do Brahmins on other-worldliness and on the fate of the soul after death. Engaged in the practical business of earning a living through manual labour, the low castes care more for health and prosperity in this life" (Gough, 1956:846). Gough's positive restatement of the outcaste image is stated psychologically, but it is set within a broader materialist analysis. The Untouchables' alternatives vary according to the image. For Dubois, Untouchables are in a state of unbridled license, while for Gough, they are in a state of psychologically healthy removal from an obsessive high-caste culture (Moffatt, 1979:13).

According to Kathleen Gough the Untouchable Pallans have a distinctive social and cultural subsystem. Gough sums up these contrasts in a personal statement about the ethos of the Pallan life: "Pallans show an almost fanatical passion for equality within their caste group. In fact, I found the equal and comradely style of life in the Palla street a great relief from the obsessive ritualism, hierarchy, and envy in the Brahmin street... (The Pallans) react to their poverty (of which they are well aware) with a combination of anger, resignation, wryness and humor" (Gough, 1973:232, 233-34). Though Gough does not make the point explicitly, the distinctive features that she discerns in the Pallans - solidarity, egalitarianism, and the weakness of traditional kinship authority might be expected to preadapt them to radical anticaste political action (Moffatt, 1979:18).

Similar views of Untouchables having their own distinctive culture are found in the works of Joan Mencher (1974), Bernard Cohn (1955), Robert Miller (1966) and Gerald Berreman (1971). According to their approach, Untouchables are seen to have demystified caste and its accompanying ideology, seeing the caste system in an objective and culture-free way for what it really is - a system of oppression. Thus Joan Mencher feels that Paraiyans in South India have a more "explicitly materialistic" view of the system and their place in it than do those at the top, and that "those at the bottom of the hierarchy have less need to rationalize its inequities" (Mencher, 1974:476).

Bernard Cohn also regards the Untouchables as the bearers of an alternate social and cultural system, different from the upper caste culture, and adapted to the needs and experiences of those at the very bottom of the system. In his analysis of the Untouchable Chamars of north India, Cohn sees the Chamars as differing from the high castes for the same reason that Gough's Pallans differ from the Brahmins, i.e. the social and spatial separation between Untouchables and higher castes. Because Untouchables cannot hear the Vedas, or be served by Brahmins, or enter high-caste temples, they suffer from a kind of communication block. The result of this block, however, is not a form of culturelessness, but the retention of a historically prior pre-Aryan little tradition. Unlike the great tradition of the higher castes and of the Brahmins in particular, the little tradition of the Chamars contains a "pre-Aryan and non-Brahmanic" religion, which emphasises the propitiation of goddesses of disease, and the use of mediums and exorcists (Cohn 1955:58). Cohn has to qualify these disjunctive contrasts considerably, however: "It is almost impossible to sort out those traits which are Sanskritic and those which are non-Sanskritic ...and ...what is idiosyncratic to the Chamars as a group and what is a common body of ritual and belief held by other low castes and high castes as well" (Cohn, 1954:175). Given this qualification, then, Cohn's analysis amounts to a set of tentatively specified contrasts within an unanalyzed framework of cultural continuities.

Robert Miller has studied the Untouchable Mahars of Central India. Unlike Cohn's Chamars, who are attempting to diminish the despised cultural disjunction between themselves and the higher castes, to be in a sense revaluing their little tradition, the Mahars, Miller writes, "have been building a tradition which can hardly be called "a distinctive variant of the Great Tradition cognate to those of the four major *varnas* of Hindu society" (quoting Singer, 1958:194). In fact, the Mahars are building on a counter-great tradition which has always existed in India, as an antithesis to the Brahmanic great tradition. In this counter tradition, "equality is opposed to inequality; individual ability is opposed to merger of the individual in the group; emotionalism is opposed to ritualism; escape from the system is opposed to movement within the system." Miller's discussion amounts to an assertion that *bhakti* devotionalism, Mahar militance, and the eventual emergence of neo-Buddhism from the Mahar caste, attest the strength of these alternate values (see Miller, 1966:26-28).

Recently, Kancha Ilaiah (1996a, 1996b) has asserted the distinctive culture of the Dalitbhaujan (lower Sudras and Ati-Sudras) in Indian society. He distinguishes and contrasts the cultural differences between the upper caste Brahmin, Baniya or Kshatriya with that of the Dalitbahujans. According to him, "Mainstream historiography has done nothing to incorporate the Dalitbahujan perspective in the writing of Indian history ...To make matters worse, recent Hindu politics - and its historiography - has sought to wipe out the possibility of Dalitbahujan perspective and a Dalitbahujan history by simply declaring that the Dalitbahujan are (fallen) Hindus. This essay seeks to challenge that Brahminical historiography by pointing to the contrariness - and differentness - of Dalitbahujan perspective and history" (1996b:165).

Gerald Berreman's "Caste School of Race"

Gerald Berreman has studied the rural Untouchables of a Himalayan village in north India. In a short critique of Louis Dumont's structural theory of caste, Berreman claims that when he presented his version of the Dumontian model to rural Untouchables, "they laughed, and one of them said, 'you have been talking with Brahmins'" (1971:16-23). Like Mencher, Berreman maintains that Untouchables in some way reject a high-caste model of the system. The Untouchables act in accordance with the system of caste because they are forced to so act, but they cannot be forced to believe.

Berreman's interpretation of Indian Untouchability is part of an explicit defense of the "caste school of race" in American Sociology founded by the work of W. Lloyd Warner (1936), John Dollard (1937), Gunnar Myrdal (1944, 1967), and others (see Beteille, 1992:15-56). In its original form, this school constructed a comparative analogy between the racial system of the American south in the 1930s and 1940s and the Indian caste system. In both systems, there are said to be two or more rigidly ranked groups between which individual mobility is impossible. Membership in each group is permanent and defined at birth (or "birth ascribed");

each group is endogamous; and each system is maintained by prohibitions on intergroup contacts, especially on sexual ones between males of the low groups and females of the high groups. Ultimately, each system is maintained by the power of the high groups - by coercion rather than consensus.

Berreman's position on Untouchables is a return to the functionalist comparison of the "caste school of race", adding insights from the more detailed anthropological fieldwork on caste carried out in the 1950s in India. Berreman compares the relationship between "touchable" and "untouchable" castes in India with the relationship between Afro-Americans and white Americans in the South of the United States.

Not all anthropologists or social scientists agree with Berreman's conclusion that "race relations" in the Southern United States constitute a caste system, the work however is important because it illustrates the value and the necessity of cross-cultural comparisons of "invidious distinctions" (Cole, 1988:467). Yet, Berreman points out that the power of high caste Indians does have a role in maintaining the caste system, and that caste is rife with manipulation and conflict. Thus it does not differ from race in terms of these sociological abstractions. He brings race and caste together as sociological equivalents (see Berreman 1960, 1972, 1988). Berreman says, "In the caste system, 'because intensive and status equal interaction is limited to the caste, a common and distinctive culture is assured. This is a function of the quality and density of communication within the group, for culture is learned, shared and transmitted'" (quoting Berreman, 1967:51; Berreman, 1972:400). From this he concludes that each social unit (each caste) is imagined as a tightly bound cultural unit (a "distinctive culture") and proceed to the following generalization: "Caste, race and ethnic stratification, like all plural systems therefore, are systems of social separation and cultural heterogeneity, maintained by common or overriding economic and political institutions rather than by agreement or consensus regarding the stratification system and its rationale" (Berreman, 1972:400).

Berreman's main point is that power alone, and consensus about power, determines caste and all other systems of structural social inequality. This position is admittedly extreme, but some of its comparative assumptions are shared by other anthropologists who have analysed Indian Untouchables disjunctively. Gough (1973), Mencher (1974), and Miller (1966), in particular, make very clear their personal distaste for caste, in all its social inequities, and its oppression.

In contrast to the above approach, Dumont does not see caste as an inexplicably "unequal" system that requires an explanation because of the way in which it violates the more fundamentally egalitarian "nature" of man. Rather, Dumont reverses the comparative question, and suggests that it is Western egalitarian ideology that is the socio-scientific puzzle, and that rank or hierarchy is more transhumanly comprehensible: "man does not only think, acts ...To adopt a value is to introduce hierarchy, and a certain consensus of values, a certain hierarchy of ideas, things and people, is indispensable to social life. ...In relation to these more or less necessary requirements of social life, the idea of equality, even if it is thought superior, is artificial" (Dumont, 1970:54-55). Caste represents the institutionalization of hierarchical values, the most elaborate known working out of a set of values that the West has been systematically denying for the last three hundred years. To understand fully the egalitarian effort in the West, Dumont says, the West must confront its polar opposite in India, hierarchy.

In this comparative epistemology, Dumont differs radically from Berreman and from other conflict theorists and functionalists. For Dumont, to compare is not to dismiss ideological specificities as unimportant detail and to search for abstract, a historical essence common to caste, race, and ethnic stratification. To compare is to construct a structural analysis of each ideological and social formation, and then to confront these fully and specifically analysed formations with one another (see Barnett, Fruzzetti, and Ostor, 1976:627-28). Dumont's comparative analyses contain a number of simple logical oppositions, but they are nevertheless interesting. Caste, Dumont says, is a homogeneous moral system that values hierarchy and does not isolate and value the individual as the "measure of all things." Racism, on the other hand, is ideologically linked to egalitarianism, individualism, and to the Western denial of hierarchy. According to Dumont, in denying hierarchy in the social realm as a legitimate innate quality of the relations between humans, Western ideology must restitute it in a rigorously differentiated natural realm as racism, referred exclusively to natural difference (see Dumont, 1960; 1970:35-55). Thus for Dumont Indian Untouchables are not the abstract sociological equivalent of racially subordinate groups in Western society.

Untouchability is a fall from the Upper-Caste Status

Pauline Kolenda has studied the Untouchable Sweepers in North India. Kolenda begins her analysis by demonstrating that the basic themes in the Sweepers' religion are common not only to higher-caste religion but to themes found in the ancient Sanskritic texts. She then deals with a single disjunction - with the question of how the Sweepers deal with one unpleasant implication of the linked doctrine of karma, *dharma* and transmigration. According to these doctrines, which the Sweepers understand in abstract form, one's caste status in a given birth is the result of the total score of one's good or bad *karma* ("action" in accord with one's *dharma*, "duty," as defined in a given caste) in past lives (Kolenda, 1964).

If the Untouchable Sweepers were to apply the *karmic* explanation to their present low status, they would be admitting that they deserved such a status - that they had been unusually wicked in past rebirths. This admission, according to Kolenda, would cause them "religious anxiety." Hence, the Sweepers refuse to apply *karma* doctrine to their own low status. Instead, they refer their present status to collective myths which state that they were once of much higher caste, and fell due to a terrible accident motivated by the best of intentions. According to one myth, for example, the original Untouchable was a Brahmin who came upon a cow mired in the mud. Intending to help the cow (a meritorious intent); he pulled on its tail. But the cow died, and since he had been in contact with a dead cow - a polluting contact - his older brothers outcast him and he became the first Untouchable (Cohn, 1954:113). Not only do myths like this protect Untouchables from the "anxiety" of *karmic* explanation, according to Kolenda, but they provide them with a positive sense of having once been much higher (see Kolenda, 1964:74-76).

Untouchability to Dalit Movement

"Dalit" which as shown earlier means ground down, downtrodden, oppressed, is now being used by the low castes in a spirit of pride and militancy. The term began to be used by politically awakened ex-Untouchables in the early 1970's when the Dalit Panthers, a youthful group of activists and writers in Bombay, came on the scene to protest injustice. The Dalit Panther organization is now scattered and important only in a few places, but the pride and militancy that has accompanied the name has created a new category of culture in India (see Zelliot, 1996:1-4). The name has achieved widespread use in book titles and in newspaper reports on both violence against Dalits and accomplishments among them.

The name *dalit* is not merely a rejection of the very idea of pollution or impurity or "untouchability," it reveals a sense of a unified class, of a movement toward equality. It speaks of a new stage in the movement of India's untouchables which is now a century old. Dalit self-assertion manifests itself today in a debate on several contrapositions: Gandhi vs Ambedkar, Harijan vs Dalit, Varna vs Jati, Manuwad vs casteless society.

In view of the social location of the Dalits, it should occasion no surprise that they were the last community in colonial India to be influenced by those liberal notions which reached out to the country as an apart of the cultural hegemony of the West. Perhaps the first modern Dalit voice was that of Jotiba Phule, a powerful advocate of social and gender equality based in Maharashtra. Another Dalit deeply influenced by liberal values was the Ezhava leader of Kerala, Narayana Guru, who attacked the institution of caste in a regional society where the Adi Shankara had argued, long centuries ago, of the essential oneness of things in his metaphysical formulation of *advaita* (non-dualism) as the true basis of reality. There was a fair sprinkling of Dalit leaders elsewhere holding out identical messages. Their principal argument was loud and clear. Humankind was made up of a vast community of individuals all of whom, in principle, were entitled to the same social status and economic and cultural dignity.

Though the dalit voice expressed itself eloquently from the outset, it was left to B.R. Ambedkar, a second generation Dalit leader, to articulate the abject condition of his community in the idiom of modern politics. Ambedkar also spelt out why Hindu discourse offered no route to liberation for the oppressed classes located within the Hindu social matrix. The Dalit communities, Ambedkar argued, were not the stratified constituents of an associational social order. Instead, they constituted the nethermost stratum of an organically integrated social body held together somewhat tightly by the world-view of Brahmanical Hinduism. The only way to liberation for the Dalits, therefore, was to opt out of the Hindu fold.

In the course of empowering his Dalit caste fellows, Ambedkar was drawn into an epic conflict with Gandhi, on the critical question of the Dalit location within the Hindu social order. Ambedkar felt that once India got freedom, his people, the untouchables, would once again be subjected to the hegemony of caste Hindus and forced to scavenge and sweep for them. To safeguard their interests, he proposed that there should be a number of special seats in the Parliament for the depressed classes which would be filled through elections from special constituencies. While drafting a new Constitution for India in the 1930s, the British extended to the Dalit communities the privilege of voting as a separate electoral constituency. Gandhi opposed this constitutional provision with all the strength at his command, since (so he believed) a separate Harijan electorate would damage Hindu society beyond repair. Instead, he offered the Dalits reserved seats in the central and provincial legislature(s) on a scale more generous than promised by the British. The so-called Poona pact of 1932 was a triumph for the Mahatma because it ensured the social cohesion of Hindu society.

According to Gandhi, "the most effective, quickest and the most unobtrusive way to destroy caste is for reformers to begin the practice with themselves ...The reform will not come by reviling the orthodox. The so-called higher classes will have to descend from their pedestal before they can make impression upon the so-called lower classes". Ambedkar on the other hand believed that India requires a cultural revolution to destroy the caste system and his call to his followers was: "'educate, organize and agitate'". Thus, Ambedkar's project rested on questioning the traditional social order in order to build a just and an equalitarian society, while Gandhi's interest was to preserve the traditional social equilibrium. In addition to providing leadership, Ambedkar engendered among the Depressed Classes the vital element of self-respect without which the untouchables movement probably could not have arisen. Under his leadership they realised that it was possible for them to organize, resistance and challenge the injustice they were suffering under.

Dr. Ambedkar's followers formed the Republican Party of India, immediately after his death, mainly for representing the interests of the Scheduled Castes and other weaker sections. But the leadership crisis in the Republican Party and the growing attacks on the Dalits have made the Dalit youths reject their leadership and adopt a militant method. These Dalits, especially the educated Dalits in Maharashtra, have come forward and taken up the task of bringing all the Scheduled Castes onto one platform and mobilising them in the struggle for their rights and justice. The caste stigma, which remained even after its legal abolition, was deeply painful to these sensitive youths. They firmly believed in that as Fanon has said: "Hunger with dignity was preferable to bread eaten in slavery" (Fanon, 1965:143). They are struggling also at various levels in villages, cities, educational institutions and working organisations by means of a number of political and social organisations like Dalit Panther, Mass Movements, Dalit Liberation Army, Youth Republican, Dalit Sangharsha Samiti, Dalit theatre, Dalit art, Dalit literature, and among Christians, Dalit theology, etc. These organizations, dominated mostly by youth wings of the Dalit force, work as pressure groups for educating and mobilising the Dalits and demonstrating in order to get their problems resolved. Dalit consciousness is also expressed in events like the formation of *Bhim Sena,* Dalit Sena, Dalit Sahitya Movement, the emergence of Dalit Rangbhoomi (Dalit Theatre) BAMCEF (The All India Backward SC, ST, OBC and Minority Communities Employees Federation), Bahujan Samaj Party and Bharatiya Republican Party.

Thus with the growth of democratic institutions and the "politics of number" the Dalits began to assume some importance in national politics in independent India. The leaders among the untouchables, in order to take due advantage of the situation and bring about their liberation, started to mobilize forces in their favour. Today the Dalit voters have successfully undercut the dominance of the upper caste and intermediate castes; and have thrown up a new leadership reflecting a social resurgence from below that provides, contemporaneously, an altogether novel complexion to democratic functioning. They are involved in mass social awakenings, providing a share in power, not only in government jobs but in all the sectors. Their politics is aimed at a cultural revolution with a belief that unless there is a cultural and social revolution there can't be a political revolution (Paswan, 1996:7). This novel politics, which is Ambedkarite in inspiration, rests on a grand strategy that seeks to turn the Indian world "upside down"; and shape an order of things wherein the hitherto deprived shall not only inherit the earth, literally and metaphorically, but also shape the principles of governance which mould the entire polity. In its strategic design, therefore, the Dalit upsurge of our times is a development of the highest significance, potentially speaking.

The current political initiative by the Dalit leaders only marks the beginning of a new era of democratic politics. In spite of its ups and downs with leadership crisis and demoralization, Dalit liberation movements have become a force to be reckoned with today. More and more Dalits speak out openly and courageously, and nobody can set their voice aside. They are actively participating in the political alliance with other influential political parties in the country.

Having this in mind, let us concentrate on the study of Mahars in Maharashtra who are Dalits, very active in politics and are found in the three major religions, namely, Christianity, Buddhism and Hinduism.

References and Bibliography

Ambedkar, B.R., 1948, *The Untouchable*, Bangalore: Dalit Sahitya Akademy.

Appadurai, Arjun, 1986, "Is Homo Hierarchicus?", *American Ethnologist* 13 (4): 745-761.

Bailey, F. G., 1957, *Caste and Economic Frontier*, Manchester: Manchester University Press.

————————, 1959, "For a Sociology of India?", *Contribution to Indian Sociology*, 3, pp.88-101.

————————, 1963, "Closed Stratification in India", *European Journal of Sociology*, 4, pp.107-24

Barnett, Steven A., Lina Fruzzetti, and Akos Ostor.

————————, 1976, "Hierarchy Purified: Notes on Dumont and His Critics," Journal *of Asian Studies* 35 (4): pp.627-646.

Berreman, Gerald, 1960, "Caste in India and the United States," *American Journal of Sociology*, 66: pp.120-127.

————————, 1967, "Stratification, Pluralism and Interaction: A Comparative Analysis of Caste," in *Caste and Race: Comparative Approaches*, A. de Reuck and J. Knight, eds. London: Churchille.

————————, 1971, "The Brahmanical View of Caste", *Contributions to Indian Sociology*, (N.S.) .5, pp.16-23; also see Dipankar Gupta (ed.) 1992 *Social Stratification*. Delhi: Oxford University Press, pp.84-92.

————————, 1972, "Race, Caste and Other Invidious Distinctions in Social Stratification," *Race* 13 (4): pp.385-414.

————————, 1988, "Race, Caste, and Other Invidious Distinctions in Social Stratification," in *Anthropology for the Nineties: Introductory Readings*, Johnnetta B.Cole Ed. New York: The Free Press, pp.484-521.

Beteille, Andre, 1992, *Society and Politics in India. Essays in a Comparative Perspective*, Delhi: Oxford University Press.

Buchanan, F., 1807, "Buchanan's Journey through Mysore, Canara and Malabar", in *Voyages and Travels to All Parts of the World*, F. Pinkerton (ed.) Vol.8, London.

Burghart, Richard, 1983, "For a Sociology of Indias: An Intracultural Approach to the Study of 'Hindu Society', Contributions *to Indian Sociology* (n.s.) 17: 275-99.

__________, 1996, The Conditions of Listening. Essays on Religion, History and Politics in South Asia (ed.) by C.J. Fuller and Jonathan Spencer, Delhi: Oxford University Press, pp.35-42.

Cole, B. Johnnetta, 1988, "Toward a New Anthropology: On Systems of Inequality," in *Anthropology for the Nineties: Introductory Readings*, Johnnetta B. Cole (ed.), New York: The Free Press, pp.463-469.

Cohn, Bernard, 1954, "The Camars of Senapur: A Study of the Changing Status of a Depressed Caste," Ph.D. Dissertation, Cornell University.

__________, 1955, "The Changing Status of a Depressed Caste," in *Village India*, McKim Marriott, (ed.), Chicago: The University of Chicago Press.

Deliege, Robert, 1992, "Replication and Consensus: Untouchability, Caste and Ideology in India", *Man* (n.s.) 27: 155-173.

__________, 1997, The World of the 'Untouchables': Paraiyars of Tamil Nadu, Delhi: Oxford, Dollard, John

__________, 1937, *Caste and Class in a Southern Town*, New York: Doubleday.

Dubois, Abbe J.A., 1959, (1815) Hindu Manners, Customs and Ceremonies, Oxford: Clarendon.

Dumont, Louis, 1957, "For a Sociology of India," *Contributions to Indian Sociology* 1: pp.1- 22.

__________, 1960, "A Rejointer to Dr. Bailey", *Contributions in Indian Sociology*, 4, pp.82-89.

__________, 1966, *Homo Hierarchicus: Essai sur le Systeme des Castes*, Paris: Gallimard.

__________, 1970, *Religion, Politics and History in India*, Paris: Mouton.

Dumont, L. and D. Pocock, 1957, "For a Sociology of India", *Contributions to Indian Sociology* 1, pp.7-22.

Fanon, Frantz, 1965, *Wretched of the Earth*, UK: Macgibbon and Kee, Penguin Books.

Freeman, J., 1979, Untouchable: An Indian Life History, London: Allen and Unwin.

Fuchs, Stephen, 1950, The Children of Hari: A Study of the Nimar Balahis in the Central *Provinces of India*, Vienna: Verlag Herold.

——————, 1981, *At the Bottom of Indian Society: The Harijan and Other Low Castes*, Delhi: Munshiram Manoharlal Pub.

Fuerer-Haimendorf, Von, 1950, "Foreword" in *Children of Hari: A Study of the Nimar Balahis in the Central Provinces of India*, Stephen Fuchs, Vienna: Verlag Herold.

Fuller, C.J. and Spencer, Jonathan (eds.), 1996, *The Conditions of Listening. Essays on Religion, History and Politics in South Asia by Richard Burghart*, Delhi Oxford University Press.

Gough, Kathleen, 1956, "Brahmin Kinship in a Tamil Village", *American Anthropologist* 58: pp.826-853.

——————, 1973, "Harijans in Thanjavur," in *Imperialism and Revolution in South Asia*, K. Gough and H.P. Sharma, (eds.), New York: Monthly Review Press.

Guru, Gopal and V.Geetha, 1997, *Dalit Intellectual Activism, Recent Trends*, Mumbai: VAK Publication.

Hutton, J.H., 1963, *Caste in India*, Oxford: Oxford University Press.

Ilaiah, Kancha, 1996a, *Why I am not a Hindu: A Sudra Critique of Hindutva Philosophy, Culture and Political Economy*, Calcutta: Samya.

——————, 1996b, "Productive Labour, Consciousness and History: The Dalitbahujan Alternative", *Subaltern Studies IX: Writings on South Asian History and Society*, (ed.) Shahid Amin and Dipesh Chakrabarty, Delhi: Oxford University Press, pp.165-200.

Juergensmeyer, Mark, 1982, *Religion as Social Vision, the Movement against Untouchability in Twentieth Century Punjab*, Berkeley: University of California Press.

Keer, Dhananjay, 1964, Mahatma Jotirao Phooley: Father of Indian social Revolution, Bombay: Popular Prakashan.

Khare, R.S., 1984, *The Untouchable as Himself: Ideology, Identity and Pragmatism among the Lucknow Chamars*, Cambridge: Cambridge University Press.

Kolenda, Pauline, 1964, "Religious Anxiety and Hindu Fate," in *Religion in South Asia*, E.B. Harper, (ed.), Berkeley and Los Angeles: University of California Press.

Lynch, Owen M., 1977, "Method and Theory in the Sociology of Louis Dumont: a reply", in Kenneth David (ed.), *The New Wind, Changing Identities in South Asia*, Paris: Mouton Publishers.

Mencher, Joan P., 1974 , "The Caste System Upside Down, or the Not-So-Mysterious East," *Current* Anthropology 15: pp.469-493.

Miller, Robert, 1966, "Button, Button … Great Tradition, Little Tradition, Whose Tradition?", *Anthropological Quarterly* 39: pp.26-42.

Moffatt, Michael, 1979, *An Untouchable Community in South India*, Princeton: Princeton University Press.

Myrdal, Gunnar, 1944, *An American Dilemma: The Negro Problem in Modern Democracy*, New York: Harper and Row.

———————, 1967, "Chairman's Introduction", *Caste and Race*, A.de Reuck and J. Knight (eds.), London: J and A. Churchill.

Paswan, Ram Vilas, 1996, "Dalit Political Figures", *Dalit International Newsletter*, Waterford: USA, Feb. 1996, p.7.

Singer, Milton, 1958, "Traditional India: Structure and Change," Journal *of American Folklore* 71: pp.191-205.

Sowell, Thomas, 1987, A Conflict of Visions: Ideological Origins of Political Struggles, New York: Quill William Morrow.

Warner, W. Lloyd, 1936, "American Caste and Class", *American Journal of Sociology*, 42, 1, 1936, pp. 234-7.

Webster, John C.B., 1994, The Dalit Christians. A History, Delhi: ISPCK.

Zelliot, Eleanor, 1996, "Dalit Movement" *in Dalit International Newsletter*, Vol.1, No.1, Feb. 1996, p.1-4.

3
Dalit Encounter with Christianity: Change and Continuity

1. Introduction

Even after sixty years of independence, the situation of the ex-untouchables, today popularly known as "Dalits", remains pathetic. Their representation in various government and private institutions is inadequate. Their social and cultural discrimination continues. All the same, there is persistent and all pervading daily struggle among them to leave behind a life tainted and broken by others and to seize the chance of a better life for a future. A call for change and an assertion of self-respect appear to be emerging from among them, and it is important to trace this highly significant struggle of the suffering humanity. This chapter studies the situation of the Dalit Christians and their struggle for equality in the Indian nation.

2. Dalit Encounter with Christianity

Of the roughly 20 million Christians in India about 14 million are of dalit origin; that is, about 70 percent of all conversions to Christianity have occurred among Dalits. Their encounter with Christianity resulted in mass movements of religious conversion, due to various socio, cultural, economic, political and religious reasons. These movements have also raised the identity question of the ethnic communities within India.

While Hindu fundamentalist organizations through their assimilation policy claim that tribals and dalits are Hindus, a large number of tribals and dalits on the other hand reject this superimposed new identity. The upper caste Hindus while trying to get the services of the dalits and tribals paid little attention to alleviate their deprived conditions. They are addressed as "Backward Hindus" (Ghurye, 1963:19). Rejecting this identity, many tribals and dalits have found their own ways to move up the social ladder of Indian society. The conversion movements among Dalits and tribals have shown the potential of social change in religion.

On the positive side, these movements represented an effort on the part of the dalits to gain dignity self-respect and the ability to choose their own destiny for themselves and their social group. There was a growing restlessness among them to have a fuller life of dignity for themselves and their children. John Webster (1992:71-76) observes that "the mass-movements constituted the first stage in the modern Dalit movement"; they were initiated and led by them, and sustained by their heroism in the face of persecution. These were group decisions to belong to a new community which not only had a religious tradition comparable to that of the caste Hindus, but which also began to distinguish itself from the traditional caste community. On the negative side, they were a revolt against a socio-religious system which failed to provide a meaningful response to their needs and aspirations (Boel, 1975).

3. Change and Continuity among Dalit Christians

If one asks a question, what is the greatest benefit the Dalit Christians have received, an affirmative answer is education. Though illiteracy rate is still high among Dalit Christians in comparison to other caste Christians, yet, the school and hostel facilities in the mission stations in several parts of India have helped the Dalit Christians in their education (see Franco, Macwan, Ramanathan, 2004:69-143). An empirical study undertaken in Bihar points out that "an overwhelming majority of Dalit Christians work as agricultural coolies as their main occupation; just a handful of dalits as cobblers, watchmen, cooks, carpenters, drivers, petty businessmen, constructions labourers, sweepers, gardeners, house servants, hostel wardens and so forth. … Consequently, the Dalit Christians, who have been looked down as `*no body*' in the society, have become `*some body*'" (Gyanoday, RTC, Patna, 2009:45).

The Dalit Vankar community in Gujarat which was infested with various social evils like child marriage and divorce after their conversion to Christianity began to reform themselves. As a result, the Catholics started the Catholic *Sudharak Mandal*. They held annual general assemblies where all the members participated. The association, in one of its general meetings, decided to institute a kind of life insurance society for its members. They also initiated a fund for promoting higher education for the children (see Valiamangalam, 2008:61). These efforts helped the Vankar Christians to improve their socio-economic conditions. Similar changes have been brought among the Dalit Christians in Tamilnadu, Andhra Pradesh and other parts of India. Though Dalit Christians have made a significant progress in their lives, their growth has been an eyesore for caste Christians and caste Hindus. Dalit Christians in many parts of India continue to be ill treated. We now take a closer look at the various struggles they undergo in their efforts towards their emancipation.

4. Carry Over of Caste Culture into Christianity in India: Inter-Caste Relations between Dalit Christians and Others

Casteism is an integral part of Hindu civilization. If a particular land is salty, the wells dug on this land also tend to be salty. Similarly, the people from Hindu civilization who embraced other religions were deeply affected by casteism. There are several studies and reports portray how Christian communities in different parts of India exhibit their feeling of caste exclusiveness and hold more tenaciously to caste customs. In many places different congregations have their own places of worship, and separate cemeteries (Koshy, 1968:1). Archbishop Casmir of Madras admitted that there is a strong caste system in the Church and he notes, "When Hindus became Christians, they kept the social structures that they belonged to, the caste system overflowed into the Church. The Church condemns the system..." (Casmir, 1991). After analyzing the continuation of the caste system in the Christian community, Bishop Azariah (CSI, Madras), says, "...the condition cannot be said to have changed very much. Most sadly, even within the world-renowned and forward-looking Church of South India there still exist the caste-ridden vestiges of Hinduism" (Azariah, 1983:10).

a.   The Origin of the Term Dalit Christians

The Dalit converts to Christianity were called the Christians of Scheduled Caste Origin (CSCO). This name became common since the First National Convention of Christian Leaders on the Plight of Christians of Scheduled Caste Origin in 1978 (see Statement, 1978). Christian circles began to use the term *dalit* for Scheduled Castes since the end of the 1970s and early 1980s. The concept and category of *Dalit Christians* and their slogan 'Dalit is dignified' were formulated by the Christian Dalit Liberation Movement in 1985. National Churches and Ecumenical Councils (World Council of Churches) became familiar with the term since 1986. Though the concept and the usage of the term *Dalit Christians* were common among the Protestants from the end of the 70s onwards, the Catholics began to use this term a little later. The National Convention of All India Catholic Union (AICU) in 1989, decided to refer to Scheduled Caste Christians, as *Dalit Christians* (see Stanislaus, 1999:44).

b.   Five Fold Discrimination

Today, Dalit Christians suffer from five fold discrimination: (i) discrimination by the Government, (ii) by the caste Hindus, (iii) by fellow Hindu Dalits, (iv) by the upper caste Christian community, and (v) by the subgroups of the Dalit Christians themselves.

i.   Government Discrimination against Dalit Christians

Before the Independence of India, as a response to the demands from the 'Untouchable' minority communities, the Government of India (Scheduled Caste) Order, 1936, gave a list of the 'Scheduled Castes.' Here the term 'Scheduled Caste' included a new specification that 'no Indian Christian shall be deemed to be a member of a Scheduled Caste.' The implication of using a religious criterion for defining a Scheduled caste was not felt immediately by the Indian Christians. In the Constitution of India, Article 341 (1) empowers the President to give a list of the Scheduled Castes. This Scheduled Castes Order of 1950, paragraph 2 says that no person who professes a religion different from Hinduism shall be deemed to be a member of a Scheduled Caste. The Christian leaders and politicians were quick to notice the discrepancy between the secular nature of the Indian Constitution and the Hindu religious bias in the functioning of Indian democracy, with regard to Scheduled Caste converts to Christianity. Thus, the discrimination against Dalit Christians is in the Constitution itself.

ii.   Discrimination by Caste Hindus

Though Christians of Dalit origin have left the caste system of the Hindus, still in the eyes of caste Hindus, the Christians of Dalit origin are still Dalits. The caste Hindus deal with Dalit Christians as they deal with Hindu Dalits. Thus, Christians of Dalit origin are not freed from the tyranny of caste system even after their conversion to Christianity.

iii.   Discrimination Fellow Hindu Dalits

The Dalit Christians suffer alienation from their own fellow Dalits in the Hindufold, because of religious and cultural differences. The hierarchical caste discriminations observed by upper caste Hindus is also followed by Hindu Dalits between themselves, because, Dalit is not one caste, but has several sub-castes which are hierarchically organized. Moreover, the Hindu Dalits frown upon the Christian Dalits as their potential competitors in the share of reservations which are given by the Government (see Kumar, 1985:6-9). Most Hindu Dalits look upon Dalit Christians with disfavor when they seek Government assistance, since they are considered already uplifted by missionary assistance.

iv.   Inter-Caste Discrimination among Upper Caste Christians and Dalit Christians

Upper castes Hindus who have converted to Christianity have retained their caste of origin within the Church. It is not uncommon that the Christian high castes append their caste suffix to their names. Such caste names are read in the Church at funerals, marriages and other occasions. Normally, Christian converts follow the caste customs and the ceremonies of their caste origin in their life cycle celebrations such as birth, puberty, marriage and funeral. For marriages, every caste follows its custom except for the nuptial blessing in the Church. They also follow the food, dressing habits, etc., as their Hindu counter-parts. In some instances, if the converts fail to comply with the caste customs, they are ostracized. Hence, the practices of social distance, untouchability and social stratification are not uncommon even among the Christians.

This is markedly seen in Tamil Nadu comparing to other parts of India. It is because Tamil Nadu has the second largest population of Christians after Kerala. Among the Christians of Tamilnadu, around 65 percent are Dalits (Statement, 1994:66; Raj, 1992: 28). Moreover, it is in Tamilnadu, the Backward Caste Movement and the Dravidian Movements are very active inspiring Dalit Christians to fight for their rights.

In the Church history of India, one can study how the caste differences and practices have permeated for the last 75 years. For example on 15th January, 1925, the Dalit Christians of Tiruchchirappalli sent a memorandum to Bishop Alexius Maria Henry Lepierier, Vicar Apostolic for India, enumerating the demands of dominant castes and the discrimination that they suffer. It stated:

> "The absurdity of their pretentions to enforce their distinctions of caste against us in the house of God is only matched by the arrogance with which they put them forward ... (1) that we

should forever be segregated as untouchables in the House of God, (2) that Holy Communion should be distributed to them, first and that after they have all been served, then and then only the officiating priest should carry the Sacrament to us. (3) that our children, under no circumstances, be admitted in St. Joseph's College, Catholic Boarding House, the Convents, the Holy Redeemer's School, the Seminaries and other institutions...The Hindu and the Mohomedan visitors are permitted to enter at every door in the church. Is it too much to ask for similar freedom for ourselves? We have waited long and patiently. As Catholics we demand our Catholic privilege for equal treatment in the House of God and for equal educational facilities" (Thattumkal, 1983:223-224).

One cannot bypass the problem as past history. The core of the problem is that caste divisions and practices still exist in the Christian community. The social discrimination they suffer within the Christian community is brought into the focus of many in the Church. The result of the research conducted by Antony Raj and his team reveal the following discriminatory practices in the Catholic and Protestant churches in Tamil Nadu as existing in some parishes: 1) The construction of two chapels, one is for the non-Dalits and other for the Dalits. In some parishes liturgical services are conducted separately, 2) Separate seating arrangements are made within the same chapel. Dalits are usually seated in the two aisles of the Church. Even if there are benches or chairs, the Dalits are asked to take their seats on the floor, 3) The existence of two separate cemeteries, two separate hearses to carry the dead bodies are found, 4) Two separate queues are formed to receive the sacred body of Christ. In some places Dalits are asked to receive communion after the non-Dalits, 5) It is forbidden to be an altar boy or lector at the sacred liturgy, 6) The non-Dalits restrict the *Corpus Christi* procession, Palm Sunday procession, and other processions only to their streets, 7) Dalits are not invited to participate in the washing of feet ceremony during Maundy Thursday, 8) For fear of equal participation in the celebration of the parish patron saint, the parish council decides not to ask any contribution from the Dalits, 9) The feast of the village patron saint is celebrated separately (Raj, 1992:213-214; Stephen and others, 1990:1-2).

The report of the late Archbishop Arokiasamy, the Chairman of the Scheduled Caste/ Scheduled Tribe Commission substantiates these discriminations against the Dalit Christians (Catholic Bishop's Conference of India 1989). He states:

> "In Tamilnadu, in the predominantly Christian villages, the Harijan colony or cheri is distinct and separate from the upper caste settlement, with all the civic and municipal amenities, such as the hospital and school, being located in the area of the caste Christians. The Church in village is cruciforum (cross shaped) as in most parts of Tamilnadu and Harijan Christians are in some places required to confine themselves to one wing of the house of God. CSCO are not allowed to assist the priest or read scriptural passages during Mass and not allowed to enter the Sanctuary. They are also denied participation in the Church choir; when Sacraments such as baptism, confirmation and marriage are being administered, the CSCO have to receive them only after the upper caste Christians have been administered the Sacraments. And they are being discriminated even in death, for CSCO are allotted their own cemeteries or a different corner of the main cemetery. In some places a wall separates the CSCOs …Interdining is a sacrilege, while intermarriage is unheard of. No caste Christian enters the home of a CSCO. During marriages in upper caste settlements CSCO are given food outside the house, served in little wicker baskets. Caste Christians never attend weddings in the cherri, as marriage or funeral processions of CSCO are banned from passing through the streets of the Upper Caste people" (Arokiasamy, 1989:53).

It is not easy to calculate the number of parishes, cemeteries and places of worship, where these divisions, distinctions and discriminations are being practiced today.

v.   Discrimination by Fellow Dalit Christians

The Dalit Christians themselves are divided into different caste subgroups which is common among the Hindu Dalits. In Tamil Nadu, there is a fourfold hierarchy of Dalits: viz., Pallans, Paraiyans, Sakkiliyans and Thottis. "Each of these has rigid and connubial restrictions. And also a general urban/rural divisions are existing, where urbanite claim superiority. On top of it, all the class divisions are added to the many subgroups of Dalits" (Danial, 1990:18). The discrimination is polarized between these subgroups.

It is a classical example of the oppressed being ruled by the values of the oppressor.

The infights are more evident in Andhra Pradesh, where Dalits are polarized mostly into the subgroups of Malas and Madigas. Azariah says, "They (Dalit Christians) are divided among themselves into different subjects like their Hindu counterparts. They observe caste discrimination against one another, equally, strongly if not more like all other Hindus" (Azariah, 1989:11; Augustine, 1984:36-42).

The Christian leaders accept the existence of the caste practices in the Christian community and they have shown a great concern for the social life of the community. The memorandum of the National Convention of the Christians of Scheduled Caste Origin (1978) states:

> "It is also found that notwithstanding conversion, caste system with all its prejudices is not destroyed but is unfortunately prevalent among the Christian converts also. They continue to be treated by their neighbours as Untouchables and are victims of the same social and economic disabilities as their Hindu brethren of the same category. These Christian converts follow the same usages, customs, manners and habits of life characteristic to each particular caste. Except in the matter of religious belief, there is absolutely no differentiation between the converts and their Hindu brethren. In a caste-ridden society as we have in India, caste practices and prejudices die hard. Hence, the Christians of Scheduled Caste origins suffer from disabilities of the practice of untouchability" (Memorandum, 1981: 2-3).

5. Commission Reports on Discrimination on Dalit Christians

The prevalence of the caste practices within Christian communities is made visible by various government commission reports.

Several Commissions appointed by the Government to study the plight of the Dalits, report that the Dalit converts to Christianity suffer from the same caste practice by the non-Dalits even after their conversion. The Kaka Khalelkar Commission Report (1955) states:

> "Even a change of religion does not destroy caste. For instance, converts to Christianity sometimes carry caste practices with them though their religion does not recognize it. A large number of people belonging to lower castes, and in particular, from among the untouchables become converts to these religions to escape the rigour and humiliation of the Hindu caste system. It is sad to note, however, that even these converts could not easily shake off their old caste disabilities" (see Raj, 1992:19).

The Kumara Pillai Commission Report (Kerala Government, 1965) too states that the caste system is found among the Christians. It observes: "…the evidence is that the degrees of segregation of the new convert from the Scheduled Castes is almost as high as before his conversion …We are convinced that in practice converts from the Scheduled Castes are treated as socially backward" (see Arokiasamy, 1992:89). While studying the conditions of the 'Harijan Christians in Tamilnadu', Chidamparam states in his Evaluation Report on Intensive Agricultural Area Programme (1975),

> "The casteism is practiced widely among the members of Christian fold as judged by the prohibition of social mobility between members of different castes, inter-marriage between them, dining with members of other castes and common work. The caste system, the most archaic but the most powerful social institution in India has also permeated into the Christian religion" (Chidambaram, 1976:43).

The Mandal Commission (1980) makes the following observation:

> "Though caste system is peculiar to Hindu society, yet in actual practice it also pervades to non-Hindu communities in India in varying degrees. There are two reasons for this phenomenon: first, caste system is a great conditioner of the mind and leaves an indelible mark on a person's social consciousness and cultural moves. Consequently, even after conversion, the ex-Hindus carried with them their deeply ingrained ideas of social hierarchy and stratification …non-Hindu minorities living in a pre-dominantly Hindu India could not escape from its dominant social cultural influences. Thus, both from within and without, castes among non-Hindu communities receive continuous substance and stimulus" (Mandal Commission Report of the Backward Classes Commission, 1991:60).

All the above references indicate the existing caste practices within the Christian community. In spite of their caste discrimination and poverty conditions, still they were not included in the Scheduled Caste list because of the presence of the Brahmin political class then dominating the Congress, and also of some right wing Hindus who feared a massive shift of dalits to Christianity if reservations were granted to them.

6.   Discrimination of Dalit Christians – Contemporary Scenario

The above said caste discrimination on various levels are felt even today. There are many fights and quarrels between different caste groups due to the appointments or transfers of priests from one parish to another. Even in the selection and appointment of Bishops, caste plays a major role. So, the Christians of the Dalit origin continue to live under the burden of oppressive forces of casteism within the Church and outside. There have been a spate of newspaper reports regarding "Christian casteism" in many parts of India (see Religion and Society, 1987 and 1990 and also Michael, 1995; Stanislaus, 1999; Raj, 1995; The New Indian Express, April 29, 2008:5; The Hindu, April 30, 2008: 8; Frontline, 2008:41; The Hindu, 2008:8; The New Indian Express, 2008:4; Dinamani, 2008:5; Sarva Viyabhi, 2008:4; The Hindu, 2008: 5; Dina Thanthi, July 17, 2008).

Understanding the dismal situation of the Dalit Christians in the Church, the Apostolic Pro-Nuncio to India, Archbishop George Zur, in his inaugural address to the Catholic Bishops Conference of India (CBCI) at their meeting held in Pune during December 1991, made the following observations, "Though Catholics of the lower castes and tribes form 60 percent of Church membership they have no place in decision-making. Scheduled caste converts are treated as low caste not only by high caste Hindus but by high caste Christians too. In rural areas they cannot own or rent houses, however well-placed they may be. Separate places are marked out for them in the parish churches and burial grounds. Inter-caste marriages are frowned upon and caste tags are still appended to the Christian names of high caste people. Casteism is rampant among the clergy and the religious. Though Dalit Christians make 65 per cent of the 10 million Christians in the South, less than 4 per cent of the parishes are entrusted to Dalit priests" (as quoted by Massey, 1995:82).

The Pro-Nuncio's observation was supported by Archbishop Alphonse Mathias, the then President of the Catholic Bishops Conference of India (CBCI). He added that the injustice meted out to Christian Dalits by the Government and the Church should be redressed fully (see Massey, 1995:82).

In spite of the above admonitions by the highest authorities of the Church, the oppressive casteism within the Church continues. On 16th February 1999, the late Archbishop Michael Augustine of Pondicherry-Cuddalore could not celebrate the funeral mass for the dead mother of a priest in the church of Eraiyur of his own Archdiocease. The only reason was that he was not simply permitted to do so by the majority Catholic non-dalit Vanniyars (about 15000) whose operative caste norms, so far, have never authorized the minority Dalits (about 1200 Catholic Dalits and 500 non-Christian Dalits) to carry their dead bodies along the main street of the village towards the parish church. These discriminatory practices have been dealt with by the Archdiocesan administration, apparently with the attitude of sitting over the fence. Only when the pressure were mounted up by the minority Dalits with the demand for a separate parish for themselves away from the clutches of Eraiyur, by some of the Dalit priests, and by the dramatic interventions by some of the Dalit political parties like *Viduthalai Chiruthaihal*, the Archdiocesan administration came out with a strong response to promote justice. The Statement of the Archbishop on Eraiyur issue sought to bring to an end the discriminatory practices. But the majority Vanniyar Catholics, though conceded to taking the dead body of a Dalit along the main street that day, they defied his directions by way of destroying the cart for carrying exclusively the dead Vanniyars. Their contention was that by no means the Vanniar corpse and the Dalit corpse could ever share the same cart on the way to the burial ground. They alerted the press that they opt for a mass conversion towards Hinduism which upholds the practice of caste discrimination and untouchability (Raja, 2008:2-3). Similar caste oppressions still continue among the Christians of different castes. The Church administration feels helpless with the caste mentality of Indian Christians which they have inherited from Hinduism.

7. Constitutional Violations against Dalit Christians

The Central Government's programmes for the Dalits, such as post-Matric scholarships and reservation of jobs, however, are restricted to Dalit Hindus, Dalit Sikhs and Dalit Buddhists only. Dalit Christians are excluded from these benefits. In Tamilnadu and some other States, the Dalit Christians are included in the category of the Backward Class (Tamilnadu, 1986).

Many Christian organizations say that the denial of 'Scheduled Caste Status' to Dalit Christians goes against their fundamental rights. For example, Letter No. 18/4/58 Act IV, dated 23-7-'59 from the Deputy Secretary of the Government of India, Ministry of Home Affairs, New Delhi, to all State Governments and Union Administrations, state that the Scheduled Castes of other religions, who reconvert themselves to Hinduism will be entitled to all the privileges of the Hindu Scheduled Castes (Massey, 1994:38; Kananaikil, 1993:73). This implies that if Christians of Dalit origin converts them to Hinduism they will be entitled to all reservation benefits of the Government, otherwise no.

There are numerous orders both from the Central and State Governments in this regard, which direct, approve and justify this practice and thus blatantly violate both the spirit and word of the Article 25 (see Kananaikil, 1984:7). In 1983, the Tamilnadu Government gave an Order demanding a Dalit person who holds a Government job to resign from the job if he changes his religion from Hinduism (Govt: TN-LET. No.21711/ADW 11/80-26 dated 16/25.8.83 to all Heads of Departments cited in J. Kananaikil, 1984:16).

According to the above interpretation, a Scheduled Caste loses his caste, once he converts to Christianity and gets it back again when reconverts himself to Hinduism. This runs contrary to the Constitutional law as prevailing in India that the State should not interfere in matters of religion. This is also against the spirit of the Constitution as contained in Article 27 and 28 which emphasizes the secular nature of the Constitution which is an undeniable right. In fact, it encourages apostasy and proselytization of Scheduled Castes Christians back to Hinduism. The Constitution of India is a deterrent to conversion to Christianity and, in fact, encourages renegadism to Hinduism. By stopping privileges to Dalit converts, it prevents Dalits from converting to Christianity.

The Dalit Christians are deprived of their human rights and equality including the constitutional fundamental rights to choose their own religion. In a civil writ petition in Court, *Soosai*[1] *vs. Union of India*, 1983, the petitioner stated that he was an Adi Dravida Dalit convert to Christianity and on conversion to Christianity, he continued to be a member of that caste and suffered from the same social and economic disabilities like other members of his community. He prayed that he is being discriminated against only on the basis of religion. This petition was dismissed by the court saying: "It is now well established that when a violation of Article 14 or any of its related provisions is alleged, the burden rests on the petitioner to establish by clear and cogent evidence that the State has been guilty of arbitrary discrimination" (see Kananaikil, 1990). The Court also said, "To establish that para 3 of the Constitution (Scheduled Castes) Order 1950 discriminates against Christians members of the enumerated castes (Scheduled Castes) it must be shown that they suffer from a comparable depth of social and economic disabilities and cultural and educational backwardness and similar levels of degradation within the Christian community necessitating intervention by the State under the provisions of the Constitution. It is not sufficient to show that the same caste continues after conversions" (Daniel, 1988:109).

---

[1] Soosai, the converted Dalit Christian is from Madras and he works as a cobbler on the pathways in the city.

This is not in consonance with the previous amendments of Dalit converts to other religions. For example, after the amendment of the Constitution, the Dalit converts to Sikhism or Buddhism are included in the list of Scheduled Castes. No proof was called for at that time to show that the Dalit converts to Sikhism or Buddhism suffered the same degree of disabilities as they did in their original religion. Why then, is different criterion used in the case of converts to other religions, ask the Dalit Christian activists.

There is also another problem connected with the laws which protect the Dalits. Although there are number of 'Untouchability Crimes' committed against Dalit Christians, the 1989 Protection of Civil Rights Act does not apply to the Dalit Christians. Thus the caste atrocities committed against the Dalit Christians do not come under them. In the absence of a comprehensive Human Rights legislation, the laws are found to be inadequate or unsuitable to deal with atrocities involving Dalit Christians. Thus "they do not even have a legal security!" (Augustine, 1991:6).

8. Secular Visionaries and Dalit Christian Movements

The secular visionaries like Jotirao Phule, B.R. Ambedkar and several others inspire Dalit Christians in their struggle for emancipation.

Jotirao Phule (1826-1890) is known as the father of the Indian social revolution (see Keer, 1964). Other than the Christian missionaries, it was Jotirao Phule who was the first Indian to start a school for the Untouchables and a girls' school in Maharashtra. It was his aim to reconstruct the social order of India on the basis of social equality, justice and reason. Today's Dalit movement draws its basic principle from Phule. He had an indelible imprint on Ambedkar's mind (Rajasekhariah, 1971:18-19; Keer, 1974:vii). Ambedkar was inspired and guided by the noble example set by Phule.

It is very important to understand that Jotirao Phule was greatly influenced by Christianity. He gratefully acknowledged this influence on his life and his commitment to the social concern of the downtrodden. Phule studied in the Scottish Mission School in Poona. He was exposed to Christ and His teachings. He was so much inspired by the Holy Bible that he used to read it and applied it to his life. His social concern to the poor, the marginalized women and untouchables rose from this Christian inspiration. He obtained much of his knowledge from the Scottish Mission School, which taught him the duties and rights of the marginalized classes (Keer, 1974:13). The impact of Christian education on Phule and his friends was such that according to Walvekar there were moments when they lost their faith in Hinduism and thought seriously of embracing Christianity (see Keer, 1974:15). Commenting on this, Keer writes: "These young students no doubt derived inspiration from the work of missionaries. Their example of service to people and their mission to spread education were worth emulating" (1974:15). The work of Phule was so much influenced by Christian ideals and ethics that some of his Brahmin critics from Poona began to "circulate a rumour among their castemen that Jotirao some day would throw them suddenly into the fold of Christianity" (1974:133).

Phule's perception on Christian mission can be delineated from his attitude towards Pandita Ramabai. There was a controversy over the conversion of Pandita Ramabai to Christianity. Many upper caste Hindus condemned her for her conversion to Christianity. Jotirao along with Rajaramshastri Bhagwat, were the two social reformers who maintained a good opinion of the Pandita even after her conversion. Phule also used this incident of her conversion to bring home the folly of Hinduism. "He said that when Ramabai had not studied other religions she made brilliant speeches in Poona in exposition of Hinduism! Poor lady, ignorant of the position to which Hinduism had assigned woman and Shudra, but in England she must have realized the true position of Hinduism" (Keer, 1974:196).

Dr. Bhimrao Ramji Ambedkar (1891-1956) was very much inspired and guided by the noble example set by Mahatma Jotiba Phule. Ambedkar's analysis of the reasons for caste and untouchability revealed that the Hindu scriptures are directly linked to the degrading status of the untouchables in Hindu society. So, in 1929 Ambedkar advised the untouchables to embrace any other religion that would regard them as human beings, give them an opportunity to break off from the oppressive structures and enable them to act, eat, walk, and live like men (see Wilkinson and Thomas, 1972:33). In spite of this suggestion, he was still emotionally tuned to Hinduism and was making efforts to reform Hinduism. When he found it is impossible to reform Hinduism he converted himself to Buddhism.

In spite of his conversion to Buddhism, Ambedkar's ideas on religious conversion and Christianity inspire the Dalit Christians in their struggle for emancipation. According to Ambedkar "there are three reasons which have impeded the growth of Christianity" in India. The first of these reasons is the bad morals of the early European settlers in India particularly Englishmen who were sent to India by the East India Company. The second impediment in the progress of Christianity in India was the struggle between the Catholic and Non-catholic Missions for supremacy in the field of proselytization. The third reason which is responsible for the slow growth of Christianity was the wrong approach made by Christian missionaries in charge of Christian propaganda. The missionary approach was Brahmin oriented. The Christian Missionary wanted to get at the Brahmin. Many schools, colleges, hospitals etc. were started to establish a contact with the Brahmin. "That the Christian Missionary has been deceived is now realized by many. The Brahmin and the higher classes have taken full advantage of the institutions maintained by the Christian Missions. But hardly any one of them has given any thought to the religion which brought these institutions into existence" (see Moon, 1989:439).

Ambedkar also critiqued Mahatma Gandhi for his attitude towards Christian Mission and conversion. Ambedkar's stand on conversion stands in sharp contrast to that of Gandhi. In 1935 Gandhi made the controversial statement "If I had power and could legislate, the first thing I would ban is conversions".

It is noteworthy to remember that in the same year when Gandhi made that statement, Dr. Ambedkar also made his historical proclamation on religious conversion at Yeola Conference of 1935, "Though I have been born a Hindu, I shall not die as Hindu".

According to Ambedkar, Mr. Gandhi's arguments against Christian Missions "are just clever. There is nothing profound about them. They are the desperate arguments of a man who is driven to wall" (see Moon, 1989:449). Ambedkar continues, "All these arguments of Mr. Gandhi are brought forth to prevent Christian Missionaries from converting the Untouchables. Ambedkar summarized his understanding of Gandhi on Christian mission: "Whatever anybody may say I have no doubt, all the Untouchables, whether they are converts or not, will agree that Mr. Gandhi has been grossly unjust to Christian Missions" (see Moon, 1989:450). Ambedkar's perception of Christian mission comes out clear in the following statement of his: "Comparatively speaking, the achievements of Christian Missions in the field of social service are very great. Of that no one except a determined opponent of every thing Christian can have any doubt" (see Moon, 1989:452).

All the same, Ambedkar was pained to realize the condition of the untouchables in spite of their conversion to Christianity. He asked, "Has Christianity been able to save the convert from the sufferings and ignominy which is the misfortune of every one who is born an untouchable? ...I am sure the answer to every one of these questions must be in the negative. In other words conversion has not brought about any change in the social status of the untouchable convert. To the general mass of the Hindus the untouchable remains an untouchable even though he becomes a Christian" (see Moon, 1989:470).

Ambedkar not only raised this issue, he also made a commendable analysis of why the Christian Dalits' negative status remained the same as before their conversion. The following observation of Ambedkar with regard the Dalit Christians is very pertinent: "It is necessary to bear in mind that Indian Christians are drawn chiefly from the Untouchables and, to much less extent from low ranking Shudra castes. The social services of Missions must therefore be judged in the light of the needs of these classes. What are those needs? The services rendered by the Missions in the fields of education and medical relief are beyond the ken of the Indian Christians. They go mostly to benefit the high caste Hindu" (as quoted by Massey, 1995:107).

Influenced by these ideologies, increasingly Dalit Christians realize today that the Church in India has not taken a credible step to evolve adequate strategies and programmes to walk with Dalits with their day today struggles. The Indian Church on the other hand has compromised the caste culture of India. Hence, the Dalit Christian has become very active in the Church for their emancipation.

The present political scenario influenced by Dalit leaders like Mayawati, Paswan, Ramadas Athawale, Krishnaswami, Thiru Ma Valavan and others influence the Dalit Christians to engage in their struggle for full humanity in the hierarchical Hindu society. For example, after a long struggle Dalit Christians in Bihar have formed "Bihar Dalit Catholic Sabha" to voice their concerns. This organization, based in Patna, is taking up the issue of reservation for Dalit Christians along with other National and state level organization of the country. It is also voicing concerns of the Dalit Christians and the poor with respect to their placement in Catholic institutions in the Archdiocese of Patna. Similar organizations are active in Tamilnadu and Andhra Pradesh.

9. Dalit Christian Interrogation of Upper Caste Sanskritic Christianity of India

In the context of caste culture entering into Christianity in India, there is a challenge by Dalit Christians at the Indian Church's attempt to indigenize Christianity in the Sanskritic culture of India. From its very inception, Christianity has been trying to indigenize itself (inculturate) in the Indian cultural soil by adopting Indian architectural styles for church buildings, rituals such as *aarti* in the service, and lighting lamps as well as candles, serve as official signs encouraging continuity with Hinduism. These attempts were in the Sanskritic culture. At the beginning stages there were not much resistance to this process. But with the awakening of Dalit consciousness, there is an increasing resistance to the Sanskritic model of indigenization of Christianity. It is because; the nature of Dalit religiosity and their rituals and religious practices have a distinct orientation. The struggles they go through in daily life for survival have infused in their religiosity a deep sense of aversion to Sanskritic rituals and symbols of the upper castes.

Let us examine the different models of indigenization that are being under discussion in the Indian Church(es). Scholars have analysed the varied approaches and identified models that are at work with regard to the relationship between Christianity and Indian Culture(s). These are not watertight compartments; often they do overlap. These approaches may be classified under different forms: Missionary, the Monastic and the Ecclesiastical Models (Theckannath, 2008:2).

The missionary model is one in which the missionary often tries to adopt high caste life-style, dress, diet customs and habits in order to be acceptable to the upper caste community, and to win them over to faith. One classical example is that of Robert de Nobili (17th century) and some missionaries even today.

The mystico-monastic model is experimented in Christian ashrams. The insights of the Hindu classical tradition are incorporated into Christian theology and life, especially the spiritual quest of contemplation and silence, coupled with hospitality for seekers, with the spiritual leadership of a Guru. Some make a distinction between *Kavi* and *Khadi* ashrams. Kavi ashrams are primarily geared toward contemplative quest and the Khadi ashrams integrate spirituality into the socio-political movements enshrined in the Ashram movement (as in the ashrams of Gandhi and Vinoba Bahve). Among the Christians the first model, i.e. the mystic-monistic model is practiced mainly by the clergy and religious men and women. This is to bring about a synthesis of Christian monoasticism and Indian form of *sanyasa* of the classical

Sanskritic tradition in ashram context of solitude, silence, austerity and asceticism, Christian yoga, and contemplation inspired by the Upanishads, Gita, etc. The examples of such indigenization are: Henri Le Saux (Swami Abhishiktananda), Jules Monchanin (Swami Parama Arubi Andannda), Vandana Mataji, Swami Amalorananda, Sara Grant and others. The primary path of spirituality is contemplation or *jnana marga*. It also includes the *Bhakti yoga* through *bhajans*, *kirthans* and *namajapa*. These ashrams also contribute to inter-religious dialogue, mainly at the level of the elite members of both communities (Theckannath, 2008:2).

The ecclesiastical model springs from the inspiration of the Second Vatican Council. The Post-Vatican II efforts in this area were initiated by ecclesiastical authorities, and designed by theologians and liturgists. It aimed at inculturating the Catholic official rituals. They emerged from the official centres and formation houses, like seminaries and pastoral centres. These efforts began to have an effect mainly on the Religious communities and were used in special celebrations. To this we can add inculturation of music, art, architecture and dance, almost all of which is related to liturgy and prayer, mostly sponsored, directed and used by the Ecclesiastical set up. These too have been to a large extent drawn from the classical traditions (Theckannath, 2008:2).

The above experiments to indigenize Christianity in India did not bring much fruit. The Dalit and Tribal Christians who form the major population of Indian Christians did not feel at home with the sanskritized rituals in the Indian Church. Moreover, the accumulating knowledge of the cultural reality of India and socio-cultural movements of the tribals and Dalits of India have added further questioning of the traditional understanding of Indian culture (see Michael, 2009). All these have added much debate among theologians with regard to the methods of indigenization of Christianity in India.

Maria Arul Raja, a theology professor in Chennai laments that the Indian Church has not taken "Dalits as their dialogical partners" (2008:138). He continues, "The system of the socio-pastoral involvement of the *Pandaraswamis* exclusively for the so-called Paraiahs is the case in point as the starter in their multiple mission experiments in South Asia. Only for the past decades, only a handful among Dalit priests, though in small number, could openly claim their cultural roots with a sense of belonging" (Raja, 2008:139).

Before Dalits were converted to Christianity, they had their own traditions, mythology, legends, proverbs, moral teachings, customs, festivals and folk religions. They had their own cultural creativity. This creativity has not vanished even after their conversion to Christianity and gradually getting familiarized with the Biblical world. Yahweh as the deity of a large family (*kula deivam*) or of an ethnic group of people (*namma saami*) evokes positive response from Dalits. They are at home with Biblical image of the Protector-God (*kaaval deivam*) and Powerful God with expression of wrath (the Lord of Hosts). The God of mobility (Ark of Covenant) is very dear to them than the God of stability (Temple at Jerusalem as God's feet). Their experience of God as Emmanuel (God-with-us) resonates their life experiences (see Raja, 2008).

The story of the death of Jesus as the result of his defiant opposition to the legalistic norms of the religious and political realms makes an easy entry into the Dalit minds and hearts as the protecting god (*kaaval deivam*) in deep solidarity with their struggle against caste repression. The symbol of crucifix more or less gives them effective impetus on a par with the spiritual energies drawn from the memory stones by them in the remote villages (Raja, 2008:3).

Dalit Christians have built their own shrines and developed their own devotional practices. This is folk Christianity. Shrines are places where Christian faith and local cultures meet and where an indigenous Christianity has become a living tradition. Most of these shrines have taken in many of the elements of Folk Religion with or without the knowledge or approval of the official Church and popularly accepted and practiced by Dalit Christians. This suited well as a continuation of their earlier faith and a meaningful expression of their Christian faith in ways that evoked a religious experience (Wilson, 2007).

This folk Christianity of Dalits has continuity with the origin of their Folk Religion traced back to Nature worship, Spirit worship, Worship of totems, Ancestor worship (Bharathi, 1999: 489-533). Dalit folk deities have been variously called in Tamil *devams, saamis, ammans, devatas*, and *peey-pisasus*, loosely translatable as "gods", "goddesses," and "demons" (see Moffatt, 1979:219). These divine beings are distinctive feature of *Shakti*, power. But in the religious world of Dalits, there is a struggle between benevolent and malevolent powers. In Christianity also there is the concept of struggle between good (God) and evil (Devil) powers. In the life of the Dalits, this struggle is an existential one between upper caste and them. Hence, the Dalit Christians easily identify themselves not with Upanisadic power of Brahman, but with the God of the *Exodus* who overpowered the power and might of the Egyptians (see Ayrookuzhiel, 1994:250-266).

Thus we see the cultural world of Dalits do not correspond to the Brahmic view of God and its cultural notions. Hence, Dalit Christians are vehemently opposed to sanskritized forms of indigenization of the Church in India. While upper caste Sanskritic Christianity attempts to adopt "*OM*" symbol in art and in chanting, the Dalit and tribal Christians do not feel at home with this symbol. For Dalit Christians, the symbol "*DRUM*" appeals. Dalit Christology takes Christ as Drum. Sathianathan Clarke explains, "The significance of the drum as an instrument of sacred power, which mediates protection and provision for the community, is quite similar to the relationship between Sakti (Divine power) and the drum in the Pariayar's religious tradition. Furthermore, the association of the drum with the well-being, health, and strength of individuals and the community points to the divine powers that are intrinsic to this religious symbol" (Clarke, 1998:145). Dalit historical experience makes them to experience the presence of Christ through the drum. Clarke explains: "The only perspective open to us (Dalits) is the one given to us by the historical situation in which we (as Dalits) find ourselves. If we cannot achieve an unobstructed view of Jesus from the vantage point of our present circumstances, then we cannot achieve an unobstructed view of him at all" (1998:197).

There are two major axes along which issues of Christian indigenization takes their inspirations. One is an idealized homogenized notion of Indian culture. The other is contrasting notion of composite culture which conceptualizes Indian culture as plural. These two axes and their ramifications are at the heart of debates on culture and identity in India today (see Robinson 2003). This debate also influences the Indian Christian Church.

The 19th and 20th century Indological approach to the understanding of Indian society as developed by the Orientalists and Colonial Administrators perceived the Sanskritic culture as the mainline culture of India. That gave the identity to the Indianness. Influenced by the above understanding of India, the efforts of the Church to indigenize the Christian life largely came from an Indological perspective without taking into consideration of the cultures of Dalits and tribals who are the main component of Indian Christians. These Christian tribals and Dalits could not oppose these movements due to the then existing cultural climate and the power structure of Indian society. But today with the increasing anthropological knowledge of India, there are several movements challenging the idea of homogenous Indianness. Despite the power and influence of Indology, with its reliance on classical texts and high culture, the bulk of the work of anthropologists and sociologists after independence has been towards empirical documentation of the enormous diversities in society and culture of India (see Robinson 2003). With the increasing anthropological knowledge on the pluralistic nature of Indian identity, today, the tribals and Dalits are asserting their cultural identity in the emerging India of 21st century. This has brought a new awakening among the Tribal and Dalit Christians in India. They question the Sanskritic oriented indigenization of Indian Church.

In the debate on the indigenization of Christianity in India, a tribal theologian comments that, "By accepting Christ tribals find a new identity in the community of men and women in the Church, with saints and with God. This identity is trying its best to maintain and develop many tribal traditional socio-cultural and religious elements. Their traditional religions are unable to provide a cultural framework to cope with the fast changing situations. However, on closer observation one finds that the old and new tribal identities harmonize well with nature and its resources, *viz. jal, jungle, jameen* (water, forest, land). With mutual dialogue, the tribals are in search of a greater, inclusive, united and collective tribal identity with a strong sense of common *tribalness* irrespective of various religious affiliations against the vigorous campaign of making different cultures part of one single Hindu culture by the Hindutva forces" (Tirkey, 2007:93).

10. Conclusion

The study points out that the situation of Dalit Christians is very bad. They are going through discrimination from all sides. The study also shows that Christians of India have become a victim to the caste system of Hinduism in their socio-cultural life. In order to stop the exodus of the Hindu Dalits to Christianity, the State has excluded the Dalit Christians from the reservation benefits of the Central and State Governments. Thus, today, Dalit Christians continue to suffer from five-fold discriminations, namely: (i) discrimination by the Government, (ii) by the caste Hindus, (iii) by fellow Hindu Dalits, (iv) by the upper caste Christian community, and (v) by the subgroups of the Dalit Christians themselves.

The Indian Church has been making efforts to indigenize itself in the cultural soil of this country. But its efforts have been under confusion due to the problem of cultural identity which is currently under heated debate between the Hindutva oriented nationalists and the Ambedkarian Dalit ideologues (see Michael 2003:78-107). Christian Dalits have been opposing the Sanskritic oriented indigenization efforts of the Indian Church.

The above study points out that the cultures of India are not extrinsic to Indian Christians. Indian Christians are insiders to and inheritors of their cultures. The social structure of caste has entered into the cultural life of Christians in India. As there is a struggle within India with regard to the cultural identity of India between Sanskrit Culture and Dalit Culture, similar struggle also exists among upper caste and Dalit Christians in the Indian Church. Only history will tell us how far the Christian world-view of equality will ultimately transform all Christians of India to shed their caste prejudices among themselves. This needs to be seen as history unfolds itself through various movements in India.

References and Bibliography

Aloysius, G. 1998, *Religion as Emancipatory Identity. A Buddhist Movement among the Tamils under Colonialism.* New Delhi: New Age International Publishers.

Ambedkar, B.R. 1945, *Annihilation of Caste.* Bangalore: Dalit Sahitya Akademy.

Arokiasamy, M. 1989, "Caste and Conversion," in *Report of the General Meeting of the CBCI* , Delhi: CBCI.

Arokiasamy, M. 1992, "Dalits," in *Report of the General Meeting of the CBCI,* Pune: Ishvani Kendra, January, 1992.

Augustine, P.A. 1984, *Andhra Church: The Caste Factors.* Jaipur: St. Xavier School.

Augustine, S.M., 1991, "The Problem of the Christians of Scheduled Caste Origin,", in *Relevance of Dr. Ambedkar for Christian Dalit Struggles in India,* ed. by M.E. Prabhakar, Bangalore: NCCR pp.1430-1437.

Ayrookuzhiel, A.M. Abraham 1994, "Dalit Theology: A Movement of Counter-Culture", in *Indigenous People: Dalits. Dalit Issues in Today's Theological Debate,* ed. James Massey, Delhi: ISPCK.

Azariah, M. 1983, *Witnessing in India Today.* Madras: UELCI.

———————————, 1989, *Mission in Christ's Way in India Today.* Madras: Christian Literature Society.

Bharathi, Bakthavatsala 1999, *Panpaattu Maanidayiyal* (Tamil), Chennai: Manicka Vashar Pathippagam.

Boel, J. 1975, *Christian Mission in India: A Sociological Analysis.* Amsterdam: ASA Publications.

Casmir, G. 1991, "Wasn't Christ a Carpenter's Son?" *The Sunday Times of India.* Bangalore, 22 December 1991.

Chatterjee, Partha 1994, *Nation and Its Fragments*. Delhi: Oxford University Press.

Chidambaram, P.1976, *Evaluation Report on Intensive Agricultural Area Programme, 1975*, Madras: Tamilnadu Government.

Clarke, Sathianathan 1998, *Dalits and Christianity. Subaltern Religion and Liberation Theology in India*. Delhi: Oxford University Press.

Daniel, D. 1988, "The Constitution (Scheduled Castes) Order 19 of 1950 and the Scheduled Caste Christians," in *Tamilnadu Christians Dharimiga Conference*. Tiruchchirappalli, 24-25, September.

Daniel, P. 1990, "Dalit Christian Experiences," in *Emerging Dalit Theology*, X. Irudayaraj, ed., Madras: Jesuit Theological Secretariat. pp. 18-54.

Dinamani, 2008, "Christian Protest", *Dinamani*, March, 2008, p.5.

Dina Thanthi, 2008, "Editorial" *Dina Thanthi*, Madurai, July 17, 2008.

Fernandes, Walter, Geeta Menon, and Philip Viegas 1988, *Forests, Environment and Tribal Economy: Deforestation, Impoverishment and Marinalisation in Orissa*. New Delhi: Indian Social Institute.

Fernandes, Walter 1988a, "The Draft Forest Policy 1987; The National Water Policy 1987", *Social Action* 38.

Franco, Fernando; Macwan, Jyotsna and Ramanathan, Suguna, 2004, *Journeys to Freedom. Dalit Narratives*. Kolkata: Samya.

Frontline, 2008, "Dalit Christians Demand" April, 15-30th, 2008.

Forrester, D.B. 1980, *Caste and Christianity: Attitudes and Policies on Caste of Anglo Saxon Protestant Mission in India*. London: Centre for South Asian Studies, University of London.

Gandhi, M.K. 1941, *Christian Missions*. Ahmedabad: Navjivan Publishing House. (1960:2nd ed.)

Ghurye, G.S. 1963, *The Scheduled Tribes*. Bombay: Popular Prakashan.

Gore, M.S. 1993, *The Social Context of an Ideology. Ambedkar's Political and Social Thought*. Delhi: Sage Publications.

Gyanoday RTC Khaspur Patna, 2009, *Dalit Christians in Bihar. Their History, Identity Struggles and Future*. Patna: Prabhat Prakashan.

Kaka Khalelkar Commission Report ,1955 , New Delhi: Government of India.

Kananaikil, J. 1984, *Consittutional Provisions for the Scheduled Castes*. New Delhi: Indian Social Institute.

___________, 1990, *Scheduled Caste Converts and Social Disabilities: A Survey of Tamilnadu*. New Delhi: Indian Social Institute.

___________, 1993, *Scheduled Caste Converts in Search of Justice: Constitution (Scheduled Castes) Orders (Amendment) Bill, 1990, Part III*. New Delhi: Indian Social Institute.

Keer, Dhananjay 1964, *Mahatma Jotirao Phooley: Father of Indian social Revolution*. Bombay, Popular Prakashan.

___________, 1974, *Dr. Ambedkar: Life and Mission*. Bombay: Popular Prakashan.

Koshy, Ninan 1968, *Caste in Kerala Churches*. Bangalore: Religion and Society Publications.

Kumar, Y. 1985, "Dalit Christians Can't Claim our Share in Reservations,", *Economic and Political Weekly*, No.18, pp.6-9.

Mandal Commission 1980, Mandal Commission Report of the Backward Classes Commission, 1980.

Reservations for Backward Classes. New Delhi: Akalank Publication, 1991.

Massey, James, 1994, *Roots: A Concise History of Dalits*. New Delhi: ISPCK.

Massey, James 1995, Dalits in India. Religion as a Source of Bondage or Liberation with Special *Reference to Christians*. New Delhi: Manohar.

Memorandum, 1981, The Memorandum prepared by the follow-up Action Committee of the National Convention on the Plight of the Christians of Scheduled Caste Origin, pp. 4-5; see An Open Letter from Catholics of Scheduled Caste Origin belonging to the Scheduled Castes Welfare Association of the Thiruvadanai Taluk of the East Ramnad District to all the Catholic Bishops and Christians in Tamilnadu, November 1981, pp.2-3.

Michael, S.M. 1995, "The Emerging Dalit Consciousness", *Indian Missiological Review*. March, Vol.17, No.1, pp.5-13.

___________, 2003, "Culture, Nationalism and Globalization: Politics of Identity in India", *Globalization and Social Movements. Struggle for a Humane Society*. Eds. P. G. Jogdand and S. M. Michael, Delhi: Rawat Publications, pp. 78-107.

___________, 2007, "Dalit Vision of a Just Society in India", *Dalits in Modern India: Vision and Values*. (ed.) S.M. Michael (2nd Edition), New Delhi: Sage Publications, First Edition 1999.

___________, 2007a, *Conversion, Social Mobility and Empowerment – View from Below*. Mumbai University: Department of Sociology. Occasional Paper Series: No.4.

___________, 2009, "Cultural Diversity and Inculturation in India", *Vidyajyoti Journal of Theological Reflection*. Vol. 73, No. 1, pp.43-56.

Moffat, Michael 1979, *An Untouchable Community in South India: Structure and Consensus*. Princeton: Princeton University Press.

Moon, Vasant 1989, *Dr. Babasaheb Ambedkar Writings and Speeches*. Vol.5, Bombay: Education Department, Government of Maharashtra.

Natarajan, Nalini 1977, *Missionary Among the Khasis*. New Delhi: Sterling Publishers.

Omvedt, Gail 1995, *Dalit Visions*. Hyderabad: Orient Longman.

Picket, J.W. 1933, *Christian Mass Movements in India*. *Lucknow*: Lucknow Publishing House (2nd Indian Edition)

Raj, A., 1992, *Children of a Lesser God (Dalit Christians)*. Madurai: DCLM.

______________, 1992, *Discrimination Against Dalit Christians in Tamilnadu*. Madurai: Ideas Centre.

______________, 1995, "The Dalit Christian Reality in Tamilnadu", *Integral Mission Dynamics. An Interdisciplinary Study of the Catholic Church in India*. ed. Augustine Kanjamala, New Delhi: Intercultural Publications.

Raja, A. Maria Arul, 2008, "Dalit Cultural Streams as Dialogical Partner with the Church", paper presented at the *CBCI Conference on Cultural Challenges to Christian Mission Today*. Pune: Ishvani Kendra, August 2-4, 2008.

Rajasekhariah, A.M. 1971, *B.R. Ambedkar: The Politics of Emancipation*. Bombay: Sindhu Publications.

Religion and Society, 1987, "Editorial: Christian Dalits and Caste in Churches," *Religion and Society*. Vol.XXXVII, No.3, p.1.

Religion and Society, 1990, "Christian Dalits in India: An Analysis", by James Massey, *Religion and Society*, Vol.XXXVII, No.3, pp.24-39.

Robinson, Rowena 2003, *Christians of India*. Delhi: Sage Publications.

Saldanha, Julian 1996, "Patterns of Conversion in Indian Mission History", *Mission and Conversion: A Reappraisal*. (eds.) Joseph Mattam and Sebastian Kim, Mumbai: St. Paul's Publications.

Sarva Viyabhi, 2008, "Christian Protest" in Tamil *Sarva Viyabhi*, Pondicherry: Archdiocesan Weekly, April 06, 2008, p.4.

Sharma, Ursula 1976 "Status-Striving and Striving to Abolish Status: The Arya Samaj and the Low Castes", *Social Action* 26.

Shetty, Rajshekar 1979, "Ambedkar and His Conversion", *Illustrated Weekly of India*. Vol.C33, November 1-24, pp.21-24.

Snaitang, O.L. 1993, *Christianity and Social Change in North East India*. Shillong: Vendrame Institute.

Stanislaus, 1999, *The Liberative Mission of the Church Among Dalit Christians*, Delhi:ISPCK.

Statement, 1978, Statement and Resolution of the National Convention of Christian Leaders on the *Plight of Christians of Christians of Scheduled Caste Origin*. Bangalore, 15-19 June, 1978, NCCL/P/CSCO/Doc.no.33,NBCLC, Bangalore.

Statement, 1994, Statement of the Tamilnadu Catholic Bishops' Conference (TNCBC), Marian Year *1987-88, in Tamilnadu Catholic Bishops' Conference Statements* (Tamil), Madurai: DCLM.

Stephen, M. and others, 1990, *The Plight of Christians of Scheduled Caste Origin (CSCO) of Roman Catholic Church in Tamilnadu*. Madras: DLET. Tamilnadu, 1986

The Tamilnadu F.O. Ms. No. 558 SWD dated 24-2-'86, in *Tamilnadu Govt. Aid to the Christians*, p.131. All the Scheduled Caste Christians are included in the Backward Class category except the Paravar, Meenavar and Kukkuvar, who are included in the Most Backward Class.

Thattumkal, J. 1983, *Caste and Catholic Church in India: A Historical-Juridical Study on the Nature of the Caste System and its Implications on the Catholic Church in India*. Rome: Pontifical Lateran University.

Theckanath, Jacob, 2008, "Inculturation in India: Review and Prospects in the Pluricultural Context of India", Paper presented at the CBCI Consultation on *Cultural Challenges to Christian Mission Today*, Pune: Ishvani Kendra, August 2-4, 2008.

The New Indian Express, 2008, "Dalit Christians Protest and Lock up 25 Churches", *The New Indian Express*, Chennai, March 17.

The New Indian Express, 2008, "Nellai Teashops Mirror Caste Divide in TN", *The New Indian Express*, Chennai, April 29, 2008, p.5.

The Hindu, 2008, "Dalit Christians Boycott Palm Sunday Celebrations", *The Hindu*, Chennai, March 17.

The Hindu, 2008, "Christians Threat to Convert", *The Hindu*. Chennai, March 28, 2008, p.5.

The Hindu, 2008 Chennai, April 30, p.8.

Tirkey, Agapit 2007, "Inculturation among Tribals", *Christ among the Tribals*. F. Hrangkhuma and Joy Thomas (eds.), FOIM XI, Bangalore: SAIACS Press, pp.79-117.

Valiamangalam, Joseph 2008, Community *in Mission. Mission Consciousness of Christian Communities. A Contextual Missiological Study*. Delhi: GVD/ISPCK.

Webster, John C.B. 1992, *Dalit Christians: A History*. Delhi: ISPCK

Wilkinson, T. and Thomas, M.M. (eds.) 1972, *Ambedkar and the Neo-Buddhist Movement*. Madras: CLS.

Wilson, Vincent B. 2007, "Folk Religions and Shrines" Paper presented at the *Consultation on Shrines and Pilgrimages*, at Bangalore: NBCLC, March 12-14, 2007.

Wingate, Andrew 1997, *The Church and Conversion. A Study of Recent Conversions to and from Christianity in the Tamil Area of South India*. Delhi: ISPCK.

Part 2 :

Hindu, Christian and Buddhist Mahars

4
Mahars in Maharashtra: A Dalit Community

In the Western India the Mahars of Maharashtra is a unique community, Mahars are found in almost every village of Maharashtra, having about 11 percent of the total population of the state, which is second to the Maratha. "Maharatta is the Pali form of Maharashtra, which with the variant reading Mallarashtra, appears in several of the Puranas, as the Vishnu. The Brahmans, looking to the name etymologically, render it by "great country", without, however, being able to explain the origin of such an alleged designation; but it is capable of another meaning. Gurjarashtra (Gujarat) is the neighboring province to the north; and the meaning of this word is the "country of Gujars". Now, Maharashtra may mean "the country of the Mahars," a tribe still known in the province, through in degraded position, and still so numerous through out the Maratha country that there runs the proverb "Wherever there is a village there is the Mahar ward" (Moleswoth's 1857:xxiii).

A Number of authors believe that the Mahars are descendants of the original inhabitants of Maharashtra, who had been dispossessed by successive waves of Aryan and post-Aryan invaders." *Wherever there is a village, there is a maharavada* "(i.e., living quarters of the Mahar community) Robertson in his valuable study about the Mahars, for example, suggest that the above mentioned proverb may be taken literally to mean - That formerly the Mahars were so great a nation that their remnants are found in every town from Bhandara to the Arabian Sea and from the

Narmada River to the middle of the Hyderabad state. They may be fragments of a folk that once owned these broad lands.

He even goes a step further and suggests that the Mahars might have given their name to the state Maharashtra.

Robertson is not the only one who believes that the Mahars were the original owners of the land and that they have given Maharashtra its name. Enthoven and Baden-powell are of the same opinion. Enthoven says that, according to popular belief, the name Mahar was derived from *mahahari*, which means *"the great eater"*. He quotes stories of the origin of the caste which explain this interpretation of the name:

Origin Myths about Mahars

The Ahmednagar Mahars claim to one of the four born castes. Their story is that the cow asked her sons how they would treat her after she died the first three sons answered they would worship her as a goddess, the fourth said he would bear her inside him as she had borne him. The horror-struck brothers called him "mahahari" or the "great eater", which according to the story, use has shortened to Mahar

Another tradition regarding the origin of the Mahars relate that once when Parvati was bathing her touch turned some drops of blood on a bela-leaf (Aegle marmelos) into a handsome babe. She took the child home and showed him to Mahamuni. One day, while still young, the child crawled out of the house and, seeing a dead cow lying, began to eat it. Mahadeva was horrified and cursed the child saying that he would live outside the village, that his food would be carcasses, that nobody would have anything to do with him, would look at him, or would allow his shadow to fall on anything pure. Parvati, who took great interest in her child, begged her lord to have pity on him, and Siva agreed that the people would employ him to supply mourners with wood and dried cow-dung cakes to burn the dead. As the child's appetite was so great, he turned his name into mahahari or the great eater.

According to a Hindu tradition, Mahars originally were night rovers whom the God Brahma turned into men list they should eat his whole creation. Others believe that the Mahars were born of the left eye of the moon. Some people said that the first Mahar had been a man by the name of Kalars, but they did not known anything else about him. *(The Mahars - A Study of their Culture, Religion and Socio-Economic Life, Traude Pillai-Vetschera)*

Ambedkar devised a theory based on anthropological data of the origin of untouchability, which he linked to the disappearance of Buddhism in India. The untouchables were earlier the broken people, sections of defeated tribes. They were victims of war, refugees whose community structure was weakened or even destroyed. These people went in search of new refuge and approached sedentary tribes.

Two things about Mahars require special comment: the traditional place of the Mahar caste, the special world of the Mahars in eastern Maharashtra. First, it must be understood that there exist hundreds of untouchable castes, and each one has a world somewhat different from the other. The Mahars of Maharashtra were ubiquitous in the Marathi – speaking area. They were present in every village, and the anthropologist *Iravati Karve* claimed, "Where there is a Mahar, there is Maharashtra". A Marathi proverb contains the same notion but has a negative meaning *"jithe gao, tithe Maharwada"* where there is a village, there are Mahars, or there's something dirty in every village. Their position in the village was as in British parlance. "Inferior village servants" and this meant a number of menial tasks in the service of the village but also a place albeit low in the village hierarchy.

The coming of the British offered new occupation in the army and on the docks and the railroads and in the mills while at the same time it destroyed the Mahar work of carrying messages, determining land boundaries and caring for government officials horses, and other such jobs. *(Growing up Untouchables in India – A Dalit Autobiography – Vasant Moon)*

The traditional role of the Mahar caste was that of village servant. Every village, almost without exception, in the Marathi - speaking area of west central India, had its Maharwada (Mahar quarters). Mahars had no special skill or craft, but performed necessary duties for the villages as watchmen, wall-menders, street-sweepers, removers of cattle carcasses, and caretakers of the burning ground, servants of any passing government official.

Grain and gifts in kind from the village, the produce from the plot of land that was his by virtue of his hereditary village service, and remuneration from field labor formed the Mahar income, Mahar service was essential for the village; his status was low, his work menial, but his place was secure. With the coming of the British and the spread of new ways of administration and communication, the Mahar place in the village grew less important. Concomitant with the diminishing of his village duties, however, were new opportunities in road and bridge building, on the railroad lines, in the mills and ammunition factories, and especially important, in the Indian armies of the British. These were all occupations that freed the Mahar from his usual subservient role. It was from the educated members of this non-traditional Mahar group that new leadership arose. Their following came from those Mahars whose identity no longer was tied to a traditional village role.

Between 1890 and 1956, the Mahar caste of Maharashtra experienced a political awakening, a development of unity, and a push for equal rights with higher castes, which mark the caste out as unique among Untouchable groups. The Mahar uniqueness does not lie in the nature of their response to 19th and 20th century political and economic forces in India; other low castes used political means to gain status, developed caste unity and asserted their rights on the social scene. The Mahar accomplishment is in the totality of their movement. The political awakening not only involved the Mahars in political processes, but also produced a series of political parties and a leader of all-India fame. The development of unity tied the village Mahar to his town brother so that mass action unprecedented among Untouchables was possible. The push for rights was not an effort to move up a notch in the social system but a leap for the top, an attempt aided not by traditional methods of social betterment but by modern means.

Given the Mahar near-worship of "Babasaheb" Ambedkar, a name given him in affection and respect, it is not difficult to overstate his part in the Mahar movement. He came to dominate the movement in all its phases - social, religious and political.

He appealed to the masses to regain their self-respect by refusing to eat the crumbs thrown away by caste Hindus, by refusing to carry the dead animals of the caste Hindus and by giving up the eating of carrion. He exhorted them to act in such a way as to assure a better future for their own children. "He further urged his people to agitate against the Government ban on their entry into the Army, Navy and Police, impressed upon them the importance of entering Government services and of education, he tweaked their self-respect by telling them that it was utterly disgraceful to sell their human rights for a few crumbs of bread, and appealed to them fervently to do away with the humiliating, enslaving traditions, to abandon their vatans and seek forest lands for agricultural pursuits". *(Socio-Political Philosophy of Dr. B.R.Ambedkar – Dr. P.V. Rathnam)*

Census figures bear out the legend of Mahar ubiquity. Alone among Untouchable castes, Mahars are found in every district, of Maharashtra.

Mahars have other myths of their origin, "they are found on the skirts of all Hindu settlements and say they belong to one of the four cow-born castes. Their story is that the cow asked her sons how they would treat her after she died. The first three sons answered they would worship her as a goddess; the fourth said he would bear her inside of him as she had borne him.

The horror-stuck brothers called him Mahahar or the Great Eater, which, according to the story, use has shortened to Mahar. According to a Hindu tradition Mahars were originally night-rovers or nishachars, whom the god Brahma turned to men lest they should eat his whole creations. Mahars have no memory of any former home. They say they sprung from the moon, and were ruled by many kings of the moon-race among whom Nak was the most famous. Mahars are commonly known as Dharniche put or sons of the soil (Maharashtra State Gazetteers 1976:235, 236). There is another myth related to its origin that, "Another tradition regarding the origin of the Mahars related that, once, when Parvati was bathing, her touch turned some drops of blood on a belleaf into a handsome babe. She took the child home and shows him to Mahadev, who named him Mahamuni. One day, while still young, the child crawled out of the house and seeing a dead cow, began to eat it. Mahadev was horrified and cursed the child, saying that he would live outside the villages, that his food would be carcasses, that nobody would have anything to do with him, would look at him or would allow his shadow to fall on anything pure. Parvati, who took great interest in her child, begged her lord to have pity on and Shiva agreed that the people would employ him to supply mourners with wood and dried cow dung cakes to burn the dead. As the child's appetite was so great, he turned his name into Mahahari or the great eater" (R. E. Enthoven 1990:402-403).

According to Doctor Bhandarkar the word Mahar is corruption the word Mrut Ahar those who live on dead meat. The scholars puts that the Mahars were the original settlers in Maharashtra that the name of the state 'Maharashtra' was originally "Mahar Rashtra" or 'the land of Mahar the Mahars in Maharashtra was an important community, which had a history of bravery and honesty, they were the original inhabitants. The anthropologist, Dr. Irawati Karve in her *Pariputri* (Fulfillment) (Pune: R.J.Deshmukh, 1951:81) in Marathi jethaparayant Mahar pochle tithaparayant Maharashtra (as far as the Mahars have gone, there is Maharashtra), in her book *Hindu Society*, she writes, 'Anthropologically they occupy a position half-way between the primitives and other Hindus, somewhat Nearer to Hindus than the primitives. They seem to belong to tribal elements very early drawn into the village economy of the Deccan'.

A Marathi proverb, jetha gao tethe Maharwada (wherever there is a village, there is a maharwada). The historical record of Mahar is not available except some scanty references. 'The origin of the term Mahar is lost in antiquity. It is popularly said to be derived from mahahari or great eater, in support of which a few traditions are quoted below. According to other it is derived through Prakrit from the Sanskrit word mritahari, which is given as the name of the lowest caste, in the Markandeya puran Chapter 35, verse 36). In verse 28 of the same puran they are also called Mritaharins. This name they are said to have earned by their occupation of removing carcasses of dead animals. The synonym Antyaja means last-born, that is. The lowest in the social scale. Atishudra means those below the Shudras, the last of the fourfold division of Manu, and is indicative of the primitive origin of the tribe (R.E. Enthoven, Vol II, 1990:401).

The puran also recognize them as a lowest caste. "According to Beden-Powell, the term "Maharashtra" is derived from the fact of the Mahar domination of Western India. This may or may not be true but there is sufficient evidence to warrant the conclusion that they were once a people with their own king, their own laws, religion and social customs. In appearance they are able-bodied and muscular, many of them handsome, intelligent and quick to assimilate and possessing physical courage. Their women many of them could have some pretensions to fine features and graceful forms, like the men can turn their hand to anything" The life of Shivram Janba Kamble, (1997:145). "In the Bombay Dacha, scattered families of Mahar or Mhar are still found - the relics of a once numerous people-now chiefly acting as hereditary guardians of village boundaries. This circumstance has led Mr. J. F. Hewitt to suggest that the position is due to their once being associated with the land as its owners, Dr. G. Oppert say that the Mahar claim to have been once the ruling race in Maharashtra (B. H. Baden-Powell, 1896:114). 'There are many indications to show that the Mahars were an ancient nation or a large community inhabiting and occupying the plains of Maharashtra. Very probably through conquest, they lost their possessions and have been treated for generations as a subject people' (W. A. Bhat, 43 C.B.K, Vol.1, 1978: 4-5).

There are different myths about Mahars, but there are no myths about their occupation, as there is for other untouchable caste, it is clear that they have no special skill or craft in their hand, they used to perform the necessary duties, which was required by the villages, with this, we can say that Mahar do not have a permanent occupation in this system as such other caste do have.

Occupation of Mahars

Mahars are landless labourers. They were working in lands which belong to the villages where the land was belonging to upper castes. Their occupation is linked to some traditional village practices.

Inam Land

An Inam land is a free land to a person in recognition of his service rendered in the past to the state on the battle field.

"The Mahars have traditions that the 52 rights claimed by him against the villages were given to them by the Muslim kings of Bedar, this can only mean that these rights were ancient and that the kings of Bedar only confirmed" BAWS, Vol 7, 1990:280.

Mahar Vatan

The vatan land is a perpetual rent free land grant made to a permanent village resident in lieu of the service he is expected to render to the village community. There was no fix time for him. If he is not available any of the family members has to give their service at that time.

Shahu in his princely state issued an order on "28th March 1919 by an order declaring that the ryots need not pay the Mahars any baluta as the latter were hence forth free from liability to compulsory service" (Chatrapati Shahu the Pillar of Social Democracy, (Ed.) P.B. Salunke, 1994:155).

On June 8th 1955, Ambedkar writes to Gaikwad, "The matter will have to be taken to the High Court and if we fail to the Supreme Court I am ready for action" (BAWS, Vol 21. 2006:220). It was abolished under the Bombay Inferior Village Vatans Abolition Act I of 1958.

"On August 31st 1955, Mumbai Rajaya Kanista Gawa Kamghar Association was founded under the Presidentship of Dr. Ambedkar" (Shankarao).

Kharat 1961:335 to see that the vatan land which Mahars were occupying should be legalized and the justice be rendering to this people.

Balutadar/ Occupation

The Mahar did not have a well-defined "traditional occupation" but his service is important at the village level. "The Mahar is emphatically called the village eye. He is the watchman and guardian of the village and the living chronicle of its concerns. His situation or curiosity makes him acquainted with everybody's affairs, and his evidence is required in every dispute. Should two cultivators quarrel respecting the boundaries of their fields, the Mahar's evidence ought to decide it; and should a similar quarrel happen between two villages, the Mahars are always the chief actors in it and to their decision alone is some times referred" R. N. Goodine 1852 Report on the Village Communities of the Deccan Bombay, Government Bombay.

Mahars was a balutedar, who use to provide service to village, which was needed in return he uses to get balut. "In the first class will be found the Mahar-one of the most useful balutedar. He is the bearer of all reports from the Patel is the district officer, and of all revenue collections when the Patel proceeds with them to the district treasury. He assembles the cultivators on occasions when they are required, either for the payment of revenue, or to give hearing to a Government notification. He attend on all travelers of note, who put up at the village, guides them to the next, and carries any loads they may have, receiving a small payment for the same. He removes all dead cattle from the stalls of the cultivators, and gives their skins, if mirasdars, to the owners; if not, he keeps them himself; but in both cases he appropriates the flesh to his own use. He sweeps the space in front of the village chowdi every morning, and, if there happens to be a district cuttchery at his village, he performs the same office in front of it. He in fact is a kind of "jack of all trade", performing all such work, as would, have required of the cultivators, encroach so much upon their time, as to prevent the possibility of their attending properly to their fields. Inasmuch as he is a very different character from the other balutedar" (The Oriental Christian Spectator June 1845:187). The Mahars are hereditary village servants and are considered authorities in all boundary matters.

In Konkan the Mahars make baskets, stone slabs, beating the drum near the temple, playing bands and doing labour work. "The Ajna-patra written by one of Shivaji's minister Ramachandra Nilakanth lays down that every caste should live by its hereditary occupation (Vritti) and nobody should change his calling" (P. N. Joshi (ed.) Ajna-patra (Marathi) 1969:28-30).

The Missionary describes the manners and customs of the people between Sholapur and Poona. "It may be as well to observer of the Mahar, that low cunning and constant attempts at dirty wit are his characteristics. Of the kind of cunning he practices, every traveler may be witness; but it is only among his companions he displays his disposition to be witty. He is extremely desirous of attaining knowledge, is much respected by his caste, when he has it, and never loses an opportunity of displaying the possession of it. It cannot be said, however, that his aptitude is greater than that of the Kunbie, and perhaps it is not so great. He is passionately fond of dress, and when it is attainable stabiles much to look respectable: yet it is beyond his power to hide his caste from the rest of the population; for his appearance seldom fails to lead to detection, and his speech always does. He is not, certainly, in general anxious to hide his descent; but when circumstances take him from his village, and place him above the horde, a degree of delicacy on this point is always discernible; and he is apt to set aside the requirements of his religion, and insult the feelings of those whom, when in his capacity of balutedar, he dared not defile by his approach. The Mahar women are sunk in a much lower state of ignorance, and moral degradation, than the rest of the female population; and this may be counted for, not only by the footing on which they stand to most of the other people, but from the circumstance of polygamy being indulged in by the males to an extent which would hardly be tolerated among the other castes" (The Oriental Christian Spectator June 1845:87).

Yeskar

Vesa is the village gate, and one of the Mahar duties was to be a gatekeeper, carrying a long stick with small bells on it and guard the village.

Other Aspects of Mahars

Honesty

He prides himself much on his honesty, and with truth it may be said that he is honest to a degree far beyond what would be expected from his degraded condition. Although, when carrying the revenue collections to the district cutchery, he has ample opportunity to abscond with the money, not even an attempt to rob, much less an actual theft, has ever been discovered and yet the temptation from the amount entrusted is often very great.

House

There are two sections in the village (i) Touchable and (ii) Untouchables, the quarters of the Untouchables must be located towards the south, since the South is the most inauspicious, so the untouchables should live outside the village. The Mahar house can't be called a house, it is just a shelter to him, the house so small when one enters, has to bow down, if not then the head will hit by the roof, most of the houses are plastered by mud and are decorated with poverty, at the door there will be earthen vessel with narrow mouth used for storing water, a broken and worn out chul (hearth) next to it a couple of earthen pots an iron griddle for roosting the bhakri, a grinding stove in the corner above the Chula the rope (Valni) on which the dry meat of the carcasses. The missionary record, "The huts of the Mahars are always without the village walls, and generally display a degree of wretchedness and filth quite humiliating. They may be known by the bones of the animals, whose carcasses the Mahars have eaten, being a it were strewn around them, and the number of naked and noisy children, mounted and dunghills, which present themselves to view at the approach of a stranger" (The Oriental Christian Spectator June 1845: 87). This can't be called as a shelter also such degraded residential quarters they had.

Chavdi

There is common meeting place in every village to look after the affairs of the village, but apart from this, there is one more Chavdi of Mahar in every village, The Mahar in this Chavdi take all the important decisions of the community in these Chavdi, it has and independent important, why Mahars had this independent meeting place, why other caste people do not have such Chavdi, This can be linked that the Mahars was once king, now it has become a halting place for the other Mahars who come from different village or passing from one village to another, the engagement, and festivals the organize in the Chavdi.

Caste among Caste Sub Castes

Mahar caste consists of 'twelve-and-a-half' sub-castes; Enthoven gives a list of fifty-three endogamous divisions within the Mahar. In Konkan there are two-sub caste Bela Mahar and Pana Mahar, Dr. Ambedkar belong to Bela Mahar though his father was follower of Kabir Panth. On 14th May 1938, at Kankavli the conference was held in the second resolution of the conference that this two sub caste should be abolished and only one cast was called that is Mahar (Vasant Moon, 2002:151). The decision to discard sub-caste among the Mahars to unit Mahars as one and the second reason unless sub-caste is not discarded the caste system will remain alive.

Caste-Oppression Status

The caste system is one of the worst, the sufferers were downtrodden they were the victims of the system. 'Relates that in some outlying villages in the early morning, the Mahars as he passes the village well, may be seen crouching that his shadow may not all on the water-drawers. The village barber will not have the Mahars, nor are they allowed to draw water from the village well. Formerly an earthen pot was hung from their necks to hold their spittle, they were made to drag thorns to wipe out their footsteps, and when a Brahmin came near, were forced to lie far off on their faces lest their shadow might fall on together, Modern means of locomotion, however, by bringing all classes together, have led to proximity of unclean classes being tolerated to an extent formerly unheard of. The Mahars live outside villages in special Mharvadas or Mahars' quarters' The Bombay Gazetteer, Vol.XVIII, Part I, p.441). "During the career of Sawai Madhavrao, the Peshwa government had directed that the Mahars, being atishudras, 'beyond Shudras' could not have their marriage rites conducted by the regular Brahmin priests. They were asked to content themselves with the services of their caste men-priests, the Medhe-Mahar" (Vad, Sawai Madhavrao, Vol. 11:280). Caste, Class and Occupation. (G. S. Ghurye:319).

Untouchability

'The Marathi Mahar, the Telugu Mala and the Tamil Paraiyan, though because of their village menial status are grouped together as field-labourers, conveyed pollution without touch, either at a specific distance or by their shadow, and were classed as impure untouchables' (G.S. Ghurye, Reprinted 1979:319). Such was the miserable condition of untouchables they were treated worse then dogs.

Death

The dead bodies are not burnt but are buried, among the Mahars.

Food

The Mahars are non-vegetarian, they eat meat, not merely goats and fowls but also of the cow irrespective whether it is dead or slaughtered, but not pig.

Salutation

The salutation of the Mahar on all occasions, and in contradistinction to the rest of the population is Johar (The Oriental Christian Spectator June 1845:187).

Education

The education to Mahars were not allowed in the Hindu caste system so they were totally kept out of the pale of education so they remain illiterate for ages, "It must be admitted that under the Peshwa's Government the Depressed Classes were entirely out of the pale of education. They did not find a place in any idea of state education, for the simple reason that the Peshwa's Government was a theocracy based upon the canons of Manu, according to which the Shudras and Atishudras (class corresponding to the Backward classes of the Education Department), if they had any right to life, liberty and property, had certainly no right to education" (BAWS, Vol 2, 1982:409). The missionary observed and writes that in the Bombay presidency that, "Through out the Bombay Presidency, Caste demands a monopoly of education, seeking to prevent low-caste children from entering the Government School" (The Oriental Christian Spectator May 1859:174). Under the chairmanship a committee was formed by the education department dated 5th November 1928 to enquire, in their report submitted its states that, "The most extreme case actually seen by any member of the committee during the investigation was in Nasik District where a Depressed Class boy was made to sit on a platform (as used by cultivators where watching their crops) exposed to the sun and rain outside the school which was held in an upper room, whilst the teacher occasionally leaned out of the window to give instruction to him. On the rainy days he had to go home" (Mr. O. H. B. Starte Report of the Committee March 1930:14). Further the committee report state that, "In the case of School held in temples, normally Depressed Class Children are not admitted. In some cases they are admitted and made to sit outside we heard of rare cases where they were admitted inside these schools" (Mr. O. H. B. Starte Report of the Committee March 1930:14). The system wants that they should not get education they should serve the upper caste people.

Dress

The clothing's, his head dress consists of rags, a black cord around his neck wearing a ear ring, a loin cloth very scanty carrying staff in has hand and wore torn sandals, they were half naked.

In Bombay the Untouchables were not permitted to wear clean or untornclothes. In fact the shopkeepers took the precaution to see that before cloth was sold to the Untouchable it was torn and soiled (Vasant Moon 1993:720).

Poverty

The system do not provide them a permanent occupation, so their, economic position were at the mercy of the upper caste so they were exploited, which lead them to an extreme poverty.

Religion

Though they were in the system of Hindus but were not allowed to access the sacred scriptures, temples and sacred places of worship they were forbidden for this, they worship the deities Khandoba, Marai, Mesai and Satvai, these temples were found in Maharwada. They had there own priest and guru to do there rituals. "At Bavda (District Poona) some Untouchables exhorted their fellow-outcastes to give up eating the leaving of higher caste people, dead animals, etc., and to refuse to do the dirty work of the people. The elders of the village have told these Mahars with new fangled notions that it is their 'Dharma' to eat what they have always been eating and do what they have been doing. Those Mahars who do not follow their ancient and eternal 'Dharma' have been thrashed by the people and threatened with expulsion from the village" (Vasant Moon 1989:55).

Punishment

Under the Peshwas distinction was observed in the punishment of the criminals according to the caste. Hard labour and death were punishments mostly visited on the Untouchables (Vasant Moon 1993:722).

Social Boycott

In the villages the orthodox classes used their economic power against the untouchables in the villages, when they dare to exercise their rights, they stopped their employment and discontinued their remuneration as the village servants, they are forced to evict from their land, refuse to sale the necessaries requirement of there daily life, fill wells with human excreta, prevent castle from grazing in the fields, not allowing to pickup fire woods - prohibiting passing through the lane located in the land of upper caste. This types of boycott is often planned on a large scale, where ever there untouchables dare to speak of their rights.

Chokhamela Saint

The saints of Maharashtra have brought untouchables, with God in the bhakti Cult marg, but "the saint has never according to on a study carried campaign against Caste and Untouchability. They were concerned with the relation between man and God. They did not preach that all men were equal. They preached that all men were equal in the eyes of God-a very different and a very innocuous proposition which nobody can find difficult to preach or dangerous to believe in" (BAWS Vol 1, 1979:87, 88). Chokhamela was a Mahar Sant from the Bhakti cult, a true devotee of Vithoba, after his death they had raised a tomb of Chokhamela at Pandharpur outside the temple of Vithoba, "But during the Peshwa period, the members of his community, the Mahar, were forbidden to approach his tomb even for paying homage to him, just because his tomb was situated very close to the Vithal temple, and there was a possibility of the Brahmin devotees to Vitthal being polluted by the touch of Mahars if they were allowed to loiter around" (Sudha V. Desai 1990:123).

The Bhakti tradition sought only personal salvation, there tradition was to protest but in course of time the Bhakti ethos become a supplement to Brahmanism.

The arrival of British; in India there was some change in the village scenario, with their arrival they bought with them the new idea which can be said the administration and communication, the Mahars depended on the villagers slowly change their way of earnings they got migrated to urban and started working as labors in building, bridge, roads, railway lines, gang men's ammunition factories and mills, the village duties which were done by him started diminishing, they were no longer attended the traditional village role.

Mahar Movement

Few factors played in the rise of the Mahar Movement in the nineteenth century. The term "nineteenth century" has been stretched to cover the early period of movement ending when Dr. Ambedkar's effective and dominant leadership began in 1920.

The essential factors in the processes by which the Mahar Movement grew were:

1. A leadership released from traditional service and followers with some economic freedom.

2. Grievances understood and felt by both the "elite" members of the caste and the masses.

3. Some from of legitimization of the new non-traditional Mahar ambition both within the caste and among members of the elite in the larger society.

4. A group of "broken" men who could serve as links between the caste and the institutions of power in society, or who knew how to use modern channels of change.

5. Channels for communication, both within the group and from the group to the public.

6.   Some form of protection for protesters when the overstepping
     of traditional boundaries brought retaliation.

Without any one of these factors, the Mahar movement would
have taken a different path, or would have remained a minor
protest. *(From Untouchables to Dalits –Essays on the Ambedkar
Movement – Eleanor Zelliot)*

The All India Republican party, the Buddhist conversion
movement, the school and colleges of the People's Education
Society all include others than Mahars but were created by the
energy and ambition of the Mahar movement.

The name Dr. Ambedkar and his vision continue to dominate
both the Dalit movement and all discussion of equality in India.
Although Mumbai is no longer the major centre of Dalit politics,
which has moved to North India, nor the only centre of Dalit
literature, the city has played a crucial role in producing the
Ambedkar movement.

Nowadays, they cannot be forced by the members of higher
castes to perform those duties, which are still required to be
performed by this community in rural areas; situation of urban
area has totally changed.

Conclusion

Though Mahars are outcaste, they carry great weight and
importance as a member of village community, the caste has
multifarious duties in the village, as a village watchmen, guarding
the village borders, knowledge of the area, also he had duty to
clean the village lanes and carry carcasses. "He was considered
the most trust worthy man in the village, and though his caste
was low, he held a highly respected position among the village
servants" (Bombay Gazetteer Vol. XVII, 438).

We can say that Mahars of Maharashtra as a caste have its
own significance, though we may add that scholar have attempted
to see the meaning but are not coming to a term, we can derive that
the Mahars in Maharashtra is the old community which they have

there own history of bravery and different culture, which may be different from today's Hindu.

References and Bibliography

Dr. B. R. Ambedkar, Buddha and his Dhamma, Siddharth Publication Mumbai, 1957.

Dhananjay Kee, Dr.Ambedkars Life and Mission, Popular Prakashan Mumbai, 1971.

Dr. Ambedkar, Annihilation of Caste Elenaor zelliot from untouchables to Dalits Essays on the Ambedkar movement, Manohar Publishers and Distributors, New Delhi, 1996.

Gail Omvedt, Dalits and the Democratic Revolution, Sage Publication India Pvt. Ltd, 1994.

J. Michael Mahar, The Untouchables in Contemporary India, (Rawat Publication, 1998.

Fernando France, Journeys to Freedom-Dalit Narratives, Popular Prakashan Pvt. Ltd. Mumbai.

Jyotsna Macwan, Delhi, Kolkata, 2004.

Suguna Ramanathan, Edited by S.M.Dahiwale, Understanding Indian Society-A Non-Brahmanic Perspective, Rawat Publications Jaipur and New Delhi.

Edited by Rowena Robinson, Religious Conversion in India-Sathianathan Clarke Modes, Motivations, and Meanings, Oxford University Press, 2003.

Dr. B. R. Ambedkar, "Writings and speeches" The Education Department Govt. of Maharashtra, Mumbai, 1987.

S. M. Michael, Dalits in Modern India-Vision and Values, Vistaar Publications, 1999.

Rowena Robinson, Christians of India, Sage Publications India Pvt. Ltd., 2003.

Traude Pillai Vetschera, The Mahar-A study of their Culture, Religion and Socio-economic life, Inter cultural Publication (p) Ltd., New Delhi.

Vasant Moon, Growing up Untouchables in India-A Dalit Autobiography, Vipul Publications, New Delhi.

K. N. Kadam, The Meaning of Ambedkarite Conversion to Buddhism and Other Essays, Popular Prakashan, Mumbai, 1997.

Gail Omvedt, Dhamma Diksha: Ambedkar's Turn to Buddhism, National Seminar on Econstructing Indian Society; Dr. B. R. Ambedkar Conversion to Buddhism.

Gopal Guru, Hindusation of Ambedkar in Maharashtra, (Economic and Political Weekly, 16 Feb., 1991.

O.D. Heggade, Economic Thought of Dr. B. R. Ambedkar, Mohit Publication, New Delhi.

Lobo Lancy, Brahmanical Social Order and Christianity in India, 2005.

Michael SM, Conversion, Empowerment, and Social Transformation, 2005.

5

Conversion Movements in India Among Mahars

Introduction

Religious conversion has become the subject of passionate debate in contemporary India. From the early 20th century onwards, it has surfaced again and again in the political realm, in the media and in the courts. During the last few decades the dispute has attained a new climax in the plethora of newspapers, journals, and books whose pages have been devoted to the question of conversion (Claerhout and Roover, 2005).

The phenomenon of religious conversion is immensely complex and varied and has been taking place all through history. Accounts of individual and group conversions that have come down to us from early days are repeated even today. All the same, this topic of religious conversion is an emotional and a sensitive one in the given political scenario of contemporary India (Michael, 1998).

The positions in the dispute are clear. On the one hand, there are those who plead for a ban on conversion, because it disturbs the social peace in plural India. This group consists mainly of Hindus. The aversion towards the proselytizing drive of Christianity and Islam is widespread among various Hindu groups – from the radical spokesmen of the Sangh parivar to the moderate Gandhians. On the other hand, there are those who argue that conversion is a fundamental human right, which should be protected in any democracy. Generally, the proponents of the right to conversion are Christians and Secularists. In spite of the clarity of these two positions, which have remained unchanged throughout the previous century, the debate has not seen significant progress. The discussions are still governed by feelings of mutual incomprehension, unease, and resentment. The participants in the debate seem to agree on one thing only: the gap between the different views on conversion is unbridgeable (Claerhout and Roover, 2005).

Sociologically, conversion is a process of change from one religion to another. The motive for a change of religion may be due to economic, social or religious reasons. Conversion could be seen as a way to gain protection, education and status. Especially in India, it has remained something that could be used by the individual to move forward in society, above all, through education and by a group to free themselves from inherited shackles, to better themselves and their children. These shackles might be those of caste, of illiteracy of economic slavery, of psychological apathy, of disease or of a religion of fears and taboos. But all these factors are always interlinked and not one of them should be considered in isolation (Michael, 1998).

Initially, conversion was not merely a religious act, but, also a search for a new social identity. Many dalits and tribals have thereby sought a religious response of conversion as a mode of upward social mobility (*Ibid*, 1998).

If a person wants to convert himself or herself to another religion as a matter of individual choice or freedom of conscience, there is no ambiguity that the Constitution of India gives every person such a right. However, conversion can be taken as a mission by religious zealots often with fixed targets to be achieved. Such religious zealots, more often than not, in their enthusiasm to achieve targets have propagated not only superiority of one's own religion, but also inferiority of other's religion, often accompanied with derogatory remarks about the other's religion. Religion being a sensitive subject for the faithful, any derogatory remarks has the potential to create tense atmosphere and often leads to outbreak of violence (see Engineer, 2003).

The Indian Constitution, as every democracy should, sees conversions matter of freedom of conscience. Freedom to convert a person from one religion to another has not been expressly specified in the Indian Constitution. It is a derivative right flowing from right to freely profess, practice and propagate religion of one's choice, an important fundamental and democratic right given to every person under **Article 25** of the Indian Constitution. Article 25 of the Constitution is as under:

Article 25: Freedom of Conscience and free profession, practice and propagation of religion:

1. Subject to public order, mortality and health and to the other provisions of this Part, all persons are equally entitled to freedom of conscience and the right to freely profess, practice and propagate religion.

2. Nothing in this article shall affect the operation of any existing law or prevent the State from making any law –

a. regulating or restricting any economic, financial, political or other secular activity which may be associated with religious practice;

b. Providing for social welfare and reform or the throwing open of Hindu religious institutions of a public character to all classes and sections of Hindus (*Ibid*, 2003).

It has been argued that right to propagate one's religion includes right to convert. Certain Christian sects believe it is their religious duty to convert others to their religion and freedom to freely practice and profess their religion would be meaningless without right to convert people of other faiths to Christianity. However, others have equally vehemently argued that the meaning of right to propagate cannot be stretched to mean right to convert. If that is the intention, right to convert would have found mention in the Constitution (*Ibid*, 2003).

Unable to find support from the Constitutional provisions for their demand of banning conversions, Sangh Parivar have been exerting themselves to achieve through legislation what the Constitution does not provide. One way of getting closer to their achieving their demand is to pass legislations to penalize conversions.

Further, the phenomenon of conversion, so far, is subjected to serious misunderstandings, misinformation and even malicious propaganda. Most stories of proselytization are spread by interested parties with a view to malign minority communities. The whole question is also highly politicized (Michael, 1998).

Hence, in order to avoid the biases of emotion and prejudice, it is necessary to study this topic objectively and dispassionately. Conversion is never an isolated event. When we study the significant conversion movements in India, we should understand the manifold factors which are operative in them, and also the potential of social change in religion (*Ibid*, 1998).

The 'scientific' study of religious conversion has been approached from various perspectives: historical, sociological, psychological and phenomenological.

Factors preceding conversion, as identified by these approaches include socio-political upheavals, psychic factors of anguish, turmoil, despair, conflict and guilt and self-realization. No single approach is adequate for a comprehensive view of the complex nature of conversion (*Ibid.*, 1998).

However, an anthropological approach is 'multi-disciplinary' and comprehensive consisting of historical and comparative methods. Therefore, the phenomenon of religious conversion in India can be looked at from an anthropological perspective.

There is a need to study the phenomenon of conversion from an anthropological perspective, because in India this has been looked at partially either from political or economic or social dimensions. While the above aspects of human behaviour may shed light in understanding the complex process of conversion in human history, this knowledge will only be partial if it is not viewed holistically or in its totality. An anthropological approach to a reality tends to be holistic. It also takes into consideration both the temporal and spatial dimensions of human beings in a culture (*Ibid*, 1998).

The purpose and significance of this study is to bring out the on-going controversy and debate on the issue of conversion. I have undertaken the stances of both the groups: pro-conversion and anti-conversion; and have tried to reach a conclusion as in whether conversion is good or bad and whether it should be banned or not? Besides, it is with the purpose of providing telescopic views of the literature pertaining to such questions that I undertook this research study, as diverse and contrast views are juxtaposed here. All these connect in different ways with one common theme— The Question of Conversion. What I have tried to do is to put forward certain fundamental aspects of 'conversion' and issues related to it.

Coming to methodology, my study mainly depends on secondary sources that include literature produced on this theme, though I have also conducted a small research as to find out various views on issues regarding conversion. This is done by the survey method, wherein the respondents answered to a questionnaire. My focus has been on qualitative data, rather than on quantitative data.

With regards to the chapter scheme, the forth-coming chapter 'Two Opposing Views on Conversion' deals with the contrasting views of Gandhi and Ambedkar and the arguments they put forth for pro/anti conversion. The next chapter 'How Hindus and Christians view Conversion: An Analysis' deals with two different set of beliefs and perception of the Hindus and Christians; and how and why they refer to two different objects while talking about religion. The subsequent chapter 'Relevance of Conversion in changing Social Status of the Converts' deals with how the socio-economic status of the converts changes, if at all, in the situations that confront them after conversion. After these, the next chapter 'Research Report' includes the findings of the research carried out, wherein a sample of 20 was taken, to find out the perceptions of the people with regards to conversion. Finally, I have concluded this study by putting forth my observations and understanding.

It is hoped that the following chapters will provide important ways of looking at how religion and conversion may be located in the fabric of contemporary Indian society.

References and Bibliography

Dhananjay Keer, Dr. Ambedkars Life and Mission, Popular Prakashan Mumbai, 1971.

Elenaor Zelliot, From Untouchables to Dalits: Essays on the Ambedkar Movement, Manohar Publishers and Distributors, New Delhi, 1996.

Gail Omvedt, Dalits and the Democratic Revolution, Sage Publication India Pvt. Ltd, 1994.)

Michael Mahar J., The Untouchables in Contemporary India, Rawat Publication, 1998.

Dahiwale, S.M. (ed.), Understanding Indian Society-A Non-Brahmanic Perspective, Rawat Publications Jaipur and New Delhi.

Rowena Robinson, Sathianathan Clarke (ed.), Religious Conversion in India-Modes, Motivations, and Meanings, Oxford University Press, 2003.

Dr. B. R. Ambedkar, "Writings and speeches" The Education Department Govt. of Maharashtra, Mumbai, 1987.

Traude Pillai Vetschera, The Mahar-A study of their Culture, Religion and Socio-economic Life, Inter cultural Publication (p) Ltd., New Delhi.

Vasant Moon, Growing up Untouchables in India-A Dalit Autobiography, Vipul Publications, New Delhi.

K.N.Kadam, The Meaning of Ambedkarite Conversion to Buddhism and Other Essays, Popular Prakashan, Mumbai, 1997.

Gail Omvedt, Dhamma Diksha: Ambedkar's Turn to Buddhism (National Seminar on Reconstructing Indian Society; Dr. B. R. Ambedkar Conversion to Buddhism.

Gopal Guru, Hindusation of Ambedkar in Maharashtra, Economic and Political Weekly, 16 Feb., 1991.

O.D. Heggade, Economic Thought of Dr. B. R. Ambedkar, Mohit Publication, New Delhi.

6
Mahar Conversion to Christianity

Arrival of Christianity in the First Century

The conversion of Mahars to Christianity by the missionary in Maharashtra can be traced from 1841, because in 1841 the first Mahar got converted to Christianity in Ahmednagar. Prior to this the record says, that the Apostle came to Maharashtra. The Apostle Bartholomew one of the twelve disciples of Jesus had a short ministry in the Kalyan area of the west coast He lived for hardly seven years in India during which time he had to face a very hostile environment. He came around 55 A.D. (Ebe Sunder Raj 1998:6). Apostle Bartholomew is the first, Apostle in Western India, Kalyan near Mumbai and the second in India. Thereafter various Christian missionary bands arrived in Maharashtra. So the mission of Christ was brought by the beginning of the first century, in Maharashtra with the arrival of Apostle Bortholomew.

The Arrival of Missionaries in Mumbai and Ahmednagar

In Mumbai, the arrival of the Protestant Missionaries was on "February 11, 1813". According to Sherring (1885:231) there were, "two American men and one American lady who entered Bombay Harbor and pledged to preach the Gospel in India. Their names were Gordon Hall, Samuel Nott and Roxana Nott. They were the first Protestant missionaries in Western India." (Ashley Brown W. 1937:131)

There were different missionary bands who were working among the dalits. It must have been very difficult to work in the caste-rigid society. In such a caste frame work, these foreign missionaries must have not seen, heard or observed about the rigidity of caste system, Dr. Ambedkar writes that "Untouchability among Hindus is thus a unique phenomenon, unknown to humanity in other parts of the world" (1990:267). So working with Mahars must have been a new experience to them when they started their work to preach the Gospel. In this atmosphere the missionaries have travelled extensively to the remote places and established their mission stations. In 1817 there were two English Methodist missionaries. In 1819 the first missionary of the Anglican Church arrived. In 1823 the first missionary of the Scottish Mission and in 1841 the first Irish Presbyterian missionaries arrived in Mumbai (Mathew Lederie 1976:38). Up to 1831, there were 13 gents and 14 ladies came to India (Adv. Santhosh Salvi 2004:14). The branch of American Marathi Mission was opened in 1831. The first Protestant Christian mission was opened in Ahmadnagar District, the heartland of Mahars in 1831 (Gazetteer Ahmadnagar 1976: 260). The American Marathi Mission in Western India did its magnificent work at Ahmednagar and its outstations. More then 130 missionaries of this Society served in Western India during the century in evangelistic, educational, medical and industrial work (W. Ashley Brown 132).

The Catholic mission in Ahmadnagar traces back to the arrival of Jesuit missionaries in this region. "A mission among the Mahars had been opened by the Jesuits at Ahmednagar in 1878. Mission Centers followed at Kendal in 1879; in Valan in 1889; in Sanguine in 1892. By the time, the number of Catholic Mahars had risen to 1,000 under Fr. Marcel D' Souza, Fr. Weishaupt, S.J. and Fr. Kraeig, S.J." (Francis Moget MSFS, 1990:219). On 28, July 1892 Fr. Weishaupt S.J came to Sangamner. In seven years he had converted sixteen hundred Mahars (Joseph Grabrial Jadhav 1994:7; Sir. D.E. Wacha, 1920:644, 645).

The Charter Act of 1813

Though the missionaries were already present in India, the official permission to preach the Gospel was only given when the Charter was passed in the House of Commons. "The Clause was inserted in The Charter Act on 2nd July 1813 by 54 votes to 32, in the House of Commons (S. M. Pathak 1967:24) thus, "After the passing of the Charter Act of 1813, Maharashtra was indeed the first place in India where the Protestant Missionary movement was launched in the early 19th century" (M. D. David 2001: 27). "By the revision of the Charter of the Company in 1813, an ecclesiastical establishment in India supported by the government was funded and the missionaries were freely allowed to come to India in large numbers. A number of measures for legal and social reforms were introduced by the government during the period 1829-1857" (T. V. Philip 1987: 21). The Charter of 1813 contained the provision that "sufficient facilities should be afforded by law, for the purpose of accomplishing those benevolent designs', i.e., the introduction among the inhabitants of India of 'useful knowledge and religious and moral improvement" (Hough J. 1845:193). John Wilson's statement of the facts, states that, "The American missionaries first came to Bombay in 1813; but the Whole of the New Testament in Marathee has been published by the Serampore missionaries in 1811. Dr. Robert Drummond published his grammar and glossary of the Gujarati and Marathi language at the Bombay Courier Press in 1808. Dr. Carey published his Marathi grammar and dictionary at Serampore 1810. All these helps were enjoyed by the American missionaries; and though they are now accessible to all students and missionaries, we would be guilty of ingratitude to those who furnished them if we overlook them. *Suum cuique tribue* should ever be our moot" (George Smith 1879:34, 35). Thus the year 1813, can be said as the beginning of the age of *modern mission*. Thus the missionary got the permission to spread the gospel.

Mahar Mission

These missionaries particularly in Maharashtra worked among the lower castes, but their major work was with Mahars. They worked actually in a particular pocket, out of 36 Jilas they mainly worked in Ahmednagar district Shrirampur, Rahuri, Sangamner, Rohit in Aurangabad district; Vaijapur and Ganagpur and other districts in Nasik; Sholapur, Kolaphur, Jalna, and Pune. No doubt, apart from Mahars, the other untouchables like Mangs, Chambhar too got converted.[1] But there were a number of upper castes also who got converted, but not as large as it has taken place in South India. The missionary not only converted people to the Christian faith but they have done good humanitarian work also. They have established schools, colleges, hospitals, Churches, orphanages, leprosy asylum and skilled job training centers etc. which led them to conversion.

"In Ahmednagar, the first Mahar was converted" (David M.D 2001:58). "On May 30, 1841 Bhagobaa Power Kinikar, took baptism from Dr, Henry Fairbank (P. D. Savarkar, 1985:91). His brother Yeshoba was baptized on October 6, 1844 (P. D. Savarkar, 1985:92). In Nasik district "in 1897, including small communities at Devlali, Igatpuri, Vadala, Pathardi and Makhakalabad, the membership of Christians was 380. In that year 12 adults and 39 children were baptized. Of the twelve adults, one was a Kunbi, one a Sonar and the rest Mahars" (Gazetteer 1975:268).

The Missionaries with the native assistants used to go to remote villages to preach the gospel and got the good result by the influence of native assistants, the record says that, "Of the Mahars who were admitted to the Church during the year, one, a man named Kandoo about 35 years of age who appears more than usually intelligent has been employed in the work of going round, with the other native assistants, to make known the truth. Thus we have now five young men, as native assistants, viz. A.F. Fonceca, Naryan, Haripunt, Ramkurshna, and Marootee, and also two older men Bhagoo and Kandoo, from among the Mahars, prepared to labour particularly among the people of their caste. With the assistance of these latter, we can generally get around us, when we visit the village; large congregation of Mahars in some respects the most interesting class we can address. In sending out our native assistants to the villages we always send one of these latter, with one or more of the former and we find great advantage in doing so." (OCS May 1843:81). The method adopted

---

[1] See the Foot Note at the end of the Chapter to see the Record on Christian Conversions.

by the missionary to preach the gospel, first they used to send the native people who have been trained, so it was very easy to preach to the new people and they turned towards the gospel.

The conversions of Mahar and the Mangs did not have so many disadvantages after becoming Christians, "By becoming Christians they do not lose their rights to their patrimonial inheritance, and they are no subject to those annoyances which, in the case of a person of a higher caste, render it almost impossible for him to live among his own people after he becomes a Christian. This probably is one cause why the gospel has made so much greater impression on the Mahars than on others. They can pursue their accustomed avocations without any interruptions. But were a poor cultivator to become a Christian we know not what he could do to attain a livelihood, unless we furnish him with employment" (M. D. David 1980:53). Apart from these basic needs they were also given some monetary help and to those who need in kind, they were also full filled so that large a number of Mahars got converted to Christianity.

The missionaries certainly had good intentions when they started their work among the downtrodden of Maharashtra, among whom the Mahars were not only the most numerous, but in many ways, the most interesting. Ernest Hull, author of the Bombay mission History considered the conversion to Christianity as the Mahars' only way to free themselves from a traditional system of suppression from which they could escape by no efforts of their own. He thought, "their pitiable and hopeless condition called for some effectual measures from outside to ameliorate and raise them" (Hull, 1930:463).

Even today, the Mahars often do not hide the fact that for them being Christian is very much connected with the idea of receiving material help from the missionaries. Mahars say; "The missionaries have deceived us. They made us Christians, and then they went away, now nobody is there to look after us and the government does not help us any more either."

The Indian government provides certain facilities for communities, which fall under the definition of Scheduled Castes. Those Mahars, who call themselves Hindus, are free to enjoy all those facilities, but Christians are not. For the 'Constitution (Scheduled Castes) Order, 1950' holds under point 3 that "...no person who professes a religion different from the Hindu or Sikh religion shall be deemed to be a member of a Scheduled Caste." Thus the Mahar Christians enjoy none of the benefits of the 'backward ' classes, like educational concessions (scholarships and free coaching classes, a large number of free places in boarding schools, and reserved places in colleges), reserved government jobs and seats in state and central government institutions.

India has seen conversion backed by political regimes or worked as forms of resistance to particular social and political regimes. We could think of sixteenth century Catholicism in Goa or modern Buddhism as instances of the different modes. India has seen both mass and individual conversion as well as conversions bolstered by varying degrees of duress and those caught in moments of dialogue and religious interchange. A point that perhaps needs some stress is that none of these differences may be easily mapped on to the divide between "insider" and "outsider" religions. At different moments of time and in different contexts, various traditions and denominations have worked in remarkably different ways.

Modes of witness and conversion to Christianity too have several and diverse. Mass conversion of Dalits, low castes and some tribal communities during the period of British colonial rule may be, in part, read as one effort among many others to come to terms with the multiple dislocations being experienced by different groups as a result of the radical social and economic shift occasioned by colonialism. The British did not back conversion with force and such movements were certainly attempts by groups to gain in social mobility, self-respect and dignity. While in Goa mass conversion across all castes took place under the shadow of a regime that saw itself both as a political and religious entity, there was also to be detected an element of collusion between the state and the high castes.

In this matter we would like to quote some questions raised by Dr. B. R. Ambedkar,

1. What has Christianity achieved by way of changing the mentality of the converts?

2. Has the untouchable converts risen to the status of the touchable?

3. Have touchable and untouchables discarded caste?

4. Have they ceased to worship their old pagan God or to adhere to their pagan superstitions?

We must say that converts have failed to reject their faith in the caste system. We came across a religious procession of Catholic Christian where the Dalit Christians were beating the drums with wooden crosses in their hands walking in front, taking every precaution of maintaining a certain distance from the mainstream.

On enquiry it was told that beating drums is the occupation of the Dalits only, be they Hindus or Christians. So conversion we may note did not change their caste profession. Another thing is that when we look at the matrimonial advertisements, we find that most of them specifically look at the pre-conversion caste and seek to marry in the same caste. A Christian converts such as a "Maratha Christian bride" wishes to seek a Maratha Christian bridegroom.

5. Publication of Missionaries

To preach the gospel among the natives the different missionaries have their own publication. "The first Christian Tract that was printed in the Marathi language was A Scripture Tract", probably one of those prepared by Gordon Hall. It consisted of eight pages, and was issued from the press on 10th March 1817, the edition consisted of 1500 copies. This was the beginning of the Marathi literature (S. M. Pinge 1960: 236). *The Oriental Christian Spectator* was started by the Scottish Missionary Society on 1830 and John Wilson was its editor; **Dynanodaya**, by Rev. Henry Ballantine, a Protestant American missionary (Camil Parkhe 2003:117).

Dynanodaya, was launched by these missionaries in 1842, in Ahmadnagar, Its cost was two anna i.e. 12 paise, this organ was launched specifically to "counter act the influence of native Papers conducted by bigoted Hindu or secret infidels who were constantly reviling Christianity and demanding proofs of its truth" (Dynanodaya 15. January 1, 1956).

Niropya was started in April 1903 in Kendal Valan by a Catholic missionary from Germany, Father Henry Doring in Marathi (Camil Parkhe 2003:117). The publications helped the missionary to reach the common people and spread the message of The Bible and know their activities. Pandit Jawaharlal Nehru writes, "The printing of books and newspapers broke the hold on classics and immediately prose literatures in the provincial languages began to develop. The early Christian missionaries, especially of the Baptist Mission of Serampur, helped in the process greatly. The first private printing presses were established by them, and their efforts to translate the Bible into the prose version of the Indian languages met with considerable success. There was no difficulty in dealing with the well-known and established languages, but the missionaries went further and tackled some of the minor and undeveloped languages and gave them shape and form, compiling grammars and dictionaries for them. They even laboured at the dialects of the primitive hill and forest tribes and reduced them in writing" (J. Nehru 1946: 318). These publications helped them to establish themselves in the new converts and preach the gospel through their publications. Also it was to counter attack the natives who used to oppose them.

The Mahars who have been converted to Christianity were called as Mahar Christians they felt as insulted or humiliated by calling themselves as Mahar Christians so there was an exchange of thoughts as to what to call them the word coined was as "Marathi Christi" which they use even today.

Birth of Marathi Kirtan and Bhakti Songs

The Annual Conference of Marathi Mission at Ahmednagar was held on October 26, 1861 where Rev. Vishunupanth Karmarkar sang the first Bhakti song. It was said to be the birth of Marathi Bhakti song on that day, and also on 31 October 1862 he started to give Kirtans (Sunil Adav. 2003: 209-210). Krihnaro Sangle of Ahmednagar composed Marathi lyrics in Indian metre and set to Indian ragas; a collection of them called *Gayanamrit* published in 1867 (C.B. Firth 2000:249).

The first Christi Samaj Marathi Sahitya Sammelan held at Sharanpur, Nasik, on April 18 and 19, 1927 (Sunil Adav 2003:209, 210). The first Dalit Christi Sahitya Sammelan was held at Ahmednagar on 26 and 24 May 1992 under the presidentship of Arvind Nirmal (Camil Parke 2003:85, 86).

The translation of The Bible in native language was done by William Carey in the year 1804 (2003:85, 86). But the whole of the New Testament in Marathi had been published by the Serampore missionaries in 1811" (George Smith 1979:34).

Impact of Education by Missionaries

The schools and colleges they established had an important role, because this was a new type of education, which was not like the traditional education. The knowledge they imparted as Science, Geography and literature and the skilled job training, made a lot of impact on the Indian masses. They also established schools in Maharwada. "The American Mission in Ahmednagar, The Marathi School was started in 1835" (OSC 1836.364; R. Tucker1980/81:137). Mahatma Jotirao Phooley opened the first primary school in Pune for Untouchable girls in 1848 (Sharad Patil 2005:270). The progress of schooling enabled girls to be skilled job trainers, so they can earn their livelihood. There was a gap in Education among the Protestant and Catholics. Cristfar Shelke states that, "If we take survey of Maharashtra, we will find that there is a lot of progress of education among the Protestants. This is because from the beginning itself they were strongly in support of education and got educated. There were different missionaries from Europe and America. From their fund, they made their progress. The community that we see today is from the urban area and cities, their percentage must be 10 percent rest 90 percent people are still in the villages. The Catholic community had not made much propagation on education, the Societies, Sanyasi, Dharma gurus and Sisters, because of funds from Europe and American. But it was among few families. Because they were scattered there was progress (Niropya 1978:261) (translation from Marathi).

Conclusion

Apart from the early contacts, proper 'Christian missionary work' in India began with the advent of the Portuguese who arrived in 1498 "to embrace Christianity as an escape from economic exploitation and social degradation. **"Their real purpose of religious conversion is not the change to a better religion, but the improvement of their economic or social situation,"** says Fuchs (*op.cit.*, 147). He cites the example of Oceania and Africa, where people change their religion to Islam or Christianity because adherence to their old tribal religion makes them appear backward and old-fashioned. He mentions tribes in Chotanagpur and Assam, who embraced Christianity in great numbers because they found their tribal religions inadequate, and also because they desired to benefit by the education and general cultural progress which the Christian missionaries offered them if they turned Christian.

Today Christians are the third major religious community in the order of numerical strength in India, comprising about 2.6 percent of the total population. The strongholds of the Christians are in the states of Kerala, Tamil Nadu and Andhra Pradesh, where we find more than sixty per cent of the total Christian population. Maharashtra has only 5.04 percent of the Christians living in India.

Mission work in Maharashtra started in 1813 when a group of missionaries of the American Board of Foreign Missions 'America's oldest Protestant Missionary Society, landed at Bombay.

In many parts of Maharashtra' the missionaries of the American Marathi Mission were the first to start work.

Christianity in Mumbai, associated with Western traditions and names, has gradually been indianised, with a growing number of Christians in the city preferring to retain not just Indian names and attire but also their own culture while adopting Christ as their savior.

Of the thousand odd Protestant church services that take place every Sunday in Mumbai, only around 150 services are in English, the rest are in Indian languages, ranging from Marathi to Malayalam and from Gujarati to Telgu, say church sources.

According to Abraham Mathai, general secretary, All Indian Christian Council, of the seven lakh Christians in the city over 70 percent have retained Indian names and surnames as well as their own culture. "Christianity in India is truly Indian, represented by people from different groups. It's an all-inclusive faith that has accepted and embraced the Gaikwads, the Kalyanpurs, the Patels, the Sunderraos and the Muthuswamys," he said.

The Prabhu Yeshu Janmotsav, an annual Christian musical festival, held on Girgaum Chowpatty drew more than 30,000 devotees from across the city. Nearly all of them defied the conventional image of Christians in the city. Clad in saris and salwar kameezes, many of the women came from traditional Maharashtrian homes and had adopted Christianity after being introduced to the religion by a neighbor, friend or relative. While many had formally converted to Christianity, there were those who simply went to church every week.

Dyaneshwar Soholkar, who is part of the Methodist Church, comes from a Brahmin family from Vidarbha. "My father converted to Christianity after reading a lot of Christian literature. However we have not forsaken our Maharashtrian culture and traditions," he said. Soholkar and his family celebrate Christmas just the way a Maharashtrian celebrates Diwali. "We even celebrate marriages with haldi and mangalsutras the way a

Maharashtrian does, except that they are held in church," he continued.

Most Maharashtrians who turn to Christianity, though, become Protestants. The majority of Catholics are Goans and Mangalorians with Portuguese surnames. "However a small number of Catholics amongst the Goans and Mangalorians are also reverting back to their Indian family names while retaining their belief in Christianity," said Fr. Anthony Charanghat, director of the Catholic Communications of the Archdiocese of Bombay.

This Indianised section of Christian society cuts across all classes. For instance, celebrated cricketer Vinod Kambli has been brought up in a family that believes in Jesus Christ as well as Sai Baba. Former Indian skipper Chandu Borde was born into a Maharashtrian Christian family in Pune. "A lot of Maharashtrian Punekars are devout Christians," he said.

Gul Kripalani, chairman of the international Trade Committee of the Indian Merchant's Chamber and president of the Rotary Club of Bombay, who adopted Christianity over two decades ago feels that Christianity is not names and surnames but about one's relationship with God and one's belief in Christ.

On the other end of the spectrum are those from poor families who have been denied education and a life of dignity and turn to Christianity for salvation.

Forty-year-old Laxmi Mane, a neo-Buddhist Maharashtrian slum dweller from Worli, knows little about her own religion or culture. She has been going to church for the last five years, as she feels her belief in Christ has helped her through a series of misfortunes that rocked her life such as the death of her husband, a major eye operation, her son's illness and continuous harassment from her brother-in-law. "**This God stands up for me**," she said,

A woman from the same chawl nearly committed suicide on Worli seaface when her husband left her for another woman, but was pulled back by her neighbors, who introduced her to Christianity. Since then, she says her burdens have lightened *(The*

Times of India dated 26 December 2006).

Church historians are generally agreed that Protestant churches succeeded far better in wiping out caste distinctions among fokkowers largely because they made a concerted effort to break all tied with a "pagan", Hinduism, and anything that smacked of Hindu practices was denounced as superstitious.

The Catholics were less successful in eradicating caste consciousness. Webster (1999:75) notes that Roman Catholics took an organic view of caste, treating it as part of Indian social stratification and till recently have chosen to work within its constraints *(Journeys to Freedom-Dalit Narratives – Fernando Franco, Jyotsna Macwan, Suguna Ramanathan).*

On the positive side, conversion movement represented an effort on the part of the Dalits to gain dignity, self-respect and the ability to choose their own dignity for themselves and their social group (*Ibid.*, 2005).

However, even now, the attitude of the upper castes and priests towards untouchables has not changed much. For example, the recent earthquake of January 26, 2001, killed thousands and rendered thousands homeless in Gujarat. But, even in this disastrous situation, the caste barriers remained firmly up. The lower castes and Dalits were not allowed to use the tents because of caste prejudices (*Ibid.*, 2005).

Lancy Lobo, in her article on "Brahmanical Social Order and Christianity in India", has tried to show how Christianity, the only rival intellectual to the traditional Brahmanical order, in bargain, has internalized some elements of the Brahmanical order (Lobo, 2005).

Over a period of time, the Dalits Christians found that their visions of seeking equality within the Church were not totally realized. Studies show that the Church and its resources dominated by the upper-caste Christians and its clergy hardly paid any attention to the felt needs of Dalits. Satisfaction of the spiritual needs alone was not sufficient. The Dalit question has brought to the surface the internal contradictions of Christianity in India (*Ibid.*, 2005).

Nearly, 50 percent of India's Christians are Dalits, ex-untouchables. Christian Dalit issue cannot be considered in isolation from those of non-Christian Dalits. Such issues relate to religious changes leading to socioeconomic mobility, identity, differentiation, stratification, urge for self-determination, and movement towards viable, sustainable communities, reservation and discrimination as well as issues relating to Dalit women, the official church and its personnel (*Ibid.*, 2005).

1. Ambedkar said in his conversion speech," Choose any religion which gives you equality of status and treatment" (*Ibid.*, 188). Group conversions to Christianity by Dalits should be seen from this point of view. The Dalits saw visions of equality in Christianity. Did the Christian Dalits achieve their visions? It is more NO than YES for the following reasons: Christian Dalits have faced four-fold discrimination:

a. *From the upper castes:* Most Dalits were economically dependent on the upper castes and on becoming Christian; there was no significant change in their economic status. The upper castes have not conceded any change. At the most, they call the Christian Dalits *sudhrela* or civilized, educated Dalits.

b. *From the Church:* The official Church has also discriminated against Dalit Christians. They are called at best neo-Christians. There are instances in some places in India of Dalit Christian being assigned a separate place during religious services, separate burial grounds, less decision making power in church matters, and facing discrimination in their recruitment for the clergy.

c. *From the State:* The state has discriminated against the Christian Dalits in the sense that anyone reverting to the Hindu religion automatically becomes eligible for the reservation benefits that are available foe scheduled castes. The argument is that Christianity, unlike Hinduism, has no caste. However, the State has granted reservations to Dalit converts to Sikhism and, later (1990), to Buddhist, but withheld it from Dalit converts to Islam and Christianity. In some states, Christian Dalits are placed in OBC category. For instance, in Gujarat, they are labeled as "Gujarati Christi". It should be stated that many religions such as Christianity, Sikhism and Islam do not believe in caste, but Sikhs, Muslims and Christians have castes. Most of the converts were from Hinduism and have not been able to shed their caste. And yet the State has thought it proper to give affirmative action to Sikh and Buddhist Dalits, but not to Christian Dalits. Perhaps political expediency has played a role in this.

d. *Against Dalit Christian as they did with non-Christian Dalits:* Non-Christian Dalits, too, discriminate against the Christian Dalits. The former are worried about encroachment by Christian Dalits on their reservation benefits. Cultural difference are also creeping in among Christian and non-Christian Dalits (*Ibid.*, 2005).

Besides, Christian Dalits have experienced partial changes. A prefix or suffix has been added to the caste tag, e.g. Christi Mahar, Wankar Christi, and so on. In the case of the Dalit Wankar caste, a comparative study shows that a creamy layer has emerged from among the Wankar Christi who is living in towns and cities, while the masses have remained in the rural areas without any socioeconomic change. However, the Christi Wankar have better literacy than the Hindu Wankars. There is some change in the living conditions and etiquette, too, among the Christi Wankars (*Ibid.*, 2005).

Very few Christian Dalits have reverted to Hindu SC status to avail of reservation benefits. Most have opted to remain Christian despite a significant lack of change of economic status. This shows that the new identity of Christian has significance and made a difference, though not to their satisfaction. One can say that the disabilities that Hindu Dalits faced in Hinduism are greater than those the Christian Dalits face in Christianity (*Ibid.*, 2005).

Record of Conversion

16 June 2007

Sr. No	Place	No's of Converts	Date	Reference Prabhuddha Bharat, Bombay, Dated
1	Nagpur	3,80,000	14.10.56	Letter to Vilasinha
2	Chandrapur	3,00,000	16.10.1956	1.6.1957
3	Akola	2,000	17-30.10.56	1.6.1957
4	Nagpur	5,000	10.11.1956	Mahabodhi Journal 1956
5	Kamathi	500	10.11.1956	"
6	Ujjain	950	14.11.1956	"
7	Sinkhand	3000	14.11.1956	"
8	Dadar Chopati Mumbai	5,00 000	07.12.1956	29.12.56
9	Manmad	5000	12.12.1956	Mahabodhi Journal 1956
10	Amravti	3,00,000	14.12.1956	"
11	Nasik	1,00,000	16.12.1956	29.12.1956 P. Bharat
12	Poona	2,00,000	18.12.1956	Mahabodhi Journal 1956
13	Wardha	90,000	27.12.1956	"
14	Wardha	2,50,000	29.12.1956	"
15	Manmad	15,000	30.12.1956	"
16	Ahmednagar	25,000	14.01.1957	Doubtful
17	Purandare Stadium Mumbai	5,00,000	26.01.1957	9.2.1957
18	Nimona	5,000	14.2.1957	23.2.1957
19	Malinagar	5.000	18.2.1956	9.3.1957
20	Akluj	2,000	18.2.1957	9.3.1957
21	Shripur	3,000	19.2.1957	9.3.1957

Contd...

22	Ambarnath (Thane)	5,000	13.4.1957	1.6.1957
23	Sholapur	20,000	16.4.1957	1.6.1957
24	Jalgaon	500	16.4.1957	1.6.1957
25	Busawal	1,000	17.41957	1.6.1957
26	Mansal Bain	*	23.4.1957	25.5.1957
27	Chandur Bazar	1,50,000	23.4.1957	25.5.1957
28	Trod (Bhandara)	10,000	24.4.1957	1.6.1957
29	Pulgaon (Wardha)	15,000	25.4.1957	1.6.1957
30	Sarand & others	1,000	28.4.1957	25.5.1957
31	Dehu	*	5.5.1957	25.5.1957
32	Wagholi (Chanda)	1,000	10.5.1957	13.7.1957
33	Poona	25,000	12.5.1957	1.6.1957
35	Triodi	10,000	15.5.1957	8.6.1957
36	Junnar (Poona)	4,000	17.5.1957	13.7.1957
37	Pipalvandi (Poona)	*	18.5.1957	13.7.1957
38	Borgaon (Chanda)	5,000	18.5.1957	13.7.1957
39	Dehuroad (Poona)	5,000	19.5.1957	15.6.1957
40	Nanda (Nagpur)	3,000	19.5.1957	8.6.1957
41	Manchar & other places (Poona)	2,000	19-20.5.1957	8.6.1957
42	Khadki	30,000	20.5.1957	15.6.1957
43	Devhali (Bhandara)	*	21.5.1957	1.6.1957
44	Aurangabad	6,000	21.5.1957	8.6.1957
45	Dhamnad	1,500	21.5.1957	8.6.1957

Contd...

46	Tumsar (Bhandara)	5,000	22.5.1957	1.6.1957
47	Ahmednagar	*	22.5.1957	1.6.1957
48	Sillod (Aurangabad)	15,000	22.5.1957	8.6.1957
49	Purna (Marathwada)	20,000	23.5.1957	8.6.1957
50	Karegaon & Kinhai (Satara)	10,000	23-24.5.1957	8.6.1957
51	Hingoli (Marathwada)	10,000	24.5.1957	8.6.1957
52	Wai (Satara)	15,000	25.5.1957	8.6.1957
53	Homgaon (Taluq Javali)	2,000	26.5.1957	8.6.1957
54	Medhe (Sholapur)	2,500	26.5.1957	8.6.1957
55	Panchgani	5,000	26.5.1957	15.6.1957
56	Shriva (Satara)	2,000	28.5.1957	8.6.1957
57	Dahiwadi	5,000	29.5.1957	15.6.1957
58	400 Villages (Satara)	2,00,000	22.51957 to1.6.1957	29.6.1957
59	Karjat	1,000	2.6.1957	15.6.1957
60	Lonavala	10,000	2,6.1957	8.6.1957
61	Neral	500	2.6.1957	15.6.1957
62	Bembal (Chand)	1,000	4.6.1957	13.7.1957
63	Chopde	500	5.6.1957	6.7.1957
64	Akola	10,000	10.6.1957	15.6.1957
65	Vijapur (Aurangabad)	3,000	16.6.1957	6.7.1957
66	Mumbai	2,00,000	16.8.1957	8.7.1957
67	Rawalgaon			

*Personal record of Shri Devaram Maloji Kadam (Wagdekar), M. H. Board, Nehru Nagar, Kurla East, Mumbai.

Sr.	Konkan Region	Date	Bhikhu	President
1	Kankavli Center	31.3.1960	Sangarakshita	J.G. Bhatankar
2	Bhirwandea Center	1.4.1960	Shiorda Sagar	
3	Jambawadae Center	1.4.1960		
4	Kasal Center	2.4.1960		
5	Nandagao Center	3.4.1960		
6	Tela Bazar	4.4.1960		
7	Metabahva	5.4.1960		
8	Cowkae	6.4.1960		
9	Wadachepath	7.4.1960		
10	Chindar	8.4.1960		
11	Devgad	24.1.1961	Shiorda Sagar	
12	Kodal	25.1.1961		
13	Kalsi (Malvan Tal)	26.1.1961		
14	Malvan	27.1.1961		
15	Adavali	28.1.1961		
16	Ramgad	29.1.1961		
17	Nandagao	30.1.1961		

References and Bibliography

1. Edited by Vasant Moon, 1979: 6, 7 and 9. Dr. Babasaheb Ambedkar Writing and Speeches Vol 1. Education Department Government of Maharashtra Mumbai 400 032.

2. Compiled by, 1987:25 Dr. Babasaheb Ambedkar Writing and Speeches Vol 3, Education Department Government of Maharashtra Mumbai 400 032.

3. Swami Vireswaranda (Tr) 1972:128 Srimad Bhagvad-Gita Vivekananda Caste, Culture and Socialism, Advaita Ashrama, Delhi 1988:27-30.

4. Gandhi - Hindu Darma the Glory and the Abuses - Orient paperbacks-pp.10,11.

5.   M..K.Gandhi, 1921. Navjeevan.

6.   The Madras Mail 30th March 1980.

7.   Compiled by Vasant Moon 1987. Dr. Babasaheb Ambedkar Writing and Speeches Vol. 4 Education Department Government of Maharashtra Mumbai 400 032, p.157.

8.   Daw May Tin, 1990:125. The Dhammapada, Sri Satguru Publications Indelogical and Oriental Publisher Indian Book Centre Shakti Nagar Delhi.

9.   Narada Maha Thera 1973:171. The Buddha and His Teaching, Singapore Buddhist Meditation Center Singapore 0511.

10. Dr. B. R. Ambedkar Book III, Part V, Section IV 1984:216. Buddha and His Dhamma, Siddharth Publication Mumbai 400 023.

11. Edited by Vasant Moon, 1990:315. Dr. Babasaheb Ambedkar Writing and Speeches Vol. 7 Education Department Government of Maharashtra Mumbai 400 032.

12. Edited by C. Lamb and M. D. Bryant 1999:51. Religious conversion Cassell Wellington House, 125 Strand, London WC2R OBB.

13. Banerjee, B.N. 1983:393, 397. "A Hindu Attitude to conversions" International Review of Missions, No. 287.

14. Jnanadeepa Vol. 3 No.1 Jan. 2000.

7
Mahar Conversion to Buddhism

Introduction

Conversion movements of Mahars to Buddhism are completely related to the leadership of Dr. B. Ambedkar. He realized the worst aspect of Hindu hegemony that basic needs of human being was denied by the Brahmincal social system since ages, under the name of caste, to revolt against the system, he had launched different social protest movement at different times and different places for the essential needs of human life, which was denied to the untouchables, these social protest was transform in to social action by way of peaceful agitation for water which was called "Water Right Agitation"

"Maha-Sangharsha" Mahad Satyagraha

"Mahad had three water tanks, Viz., Cavadar Tale, Viresvar Tale and Hapus Tale. It is said there are 14 wells beneath Cavadhar Tale" [1] (Maharashtra State Gazetteers Kolaba District Revised Edition Government Press Bombay – 400 004 1964, p.854). At this Cavadhar Tale the non-violent agitation for the right to take water, was launched, against the ban for the use of water from the tank for untouchable by the orthodox Hindus.

The agitation was launched on March 20, 1927 which was the first step in the direction of creating confidence among the depressed class, this first movement which united the untouchable under his leadership, these was not only a protest movement of Untouchables it was an action program, where the water was drank, from the water tank, which was denied to untouchables.

Herewith this act he challenged the rigid caste social system and showed to the world what the social system is to get the basic human needs. This resulted in confrontation with caste Hindus and he won the legal battle. This attempt made to vindicate the right to take water from the public place.

In this context, the first conference of the Untouchable was held on 18th and 20th March 1927, in the Kolaba District, where 2,500 people attended the conference and there was great enthusiasm. Dr. Ambedkar exhorted them to fight for their rights, give up their dirty and vicious habits and rise to full manhood. On the next day 20th the Conference met at 9 in the morning, it took about 3 hours to do the business and pass the resolutions, including the "Declaration of the rights of a Hindu", which asserted the following principles:

i.   All Hindus have the same social status from birth.

ii.   The ultimate aim of political, economic or social changes should be to maintain intact the equal status of all Hindus.

iii. All power is derived from the people.

iv.   Every person is entitled as his birth right to liberty of action and speech as his birthright.

v.   Hindus can be deprived of their rights other than their birthrights only by law.

vi.   Law is not a command of an individual or a body of individuals. "Law is the people's prescription for change" (Compiled by Vasant Moon, BAWS, 1989:253, 254).

What are object of resolution he said "these resolutions was two fold. The one object to foster among the untouchables self respect and self-esteem. This was a minor object. The major object was to strike a blow at the Hindu Social order" (Vasant Moon, BAWS, 1989:258). He wanted to revolt against the Hindu Social order so he had organized a mass movement on a large scale.

The Bonfire of Manusmriti

The Manusmriti is composed of 2685 Verses (slocks) which governs the so called Brahminical social system. The Law book had code that how life should be lived, in public and in private by the Untouchables, Unapproachable, and Unseeable which made the life of these people miserable, to live like a human being, they were treated worse then an animal, these divine laws of the Hindus, has a pride in this doctrine, which discriminate, extort, conspiracy and, murder which was called in the name of system of Varna which later came into existence as caste. He called conference at Mahad, where the resolution was passed by the conference that, to burn the Manusmriti, he said: "Taking in to consideration the fact that the laws which are proclaimed in the name of Man, the Hindu law giver, and which are contained in the Mansmriti and which are recognized as the Code for the Hindus are insulting to persons of low caste, are calculated to deprive them of the rights of a human being and crush their personality. Comparing them in the light of the rights of men recognized all over the civilized world, this conference is of opinion that this Manusmriti is not entitled to any respect and is undeserving of being called a sacred book to show its deep and profound contempt for it, the Conference resolves to burn a copy thereof, at the end of the proceedings, as a protest against the system of social inequality it embodies in the guise of religion" (Edited by Vasant Moon, BAWS, 1989:254).

Manusmriti, the law book of Brahmincal Hindus, which had influenced the behavior of Hindus, on 25th December 1927 at 9 p.m. that the book Manusmriti was placed on a pyre, in a specially dug pit, in front of the pandal and publicly burnt by six Dalit Sadhus, the symbol of inequality, cruelty and injustice, a Bible of slavery, was burnt and thus started a rebel against Hinduism. "This act, as Keer states, was one of the greatest sacrilegious blows ever since the days of Luther upon the egoistic bigots, cusom-mongers and no changers on earth. December 25, 1927 is, a red-letter day in the annals of India as it was on this day Ambedkar burnt the old Smriti and demanded a new one in order to reshape the Hindu code governing the life of so vast a people. Mahad thus became the Wittenberg of India" (D. Keer, 1981, 101).

Ambedkar gave an interview in this matter and said to T.V Parvate in 1938, "The bonfire of Manusmriti was quite intentional. It was very cautious and drastic step, but was taken with a view of forcing the attention of caste Hindu. At intervals such drastic remedies are necessary. If you did not knock at the door, none opens it. It is not that all the parts of the Manusmriti are condemnable, that it does not contain good principles and that Manu himself was not a sociologist and was a mere fool. We made a bonfire of it because we view it as a symbol of injustice under which we have been crushed for centuries. Because of its teachings we have been ground down under despicable poverty and so we made the dash staked all, took our lives in our hands and performed the deed" (Parvate T.V., Mi Gethlelya Mulakhati (Marathi) pp.58.59), quoted in Keer Dr. Ambedkar L.M., 1981:106.

He states that these scriptures, "The rock on which the Hindu Social Order has been built is the Manusmriti. It is a part of the Hindu Scriptures and is therefore sacred to all Hindus. Being sacred it is infallible. Every Hindu believes in its sanctity and obeys its injunctions. Manu not only upholds caste and untouchability but also gives them a legal sanction. The burning of Manusmriti was a deed of great daring. It was an attack on the very citadel of Hinduism. The Manusmriti embodied the spirit of inequality which is at the base of Hindu life and thought just as the Bastille was the embodiment of the spirit of the Ancient regime in France. The burning of the Manu Smriti by the Untouchables at Mahad in 1927 is an event which has the same significance and importance in the history of the emancipation of the untouchables which the Fall of Bastille had in the liberation of the masses in France and Europe" (Compiled by Vasant Moon, BAWS, 1989:255). This act shows that they are no longer prepared to abide by the religious and ritual confinement, of the Brahmincal social order, thus the age long oppression and exploitation of the untouchable by the order of high caste, the Smriti deserved to be burnt long before, but the so called ghost was burnt by Dr. Ambedkar.

Jhotirao Poole was against the Brahmincal social order; he realized that it was the greatest stumbling block in the way of social change he too wanted that the Manusmriti to be burnt, whoever raised the banner of social equality, has condemned the Manusmriti, the divine law of Hindus.

Poole, writes in one of his akand, Manu is consigned to flame (Y.D Phadke, 1991:191). Poole writes and Dr. Ambedkar implemented. Poole established the Satya Shodak Samaj (Society for Truth Seekers) an organization which proclaimed the need to save the lower caste from the "hypocritical Brahmins and their opportunistic scripture."

The next agitation was for temple entry movement.

Kalaram Mandir Satyagraha: Right for Worship at Nasik

Kalaram Mandir Satyagraha was launched on, March 2, 1930, and the struggle was going on for five years seven months and eleven days this was the longest struggle of Ambedkar movement, this was to secure right for entry in to the temple of Rama. The struggle continued but it failed to bend the orthodox Hindus, so he taught to stop the agitation, he writes to one of his activist Dadasaheb alias Bhaurao Gaikwad letter dated 3.3.1934 "…I have no position in saying that such a move would be quite uncalled for and should not merely be suspended but should be stopped altogether. This may appear strange and surprising coming as it does from one who was the author of the Satyagraha. But I am afraid to declare this change of front. I did not launch the temple entry movement because I wanted the Depressed Class to become worshippers of idols which they were prevented from worshipping or because I believed that temple entry would make them equal members in and an integral part of the Hindu Society. So far as this aspect of the case is concerned I would advise the Depressed Class to insist upon a complete overhauling of Hindu Society and Hindu theology before they consent to become an integral part of Hindu Society. I started temple entry Satyagraha only because I felt that was the best way of energizing the Depressed Class and making them conscious of their position. As I believe I have achieved that purpose, I have no more use of temple entry. I want the Depressed Class to concentrate their energy and resources on politics and education and I hope that they will realize the importance of both. The sangarsha was not for worship but to make the untouchables conscious of their position" (Vijay Surwade, 1986:180), he stopped the temple entry movement.

The water right and temple right movements, these two movements gave the direction for the further course of action for the strategy or the turning point for the movement, by drinking the water from the tank they were not going to drink (nectar) or by temple entry all questions of untouchable were not going to solve, Dr. Ambedkar was aware, he wanted the movement to make them realize their strength of there united effort to achieve their goal and make them aware of their social position the agitation was to show them where they stand in this social system, and the agitation was to achieve the social equality and social justice with this act.

Analysis of Caste System – Annihilation of Caste: An undelivered Presidential Address

The Punjab Arya Samajist invited Dr. Babasaheb by the Jat Pat Todak Mandal to deliver the presidential address in their Annual Conference. The invitation was accepted; he prepared his well-documented address and got it printed on his own. But his revolutionary thoughts were unbearable to the members of the Mandal, the request was made to delete some controversial portion which was refused by him, the speech remains undelivered which took a shape of book called *Annihilation of Caste*.

With his opening title:

"Know Truth as Truth and Untruth as Untruth"
- BUDDHA
"He that WILL NOT reason is a bigot
He that CAN NOT reason is a fool
He that DARE NOT reason is a slave"
- H. DRUMMOND

Ambedkar asserts that, "Caste System is not merely a division of labour. *It is also a division of labourers* - it is a hierarchy in which the divisions of labourers are graded one above the other". He says further, "This division of labour is not spontaneous; it is not based on natural aptitudes". Further he writes, "The division of labour brought about by Caste System is a division based on choice. Individual sentiment, individual preference has no place in it. It is based on the dogma of predination" (BAWS, 1979:47:48). In this system there is no choice, once one takes birth, it is very hard to destroy the stigma in one who is born. His intention was to change the attitude, make them realize that they too are Hindu. In his address he wanted to make the Hindu religion a more dynamic one and also Ambedkar wanted to suggest the reforms in the Hindu religion: "1) There should be one and only one standard book of Hindu Religion, acceptable to all Hindu and recognized by all Hindus. 2) It should be better if priesthood among Hindus was abolished. 3) No ceremony performed by a priest who does not hold a *sanad* shall be deemed to be valid in law and it should be made penal for a person who has no *sanad* to officiate as a priest. 4) A priest should be the servant of the state and should be subject to the disciplinary action by the State in the matter of his morals, beliefs and worship, in addition to his being subject along with other citizens to the ordinary law of the land. 5) The number of priests should be limited by law according to the requirements of the state as is done in the case of the I.C.S" further he says, it will prevent it from doing mischief and from misguiding people. "It will democratize it by throwing it open to every one. It will certainly help to kill the Brahmanism and will also help to kill Caste, which is nothing but Brahmanism incarnate. Brahmanism is the poison which spoiled Hinduism. You will succeed in saving Hinduism if you will kill Brahmanism" (BAWS, Vo.1, 1979:76, 77). By these he wants to kill the hereditary system of Brahmanism. The Annihilation of Caste "was logic on fire, pinching and pungent, piercing and fiery, provocative and explosive. It was to the mind of the caste Hindu leader what silver-nitrate is to gangrene" (D. Keer, 1981:269). Reaction of Gandhi said: No reformer can ignore the address. The orthodox will gain by reading it. This is not to say that the address is not open to objection. It has to be read only because it is open to serious objection. Dr. Ambedkar is a challenge to Hinduism. Brought up a Hindu, educated by a Hindu potentate, he has become so disgusted with the so-called savarna Hindus for the treatment that he and his people have received at their hands that he proposes to leave not only them but the very religion that is his and their common heritage. He has transferred to that religion, his disgust against a part of its professors (*BAWS*, Vol.1, 1979:81). The question of caste in his Annihilation of Caste he examines it in relation with social significance, and gives a solution to destroy the caste system. This rigid system has become the barrier in developing an Indian society.

Riddles in Hinduism

Riddles in Hinduism (An Exposition to Enlighten the Masses): In Introduction, he writes, "this book is an exposition of the beliefs propounded by what might be called Brahmanic theology. It is intended for the common mass of Hindus who need to be awakened to know in what quagmire the Brahmins have placed them and to lead them on to the road of rational thinking". Further he states: "I want to make the mass of people to realize that Hindu religion is not Sanatan. The second purpose of this book is to draw attention of the Hindu masses to the devices of the Brahmins and to make them think for themselves how they have been deceived and misguided by the Brahmins" (BAWS, Vol. 4, 1987:5). Further he says "the Brahmins have left no room for doubt, for they have propounded a most mischievous dogma which the Brahmins have spread among the masses, is the dogma of the infallibility of the Vedas. If the Hindus intellect has ceased to grow and if the Hindu civilization and culture has become a stagnant and stinking pool, this dogma must be destroyed root and branch if India is to progress. The Vedas are worthless set of books. There is no reason either to call them sacred or infallible. The Brahmins have invested it with sanctity and infallibility only because by a later interpolation of what is called the Purush-Sukta, the Vedas have made them the lord of the Earth" (BAWS, Vol. 4, 1987:8). It is nearly books on dogma and rituals.

Riddles of Ram, According to Buddha Ramayan, Sita was the sister of Rama, both were the children of Dasharatha. The Ramayana if Valmiki does not agree with the relationship mentioned in Buddha Ramayana, According to Valmiki, Sita was the daughter of the king Janaka of Videha and therefore not a sister of Rama. This is not convincing for even according to Valmiki she is not the natural born daughter of Janaka but a child found by a farmer in his field while ploughing it and presented by him to king Janaka and brought up by Janaka. It was therefore in a superficial sense that Sita could be said to be the daughter of Janaka" (BAWS, Vol.4, 1978:325). The episode of kidnap of Sita by Ravana after killing Ravana when Sita was brought to him what he says to her? "I have got you at a prize in war after conquering my enemy your captor. I have recovered my honour and punished my enemy. People have witnessed my military prowess and I am glad my labours have been rewarded. I came here to kill Ravana and wash off the dishonour. I did not take this trouble for your sake". He does not stop there. He proceeded to tell her: "I suspect your conduct. You must have been spoiled by Ravana". Ambedkar say's "Such is Ram" (BAWS, Vol.4, 1987:327). The motive of such writing is to deceive and misguide the society were they can rule over their head without calling a revolt by giving such epic by exposing such writing he wanted to have revolt against Hinduism which is a need of nation and time.

Education Institution

He wanted to have an education institution to educate the suppressed people which was denied to them for ages, so on February 1, 1945, Ambedkar writes to the Sardar Sir Jogendra Singh, Member-in-charge of the Department of Education, Health and Lands New Delhi. Requesting the Government of India for a loan of Rs. 6,00,000 (Six Lakhs) for setting a College in Bombay for the promotion of Education among the Scheduled Castes, further stating that, "From the point of view of raising the status of the Scheduled Castes and from the point of view of giving them social security from those elements in Indian Society which are hostile to them higher education particularly College education is more important to them than primary education. The welfare of the Scheduled Castes depends entirely upon a systematic public service and that the public service if it is to be sympathetic must be representative of the different elements in the national life of the country, and particularly of the Scheduled Castes." he emphasis, "Primary and secondary education for a Scheduled Caste student may be good from the standpoint of providing a career for an individual. But it cannot raise the condition of the Scheduled Castes. The status and condition of the Scheduled Castes will be improved only when the representatives of the Scheduled Castes come to occupy executive post as distinguished from ministerial posts. Executive posts are strategic posts, posts from which a new direction can be given to the affairs of the State. The attainment of Executive post, it is obvious requires a high degree of education. Consequently, the primary aim in the education of the Scheduled Castes should be to make provision for those students who reach the College stage so that they may be able to complete it and thereby fit themselves for Executive posts", the reason for dropout was that, "there are a number of reasons why the Scheduled Castes students drop out when they have reached the College stage. The first and foremost reasons is their poverty, second is difficulty in getting admission in College, third is absence of freeship and fourth is want of hostel accommodation." Adding the reason, "it hits hard the Scheduled Castes students far more than it does students of other Communities. This is due to the fact that College education is in Private hands, and most of the College run by private bodies which are communal in their organization and in the matter of their staff. The outlook of the Colleges is on this account largely communal. This communal outlook has its effect on granting admissions. The result is students belonging to special communities or higher communities get preference in the matter of admissions and student belonging to the Scheduled Castes are either refused admissions on the ground that the numbers are full or are considered last when only a few vacancies are left", he gives the remedy, "the only effective remedy seems to be to establish Colleges in Selected Centers which have education of the Scheduled Castes as its primary aim" he also indicates how it will function, "(I), It will be managed by a duly constituted body registered under the Charitable Society Act. (II), it will have two side Arts and Science. III It will be non-communal in as much as: (1) It will be open to students of all Castes and Creeds, only it will pay special regard to the educational interest of the Schedule Castes students (2) The teaching staff will be mixed staff. There will be no bar on the ground of race, religion or community. (3) Subject to the Regulation of the Universities in India it will be open to Scheduled Castes students of all Provinces without any kind of discrimination" (BAWS, Vol.17, Part II, 2003:423-427).

People's Education Society

So he established The People Education Society, on July 8, 1945. The first college of the society was Siddharth College of Arts and Sciences in Mumbai on 1945, then the number of colleges and hostels went on adding. Siddharth College of Commerce and Economics Mumbai 1953, Siddharth College of Law Mumbai 1956, Siddharth College of Mass Communication and Media Mumbai 1965, Milind College of Science Aurangabad 1950, Siddharth Night High School Bombay (Mumbai) 1948, Milind Multipurpose High School Aurangabad 1955, Backward Classes Hostels-Shri Gadge Maharaj Vidyarthigriha Pandarpur (take over by the Society in 1949), Dr. Ambedkar College of Art, Science and Commerce June 1961 Mahad.

The institution not only helped the depressed classes to get higher Education but, it helped all the stature of the society. The Mumbai College of Arts side: Its achievements are more creditable because in the morning session those who struggle hard against heavy odds, especially against the time factor were more benefited by learning while earning so the college was a pioneer institution in starting morning classes right from its inception. The Secretary of the Society of Shri Talwatkar writes. "All these institutions are established by Dr. Babasaheb Ambedkar and are a great legacy to the down-trodden community. His followers have now to shoulder the onerous responsibilities of safeguarding this legacy and promoting it and passing it on to the future generations. The educational institutions founded by him are cultural centers which will help to carry out successfully the great task of reconstruction of the present social order into a casteless society based on social, political and economic equality. These institutions will serve as light-houses which will always show the new way of life based on the three principles preached by Lord Buddha namely, knowledge, character and compassion" (Silver Jubilee, Number PES, 1973:83).

It is observed that thousands of students have been benefited by the People Education Society institution, from all stature of the society got the benefit of higher education they achieved social status in the society being educated.

Reasons for Conversion

In his word "Caste is a state of mind. It is a disease of the mind. The teachings of the Hindu religion are the root cause of this disease. We practice casteism and we observe untouchability because we are enjoined upon to do so by the Hindu religion in which we live. A bitter thing can be made sweet. The taste of anything can be changed. But poison cannot be turned into nectar.

To talk of reforming caste is like talking of changing the poison into "*Amrit.*" In short, so long as we remain in a religion which teaches a man to treat another man as a social leper, the sense of discrimination on account of caste which is deeply rooted in our minds cannot go. For annihilating caste and untouchability so far as the untouchables are concerned change of religion is only remedy" (Bhagawan Das, Thus spoke Ambedkar, Vol. 4, pp.38, 39).

He reasons in his words: "The Hindu religion which forced your forefathers to lead of degradation, and heaped all sorts of indignities on them, kept them poor and ignorant, why should you remain within the fold of such a diabolical creed? If, like your forefathers, you too, continue to accept a degraded and lowly position, and humiliation, you will continue to be hated. Nobody will respect you and nobody will help you.

It is for these reasons that the question of conversion has become important for us. If you continue to remain within the fold of Hinduism, you cannot attain a status higher than that of a slave. For me, personally, there is no bar. If I continue to remain an Untouchable I can attain a position that a Hindu can. Whether I remain a Hindu or not, it makes little difference to me. I can become a Judge of the Hindu Court, a Member of the Legislative Assembly or even a Minister. But, it is for your emancipation and advancement, that conversion appears to be very necessary to me.

To change this degraded and disgraceful existence into a golden life, conversion is absolutely necessary. You will certainly get assistance and co-operation to improve your condition, from friends and well-wishers, I hope. I have to start conversion in order to improve your lot. I am not at all worried about the question of my personal interest or progress. Whatever I am doing today, it is for your betterment and in your interest.

You look upon me as 'God' but I am not a god. I am a human being like you all. Whatever help you want form me, I am prepared to give you. I have decided to liberate you from your present hopeless and degraded condition. I am not doing anything for my personal gain. I will continue to struggle for your upliftment and to make your life useful and meaningful. You must realize your responsibility and follow the path which I am showing you. If you follow it earnestly, it would not be difficult to achieve your goal" (BAWS, Vol.17, 2001:344,345).

The reason of his conversion to make their life meaningful by changing the degraded and disgraceful life, to change this he started searching a religion which will satisfy his needs.

Search for New Identity and Religion
Phoole has refused the Vedas as sacrosanct. He denounced the Varna system in his book *Sarvajanik Satya Dharma* his views on religion. One of the followers Surba Tipnis asked Ambedkar, "Instead of conversion, why do you not establish a new religion?" Ambedkar replied "I am a Mahar and not a Shankaracharya. Who

will follow the religion established by a Mahar?" (S.G. Tipnis, Mahad College Magazine, March, 1962). On May 17, 1924, at Sholapur Dr. Ambedkar, address is to be seen as a first step or the seed sown for the conversion he said, to get-out of the clutches of Hindu religion, he suggested the three different ways, namely: "Deshantar, i.e. Change of Country, Dharmantar, i.e. Conversion or Namantar i.e. Change of Name." (BAWS, Vol.18, Part 1, 2002:14).

The news flashed in Nasik "Kohinoor", which Ambedkar reads, that 500 untouchables peoples were going to accept Islam, he said, that I have learnt we may give an opportunity to change the mind of Hindus (Shankarao R. Kharat, 1961:156, 157). He appeals, to his people, that to wait and not to go for conversion in such a haste, he said that, we will give an opportunity to Hindus to change their mind, and see that they give equal status in the social system and stop atrocity on the downtrodden people. There was a rumor in the middle of 1933 that Ambedkar intended to embrace Islam, some of the Mahars got converted to Islam faith, but letter addressed to Subhedar Savadkar from London dated 13.9.33 states that he had talked to Gavai G.A. regarding conversion, "that not going; to become Muslim nor remain Hindu, but inclined to Buddhism" (Vijay Surwade 1986:174). But already some got converted to Islam faith.

The Mahars of Maharashtra were in no mood to wait. Which can be seen the conversion to Islam by 12 peoples in Jalgaon (Bahiskhrut Bharat, 21.6.1927, pp.288 [4]). Source Material on Dr. Babasaheb Ambedkar, Vol II, 1990, and many more are waiting to get converted.

Declaration at Yeola Nasik Bye to Hinduism 13th October 1935
A conference was called at on 13th October 1935, to decide the future course of action. He said, "To secure the bear human rights as members of the same community under aegis of Hinduism" (Edited by Hari Narke, BAWS, 2002:431). Now the time has come to decide for betterment to abjure Hinduism and embrace any other faith that would give them equal status, a secure position and

rightful treatment. Further added, "Unfortunately, I was born a Hindu. It was beyond my power to prevent that, but I solemnly assure you that I would not die a Hindu." (Edited by Vasant Moon, BAWS, Vol.18, Part 1, 2002:432).

This declaration shocked all Hindu leaders including Mahatma Gandhi, in an interview with the Associated Press representative Gandhi said: "The speech attributed to Dr. Ambedkar seems unbelievable. If, however, he has made such a speech and the Conference had adopted the resolution of complete severance from Hinduism and acceptance of any faith that would guarantee equality I regard both as unfortunate events" (D.G.Tendulkar, 1930:50).

A deputation consisting of five Progressive caste Hindu, headed by Mr. R.G. Pradhan, former M.L.C meets Ambedkar at his residence on November 10, 1935, and the interview which lasted over three hours, the deputations placed before Ambedkar the resolution "(a) The question regarding public temples, public places of pilgrimage and thirtas being extremely controversial and outside the sphere of immediate practical achievement, every possible effort should be made to bring about a change of public opinion with regard to that question. (b) Barring the above question except to the extent of bringing about a change of public opinion with regard to, continuance and unflinching efforts should be made both individually and collectively by propaganda, constructive work and in other ways for securing for the *Harijans*, freedom to reside and settle in localities inhabited by non-Harijan Hindu for abolishing Untouchability in public places, such as wells, schools, dharamshalas and hotels and in general for doing away with Untouchability in the Hindu society with regard to all other matter" (Edited by Hare Narke, BAWS, 2003:235, 237).

The delegates were anxious to solve the problem arising out of Dr. Ambedkar's speech at Yeola. In the course of the interview Ambedkar said: "Though Hinduism is based on the conception of Absolute Brahma the practices of the Hindu community as a whole are founded on the doctrines of inequality as pronounced in

"Manusmriti". Some people think that religion is not essential to society. I do not hold this view. I consider the foundation of religion to be essential to the life and practices of society. At the root of the Hindu Social System lies *Dharma* as prescribed in "Manusmriti". Such being the case I do not think it possible to abolish inequality in the Hindu society unless the existing foundation of the "Smriti" religion is removed and a better one laid in its place. I, however, despair of the Hindu Society being able to reconstruct on such a better foundation." Referring to the position of Harijans in the coming constitution, he said the cause of removal of Untouchability and social reform would not advance with the help of the legislature under the new constitution. About adjuring the Hindu religion, Dr. Ambedkar declared: "Personally, I have made up my mind to change my religion. I am not able to tell you today what other religion I will accept. But I do not intend to secure any personal gain by the change of religion. It is not a personal question and I desire to carry with me the whole Untouchable community at all events the majority of that community. I do not want it to be split up by some joining one religion or sect and other another. From the point of view of the interests to my community it is necessary that it should be united with the absorbed into some powerful and living community. It is my intention to make this movement for change of religion an all India one. If my community does not follow me than I will alone change my religion. This may take at least four or five years and you will period for doing what you can. Before the final decision is made we shall of course consider what success your efforts may have met with. I admit the work before you is tremendous. But if it cannot be accomplished except after a very long period, we are not prepared to wait for such a length of time" (BAWS, Vol.17, Part I, 2003:235-237). It is clear that he is waiting that Hindus should change their mind or there is no other goes then to go for conversion to change the system. An angry youth writes if Ambedkar converted with depressed class, he will face death.

"Listen Doctor, if you are other than Harijan leave our own Religion-Hinduism and are converted onto another religion by the will of God, The Gods and Goddesses of the Hindus are the

Masters of Hinduism. This hand of mine shall forever knock you down dead" (Edited by Vijay G. Surwade, Part I, 2002:143), such were threat to his life when he declared that he will not remain Hindu.

He was very kin to know that what he has said, whether it is implemented or not, he came to know that some peoples are not following as per the resolution, so at Bandra on August 28, 1937, the resolution was passed in the meeting, "as per the resolution passed at Mahar Ialka Parishad that as per Hindu religion festivals, etc., religious rites and fasts etc., Hindu religious system should not be followed" (BAWS, Vol.18, Part II, 2002:45). At the same place he has started in his speech that, "It is observed by the people that the conversion movement is stopped, but it is not, the conversion will take place, the movement I have not left it mind it" further he says that Hindu people say that your conversion question has opened our eyes, we have become alert about your issue we will forget our duty, so you stop the conversion movement. Till today whatever I have said it is for doing purpose, so the movement is not to be taken back, you people think it over" (BAWS Vol 18 Part II, 2002:47).

On July 2, 1939, while clearing his stand on conversion, he states that, "I agree to get converted, so that within us caste such as Mahar, Mang, Chambar etc., will be destroyed, this is one of the intention, when we get converted, Mahar, Mang, Chambar names will not stick to us" (BAWS, Vol.18, Part II, 2002:274).

The intention of Ambedkar is to get converted, without a mark of caste into label of caste the identity of caste to be destroyed was in his mind.

Different Religious Heads and Organizations

The approach from different religious groups, to request him to join them, the first one to approach was from the Buddhist, to follow Buddhism. The secretary of the Mahabodhi society Benaras in a telegram to Dr. Ambedkar, stating that, "If you persist in embracing another religion, you with your community, are most cordially welcome to embrace Buddhism, which is professed by the greater part of Asia. Among Buddhism there is no religion or social disabilities amongst us. We are willing to send workers" (The Times of India, October 18, 1935).

Italian Buddhist Monk Bhikkhu Lokanatha wrote a letter to Dr. Ambedkar on July 4, 1936 from Colombo, "The Depressed class must leave the Hindu fold and join some other Religion that gives social and religious equality to them". Emphasizing to chose Buddhism, further stating, "Let your prophetic vision look into the future and embrace Buddhism, The FINSEST RELIGION IN THE WORLD' In his second letter, August 12, 1936 Bhikkhu Lokanatha, state's "please remember that there is only one religion which will raise the untouchables to the highest level and give them the social and religious equality they; and that Religion is Buddhism" (D.C. Ahire, 1982:11, 13).

There was strong reaction by the orthodox section, to this statement, the different religious leaders and heads approach to follow their religion, not only in the India from abroad, also there was request to follow their religion.

"What religion we shall belong to have is not decided; what ways and means we shall adopt, we have not thought out; but we have decided one thing, and that after due deliberations and with deep conviction, that Hindu religion is not good for us" declared Dr. Ambedkar when shown by the Associated Press representative Gandhiji comment on his Nasik speech.

Asked whether it would be an individual action or mass action Dr. Ambedkar said, "I have made up my mind to change my religion. I do not care if the masses do not come. It is for them to decide. If they feel it is good they will follow me; but on the contrary, if they feel it is not they will not follow my example. My own advice is that Gandhiji should allow the Depressed Classes to chalk out their own line of action" (Source Materials, 1982:135). He was very clear about his action.

Muslim Approach

The Muslim organization too started to take interest in depressed classes, they wanted that entire lot in there fold, so there was all sought of attempt to win them on there side, Khalid Latif Gauba telegraphed to Dr. Ambedkar, "All Muslim India is ready to welcome and honour you and the untouchables, promising the fullest equality and rights in every sphere, political, social economic and religious. If you wish to discuss any matter with the Muslims come to the Badaun Conference on Sunday" (The Times of India October 18, 1935).

The Pune Muslim community was thinking that Dr. Ambedkar and his community were going to convert to Islam, the news published in this regard in The Times of India 'Dr. Ambedkar May Embrace Islam! Hope of Muslim Deputation', "Mr. Gulam Bheek Nairang, M.L.A., Secretary of the Central Tabligh Committee, Ambala, with Dr. Durani, Maulvi Zakeria, Maniar and Maulvi Khujandi, who were deputed in connection with recent Depressed Classes Youth conference to watch the situation arising out of Dr. Ambedkar's proposed intention to embrace another faith, met at the residence of H. H. Moledina last evening and discussed the situation. Many prominent local Muslims were also present. The deputation expressed the view that although Dr. Ambedkar has not openly intended that he would embrace Islam together with his followers, still there was indication that he would ultimately decide in favour of the Islamic Faith. It was therefore decided that the community should be prepared for the eventuality and propagate the cause of Tabligh in Maharashtra. A meeting was also held in the city under the presidentship of Mr. A.A. Khan, Advocate" (C.B.K, 1998:83). The Times of India 16.1.1936 there was lot of discussion on conversion among the main religion, each one were making all attempt that the depressed class should convert to their faith.

"Islam seems to give the Depressed Classes all that they need. Financially, the resources behind Islam are boundless. Socially, the Mohammedans are spread all over India. There are Mohammedans in the province and they can take care of the new converts from the

Depressed Classes and render all help. Politically the Depressed Classes will get all the rights, which Mohammedans are entitled to. Conversion to Islam does not involve loss of such political right to services, etc." (Edited by Vasant Moon, BAWS, Vol.17, 2001:426). Nizam - promised to pay 7 crores, if he converts to Islam faith (Keer, 1981:263).

Although Islam is the one religion which can transcend race and colour and unite diverse people into compact brotherhood, yet Islam in India has not succeeded in uprooting caste from among the Indian Musalmans. Caste feeling among the Musalmans is not a virulent as it is among the Hindus. But the fact is that, it exists. That this caste feeling among the Musalmans leads to social gradation, a feature of the Muslim community in India, has been noticed by all those who have had an occasion to study subject (BAWS, Vol.5, 1989:245). It is true that in doctrine there is no caste as such but in reality they observed.

Christianity

Bishop and the missionary approached Ambedkar and made a request to convert to Christian faith. Bishop J. W. Pickett and E. Stanley Jones met Dr. Ambedkar on several occasions and requested him to consider the claim of Christianity (T.S.W and MMT, 1972:29).

Dr. Ambedkar acknowledges the work of Christian Mission; he said "That Christian Missions have been endeavoring to provide the *corpus sanum* for the people of India and to create *Mens Sana* among those who have entered the fold is undeniable" (BAWS, Vasant Moon, Vol.5, 1989:450). He further observes, "The achievement of Christian Mission in the field of social service is very great" (BAWS, Vasant Moon, Vol.5, 1989:452). To him, further he observed that, "Christianity seems equally attractive. If Indian Christians are too small numerically to provide financial resources necessary for the conversion of the Depressed Classes, the Christian countries such as America and England will pour their immense resources in if the Depressed Class shows their readiness to embrace Christianity. Socially, the Christian community is numerically too weak to render much support to the converts from the Depressed Classes but Christianity has the Government behind it" (BAWS, Vol.17, 2001:426, 427).

Dr. Ambedkar said to Dr. Stanley Jones, "If you Christians had succeeded in wholly wiping out caste distinction we should turn toward you, but you have not done it particularly in south India, and the ace stings, for it is true" (Godfray Philip, The Untouchable's Questions 88) (C.B. Khairmode, Vol.6, 1998:79, 80). Further he observes, "As a community never fought for the removal of social injustice" (The Janata, February 5, 1938). One of the reason for not going to Christian religion that the missionary has not fought strongly for the social cause, which is called as caste so from social point of view he rejected to convert to Christian faith.

Sikhism

Caste system is rejected by Guru Nanak too in Adi Granth it says "be there the lowest among the low, or even the lower, Nanak is with them (Adi Granth, 15). "Every Sikh was equal in the presence of the Granth Sahib, in the samgat and the langar, but in the life outside, social differences was legitimized" (Grewal, 1994:118) so in practice it is there.

The Hindu Mahasabha Dr. Moonje had a talk, with Dr. Ambedkar on June 18, 1936, where they have issued a statement, "Sikhism is the best" (Edited by Hari Narke, BAWS, Vol. 17, Part I, 2003:240). For some time he was under the influence of Sikh religion and wanted to attend one of the celebration, he invited one of his supporter to attend the celebration with him, letter dated November 8, 1935, addressed to B.K. Gaiwad, in its note he states that, "The Sikhs have invited to the celebration they are holding in Bombay in honour of Guru Nanak on Sunday next in the morning. I am thinking of going. Would you like to come? (Edited by V. G. Surwade, 1986:193). Dr. Ambedkar showed some interest in Sikhism and had activities with Sikhs Mission and planned of Khalsa College in Bombay. But Gandhi had some different view in this matter, in a letter dated September 7, 1936, to Mr. Juggal Kishore

Birla, Mr. Gandhi wrote, "today I will only say that to me Sikhism is a part of Hinduism. But the situation is different from the legal point of view. Dr. Ambedkar wants a change of religion. If becoming a Sikh amounts to conversion, then this kind of conversion on the part of Harijans is dangerous. If you can persuade the Sikhs to accept that Sikhism is a part of Hinduism and if you can make them give up the separate electorate, then I will have no objection to Harijans calling themselves Sikhs" (The Sikhs in History by Dr. Sangar Singh).

Gandhi sees that Untouchables were not converting to Sikh religion, he made all attempt that the depressed class people will not get converted to Sikhism. "Sikhism has few attractions. Being a small community to forty lakhs, the Sikhs cannot provide finance. They are confined to the Punjab and as far as the majority of the Depressed Classes are concerned, the Sikhs can give them no social support. Politically, Sikhism is at a positive disadvantage as compared with Islam or Christianity. Outside the Punjab, the Sikhs are not recognized for special representation in the Legislature and in the services" (BAWS, Vasant Moon, 2001:427) even though, Ambedkar Deputed on 18th September 1936, a group of his followers to the Sikh Mission at Amritsar to study Sikhs religion, a batch of thirteen men (D. Keer, 1981:284).

Caste in Sikh Social Order

Every Sikh is equal in the presence of the Granth Sahib, in the samgat and the langar, but in practice they observe caste discrimination. "On 28th November 1947, the tyranny and oppression that is being practiced upon the Scheduled Caste in East Punjab by the Sikh and Jat who have come from West Punjab have been equally unbearable" (Dr. Babasaheb Source Material, Vol.1, 1982:349).

"The Untouchables of Punjab had conveyed to Ambedkar the atrocities they suffered at the hand of the dominant community of Jat Sikhs and appealed to him ensure that the untouchables never become Sikhs" (L. R. Bally, 2006:193). "Kaminas, that is to say belonged to a low class, and they are not entitled to share in the land. Consequently, they could not build their houses in 'pucca' form on the land on which they stayed. They are always afraid the zamindars of Punjab may, at any time, turn them out" (Vasant Moon, BAWS, Vol.15, 1997: 928).

Shankaracharya Dr. Kurtakoti and other prominent Hindu leaders have favored the idea of Untouchable embracing Sikhism (Edited by Vasant Moon, BAWS, Vol.17, 2001:56). Regarding practice of ritual purity and pollution in the nineteenth century, the injunction from the Khalsa Dharma Shasta, Amritsar, 1914, it reads: Those Sikhs who belong to the untouchable groups (like Mazhbi, Rahtia and Ramdasia Sikhs) constitute a separate caste. These untouchable castes do not have the right to precede the fourth step in Sri Amritsar (Golden Temple). Member of the high caste should take care not to mix with persons belonging to the lower castes. If someone seeks to do so he forfeits his claim to belonging to the higher caste (Harjot Oberoi, 1994:106). Why Ambedkar had not converted to Sikh religion? Why he had stopped the relation with Sikh community, of the main reason a Sikh political class. Sardar Kapur Singh in book Saachi Sakhi According to him "there was an apprehension that once Ambedkar become a Sikh with all his followers, no one from the existing Sikh leaders like Baldev Singh would be nominated to the Viceroy's executive council as a representative of the Sikh community Master Tara Singh and his supporters had to consider their position and that of other leaders in the Sikh community and the Shiromani Akali Dal, the SPGC and control of gurdwaras. Kapur Singh recounted a story told by Sardar Inder Singh Karwal, an advocate and Akali leader to a small gathering of advocates in the bar room of Punjab High Court at Chandigarh in September 1964. He stated that when, because of differences between Akali leaders and Ambedkar, the six crore untouchables publicly dropped the idea of adopting Sikh religion, he asked his neighbour in Lahore, Sardar Harnam Singh Jhalla, MA, LLB advocate (judge of high court), who was at that time a prominent Akali leader, the real reason or cause, of this 'tragedy'. Sardar Harnam Singh then replied, "O you don't have an understanding of these matters. By making six crore of untouchables, Sikh, should we hand over the Darbar Sahib to Chuhras"? 'This way', says Kapur Singh "six crore of *Rangretas-Guru Ka-Betas*, who had come to the door of the Guru were pushed out; the same way as Guru Tegh Bahadur was not allowed to enter Harimandir Sahib (Golden Temple)". But, according to him, the actual truth of the matter is even "more crude and despicable." His argument is that when the 'Akali party' understood the full implications of six crores entering the Sikh community, they unanimously devised a strategy to deal with this 'emergency'. Then "they unanimously decided that Ambedkar and his follower untouchables must be dissuaded and stopped from becoming Sikhs for all time". Master Tara Singh, whose leadership of the Sikh community was threatened by Ambedkar's entry, sent Sardar Sujan Singh to Bombay, 'with specific instruction' to tell Ambedkar 'clearly' the mind of the Akali leaders, so that he dropped the idea" (Sardar Kapur Singh, 1972:72,75). There were several offers made by the different religious head, but Ambedkar refused their offer and waited for the time to come for conversion.

Impression, Interest in Buddhism

Keluskar Gurji presented Ambedkar a book *Life of Gautam Buddha (1908)*. Ambedkar learned the history and the teachings of Buddha. Already in his letter dated September 13, 1933, Ambedkar expressed his desire to embrace Buddhism. The house he built was named as Rajgriha. Between 1934-1945 the Meeting-Pandal at Ahmednagar was named as Buddha Mahar. In 1948, he reprinted the book *The Essence of Buddhism* written by Prof. P. Lakshmi Narasu, and recommended it for study. In the preface he mentioned that he himself wrote a book on Buddhism. He visited the Ajanta Ellora, the Buddhist caves in 1949.

The World Fellowship of Buddhist conference was held at Sri Lanka in May 1950, addressing the gathering of the Buddhist from all over the world he said, "I came here with some serious purpose. You probably know that there are people in India who thought the time had come when an effort might be made to revive Buddhism in India. I am one of them. The definite objects of my visit are first, to see Buddhist ceremonial. Ceremonial is an important part of religion. By coming here I thought I would be able to see the ritual that formed part and parcel of Buddhism" (Vasant Moon, BAWS, 2001:442).

At Buddha Vihar in Delhi on May 20, 1951, "Buddhism as a sure cure for India's numerous ills social and economic" he said "if the rest of the Hindu society does not co-operate then we the members of the Schedule Caste, will go on our own and try once again to bring back Buddhism to its former glory and prestige in the land of its birth" (Presented by D. C. Ahir, 1997:54) the Bhartiya Buddha Jansangh, July 1951. A Buddhist prayer book *Buddha Upasena Patha* was completed by him in 1951. December 1954, he participated in the Third Conference of the World Fellowship of Buddhists at Rangoon, he said, "I have to say this with great anguish that in the land where the Great Buddha was born, His religion had declined. How such a thing happened is beyond only one's comprehension". His emphasis "I am keen that India should re-adopt Buddhism. I have already taken some step in this direction, further he said, I shall continue to work for its revival whether anybody helps me or not" (D.C. Ahir, 1997:107, 108).

As he was leaning towards Buddhism, he has written several articles and for the propagation of Buddhism, he established The Buddhist Society of India and it was registered on May 4, 1955, the formal announcement was made at Nare Park on May 8, 1955. The temple at Dehu Road Pune was under construction and the committee of the temple went to install the statue of Mahar Saint Chokoba, but the movement of conversion was taking grip, Ambedkar had bought a statue of Lord Buddha from Rangoon (Myanmar) on December 25, 1955. In this temple Ambedkar installed the statue and said, "After twelve hundred years, we got the opportunity to install the image, this event will be recorded in the history (BAWS, Vol.18, Part 3, 2002:424).

Talk on B.B.C on May 12, 1956, 'Why I like Buddhism', "I prefer Buddhism, he said, because it gives three principles in combination which no other religion does. Buddhism teaches *prajna* (understanding as against superstition and supernaturalism), *karuna* (love), and *samata* (equality).

This is what man wants for a good and happy life on earth" (BAWS, Vol.17 2001:449).

A book *The Buddha and His Dhamma* as written by him, which is the Bible for the converts, because he knew that for an ordinary layman to read the whole of Tripitaka is not possible, he apply to meet the needs of modern world, the book emphasis on the social gospel of Buddha. He also compiled prayer book on 23/2/1956 'Bouddha Pooja Patha', to satisfy the spiritual need for the followers of Buddhism.

Why Religion is necessary, as there is some criticism (*Translation Marathi*) April 3, 1955 (BAWS, Vol.18, Part 3, 2002:437).

Why Ambedkar Chooses Buddhism?

In his words he states that, "i) Buddha stood for equality. He was the greatest opponent of Chaturvarna. He not only preached against it, fought against it but did everything to uproot it; ii) in the Mahaparinibbana Sutta he told Anand that his religion was based on reason and experience and that his followers should not accept his teaching as correct and binding merely because the emanated from him. Being based on reason and experience they were free to modify or even to abandon any of his teachings if it was found that at a given time and in given circumstances they do not apply. He wished, his religion not be encumbered with the dead wood of the past; iii) the religion of the Buddha is morality. It is imbedded in religion. Buddhist religion is nothing if not morality; iv) that religion as defined in the proposition must be in accord with science. Religion is bound to lose its respect and therefore become the subject of ridicule and there by not merely lose its force as a governing principle of life but might in course of time disintegrate and lapse if it is not in accord with science. In other words is merely another name for science; v) that religion as a code of social morality must recognize fundamental tenets of liberty, equality and fraternity" (Vasant Moon, BAWS, Vol.17, 2001:432,434,438). Explaining the foundation of Buddha's religion, Ambedkar said, "That I am going to give the depressed classes is Buddhism. Be everybody happy over it. There is no conflict of Soul, God or even the gods in it. There exist in it universal brotherhood, justice, equality and fraternity to serve the humanity" (N.C. Rathu, 1997:131). Prabuddha Bharat a Marathi magazine started by him, on the occasion of 2500 years of Buddha Jayanti, there appeared several articles.

Conversion Movement: En-mass Conversion to Buddhism 1956
On 23/9/1956 Press note was issued to press announcing the day, date and place of conversion, "The date and place of Dr, Ambedkar conversion to Buddhism has now been finally fixed. It will take place at Nagpur on Dusshera Day i.e. 14 October 1956. The conversion ceremony of Conversion will take place between 9 and 11 am" (BAWS, Vol.18, Part 3, 2002:482).

On October 13 1956 in the evening the press conference was held, asked by press reporter why he was embracing Buddhism he said angrily: "Why cannot you ask this question to yourself and to your forefather as why I am getting out of the Hindu fold and embracing Buddhism?" (D. Keer, 1981:498). Such strong reaction was given from him.

Bhikkhu U. Chandramani of Kushinagar a senior Buddhist monk, age 80 gave Trisarana and Panchasila i.e., five precepts to Ambedkar and his wife, then it was announced that he has become Buddhist, Ambedkar then administered to them the twenty-two vow which he had specially prepared to ensure that his followers renouncing their old religion fully and become a good Buddhist.

These twenty two vows are as follows:

1. I shall have no faith in Brahma, Vishnu and Mahesh nor shall I worship them.

2. I shall have no faith in Rama and Krishna who are believed to be incarnation of God nor shall I worship them.

3. I shall have no faith in Gouri, Ganpathi and other gods and goddesses of Hindus nor shall I worship them.

4. I do not believe in the incarnation of God.

5. I do not and shall not believe that Lord Buddha was the incarnation of Vishnu. I believe this to be sheer madness and false propaganda.

6. I shall not perform Shraddha nor shall I give pind-dan.

7. I shall not act in a manner violating the principles and teaching of the Buddha.

8. I shall not allow any ceremonies to be performed by Brahmins.

9. I shall believe in the equality of man.

10. I shall endeavour to establish equality.

11. I shall follow the noble eightfold path of the Buddha.

12. I shall follow the paramitas prescribed by the Buddha.

13. I shall have compassion and loving kindness for all living being and protect them.

14. I shall not steal.

15. I shall not tell lies.

16. I shall not commit carnal sins.

17. I shall not take intoxicants like liquor, drugs etc.

18. I shall endeavour to follow the noble eightfold path and practice compassion and loving kindness in everyday life.

19. I renounce Hinduism which is harmful for humanity and impedes the advancement and development of humanity because it is based on inequality, and adopt Buddhism as my religion.

20. I firmly believe that the Dhamma of the Buddha is the only true religion.

21. I believe that I am having a re-birth.

22. I solemnly declare and affirm that I shall hereafter lead my life according to the principles and teaching of the Buddha and his Dhamma.

Devapriya Valisinha, General Secretary of the Mahabodhi Society writes, about this historical moment, that "Never did I see such an enthusiastic gathering in all life. Throughout the previous night and the whole of the morning of the 14th, the sky was rent with cries of "Bhagawan Buddha ki Jay" (Victory to Lord Buddha). Large and small batches of men, women, and children, and some with babies in their arms, some with flags in the hands, came in never ending streams from all parts of the country and poured in to the enclosure. Thousands were seen squatting on the roadside waiting to take their places in the enclosure. We went round the city and wherever we went we saw procession after procession wending its way to the places of meeting. When we reached the place was with difficulty that the large force of volunteers made a way for our car to reach the back of the platform. As I looked round from the platform I saw nothing but a sea of human heads and the scene was indeed heart lifting. This was unique for never in the living memory had such a mass conversion taken place" (Dr. Ambedkar and his contribution to Buddhism, Editor Verinder Grover, 1998:271).

This oath and the resolution passed in Mahar Ilka Parishad it is a detail of it.

"The twenty two oaths stuck a blow at the roots of Hindu beliefs and practices. These could serve as a bulwark to protect Buddhism from confusion and contradictions. These oaths could also liberate converts from superstition, wasteful and meaningless rituals which have led to paurperization of masses and enrichment of upper Castes of Hindus" (Bhagwan Das, Revival of Buddhism in India, 1998:65).

Referring to his declaration in 1935, Ambedkar said, "This conversion has given me enormous satisfaction and pleasure unimaginable. I feel as if I have been liberated from hell."

Next day speech

The important feature of such movements has been the change of religion by the large number and not individual, as a result of it its shows the change and the social solidarity of the group.

An estimated 3,80,000 men, women and children in the presence of other Bhikkhus have taken diksha, as stated by him, to Devapriya Valisinha, the General Secretary of the Mahabodhi Society, dated 30 October 1956 (Edited by Hari Narke, BAWS, Vol.17, Part I, 2003:447).

He wanted that not only Mahars and Untouchables should get converted to Buddhist religion but all people irrespective of caste. "Not only the people treated as Untouchables but all people irrespective of caste or religion, who believes in the teaching of the Buddha, should participate in this Deeksha ceremony and embrace Buddhism" (Edited by Hari Narke, BAWS, Vol.17, Part I, 2003:449). He said, "if you follow Buddhism the world will recognize you, not only this, you will get strength and your children's future will be bright, they will have equality and fill proud of it, they will be thankful to you" (BAWS Vol. 18, Part III, 2002:475).

The Buddhist follows simple conversion, if one desires he/ she in the presence of Monk or Upasaka one recite five precept and take vow to abide by the 22 oaths laid by him.

"The danger to Buddhism from Islam no longer exists but the danger form exists. It will be its toughest opponent. A Brahmin will remain a Brahmin no matter what colour he assumes or what party he joins. That is because Brahmins want to maintain the system of graded, social inequality, for it is this on the top of everybody. Buddhism believes inequality. Buddhism strikes at the very root of their prestige and power. That is why the Brahmins hate it. It is quite possible that if the Brahmins are allowed to lead the movement of revival of Buddhism they may use their power to sabotage it or misdirect it. The precaution to exclude them from position of power at least in the early stages of our movement is, therefore, very necessary" (BAWS Vol 17 2001: 465). He also sees that danger in Buddhism if Brahmin skips in.

Buddhism

The conversion movement of Ambedkar, was not to establish a new religion, but to convert to destroy caste system which he saw answer in Buddhism so his conversion means not to form any new religion, when he was asked why you are not establishing a new religion he replied to it, "I am a Mahar and not a Shankaracharya. Who will follow the religion established by a Mahar?" So the conversion to Buddhism is not to establish a new sect calling Ambedkaryana, Bhimyana, Navayana or Ambedkar and his Dhamma, but Buddhism.

The Buddha and His Dhamma

The book he has written on Buddhism is *Buddha and his Dhamma*, in the Preface of The Buddha and His Dhamma dated March 15, 1956, which was not published he writes "that I claim no originality for the book. It is a compilation and assembly plant. The material has been gathered from various books" further he adds that, "I may mention that this is one of three books which will form a group for the proper understanding of Buddhism. The other two books are (1) Buddha and Karl Mark and (2) Revolution and counter Revolution in ancient India. They are written out in parts. I hope to publish them soon" (1991:282). The book was posthumously published in November 1957. Dr. Bhikkhu Anand Kausalyayan translated the book into Hindi and published in 1961, he had attempted to provide as many sources from the original text. Mrs. Adele M. Fiske for her Master of Art dissertation she submitted her paper entitled "The use of Buddhist scripture in Dr. Ambedkar's Buddha and His Dhamma" for her degree to the University of Pennsylvania. She states "The format of his book reveals Ambedkar's aim: to create a "Bible" for his people. The text is divided into books, subsections, chapters and verses. His people were and still are largely uneducated, very simple folk, whom he seeks to vein from Hinduism. He writes as a teacher of the simple, although not a teacher whose own background is simple" (1965:4). In this treatise, he re-interprets the Dhamma in order to show that Buddhism can amply meet the need of modern world and it is a social gospel, the book is like to emptying the water of ocean in a bucket. The traditional (orthodox) Buddhist may not be satisfy, or quench their thirst by this book. But for the new convert the book is for them a "Bible". The book was published in some regional languages like Marathi, Hindi, Punjabi, Gujarati and Tamil and the original book he has written in English.

Other Major Conversion Movements till Date

After the conversion of Nagpur Dr. Babasaheb went to Chandrapur on 16th October with Rajabhau Khobragade and Bahurao Gaikwad where two lakhs people got converted, the next date of conversion was decided to be conduct at Mahlaxmai Race Course ground Mumbai on 16th of December 1956, but due to sudden demise of Dr. Babasaheb on 6th December at Delhi, the program could not take place, but on 7th December at Dadar at cremation ground, Bahurao Gaikwad with a heavy thought asked that those who want to convert to Buddhism may please raise your hand in a second 10 lakh of hands went up then Bhadant Anandkausalyayan a Buddhist monk administered the three refuges and five precepts to the gathering, "The Buddhists were thereafter given a code of conduct in Hindi which stressed, among other things, the following:

We swear we shall not recognize any Hindu God or deity.

We swear we shall not worship any Hindu God or Goddess in any manner.

We denounce the worship of any Hindu God like Rama, Krishna, Ganesh, Mahadev and Satyanarayan, and we swear we shall not perform any Hindu ceremonies like Satyanarayan puja, Mangal-Gaur and Ganesh Puja (Last Few Years of Dr. Ambedkar Nanak Chand Rattu, pp.131).

In a stroke lakhs were converted to Buddhist faith.

After that the conversion movement started taking place in villages and cities, the conversion continued unabated, there was so much enthusiasm for conversion that it continued for years together, in different region and states the conversion movement took place in Konkan, they had committee and the committee took program at different talukas where they had centers. The first conversion in Konkan took place at Kankavli on 31.3.1960 under the presidentship of Shri J.G Bhatankar, Bhikkhu Sangrakishata gave the Panch shila and then Shri Bhatankar gave 22 oaths. The second conversion was at Bhirwad Center on 1.4.1960, from Vengurla, on the same day in the evening the conversion took place at Jambavade center, then on 2.4.1960 at Kasal center, then on 3.4.1960 at Nandgao center on 4.4.1960 at Tal Bazaar center on 5.4.1960 at Mitbau Deavagad center, on 6.4.1960 at Chowka center, on 7.4.1960 at Wadacha Pan and on 8.4.1960 at Chindarthe second phase was started from 24.1.1960 to 30.1. 1960.

Census figure of 1951 of Buddhist population was 2,487 it rose to 27,89,501 in 1961 census, people who have converted started following the twenty two oaths and throwing the gods and goddess from their houses and new way of life they have started to live they observe the fresh sense of identity and acquired confidence. There is new cultural and social change; they started to build Buddha Vihars in their locality, among the converts that name was changed indicating of the affinity to the Buddhist culture and tradition and gave them new identity. Census report 2001 of Maharashtra states that there are 58,38,710, Buddhist where its 6.1 percent.

Conversion in Konkan Region

2.8.1959, Bhoiwad Dadar, Buddha Natipanchat Hall meetings was held and decides that every Taluka should form 10 village groups, for conversion ceremony. Shri J. G. Bhatankar organized the program after late Dr. Ambedkar, 4 Jila, 15 day Sindudurgta Jila 8 days and next year 8 days. It is observed that in Konkan particularly the exuntouchables have their own caste organization, so for the conversion they use to come in groups, for conversion program. The conversion movement started on October 14, 1956, is going on either in small number or in large number, the pattern of conversion remain same, as given by him, wherever there is a conversion, they take five precept and 22 oaths either the Bhikkhu or a lay men gives it.

Conclusion

Today, the Buddhist Mahars are active in politics and challenging the existing caste system. There are political parties which work for the welfare of Mahar Buddhists.

8
A Comparative Study of the Mahars of Mumbai

This study is based on in-depth interviews, which takes account of changes and continuity Among Mahars - A comparative study of Hindu, Christian, and Buddhist Mahars in Maharashtra.

Migration has traditionally been one of the means through which families and groups have left their original moorings in search of better economic opportunities. But in case of Mahar, this is not the case as the Mahars did not have any specific occupation in the village. So they were the first to migrate when Britishers came to India.

Conversion is an issue that goes to the heart of the problem for it raises the question of why anyone, short of a personal relation would want to change the religion into which she or he has been born. The interviews reveal a rich complexity regarding the role of religion in the lives of both those who convert and those who do not.

Mahars got converted often because of educational opportunities, sometimes they reconverted for constitutional benefits, and members of the same family may follow different religion. Some people turn to attracted not religion – Christianity – attracted not only by material benefits and promise that education will change their lives but also because they developed a new sense of self respect through conversion.

However conversion is a conflicted issue: - a new religious identity is not that easy, competing with an older caste identity, and not recognized as new by the other communities. The creed of the new religion (promising equality and dignity) has not always translated into social practice nor has caste society allowed these changes to go unpunished

One of the strategies adopted by duties to deal; with an oppressive history is conversion to another faith that gives them an alternative history. In 1951 there were 1,80,823 Buddhists in India, chiefly along the northeastern border, they were not in any way associated to with Ambedkar but were Buddhists by tradition. In 1961 there were 32,00,333 Buddhists in the country, the result of mass conversion by Mahar in Maharashtra (Webster:1999) Ambedkar's influence in religious matters is generally discussed in terms of the large groups of Mahars in Maharashtra who followed his example and converted to Buddhism. According to him Hinduism, neither has morality, nor revolutionary force, nor social utility, instead it promoted the interests of a particular class.

We need to see Ambedkar's choice of conversion as a step into the modern world in that he exercised choice, and through his conversion, asserted his right to equality (Vishwana than 1998). The liberation that he sought was thus political and social; nirvana was interpreted to mean liberation not from a cycle of rebirths but from oppression in this world. Buddhism was to be the foundation of a new social order and the right to convert was based on the political principle of freedom of religion guaranteed by the constitution he himself had drafted. His act of conversion was a public act and was meant to send out a clear signal that he was rejecting Hinduism into which he had been born but within.

Ambedkar wanted to build an ideal society, and his ideal society is based on liberty, equality and fraternity. Ambedkar gave two ideas to get rid of caste system:-

1. Inter-caste marriage

2. Leave that religion

One discovers that dalits, in living out their new identity, or in following Ambedkar, interpret and re-interpret the doctrine according to their convenience. They are Buddhists, but they retain Hindu popular Gods. They are Buddhists, but will participate in, and use popular local (religious) festivals and fairs to propagate their new ideology. They may explain the weak hold Buddhism has on them, those who got converted. They just want to live a more human and dignified life.

However in some cases we see that those who got converted to Buddhism totally reject Hindu rituals and practices. At the same time it is also noticed that converts to Buddhism often celebrated Hindu festivals as well as the birth anniversary of the Buddha, Buddha Jayanti. We also noticed that Buddhists no longer carry out what they feel are ritually submissive, degrading, or impure practices. But there are contradictions where many still worship Hindu gods and Buddha and Dr. Ambedkar. They have photo frames of Buddha, Dr. Ambedkar, and Lakshmi. When asked that why do they worship Hindu Goddesses, they say that there is no harm in doing that. Some of them fast, especially on Thursday in the month of Margishish

Educated youth however refuse to worship Hindu deities and also do not celebrate Hindu festivals. According to them the important way of maintaining identity is to adhere and propagate the doctrine of Buddhism at the same time they have also rejected Hinduism. They have strong sense of belonging to Buddhism.

The Buddhists who are more aware, irrespective of their level of education, occupation, income and age, they maintain their identity very strongly, they adhere to their Buddhist culture and display their cultural identity through cultural symbols. They have built the Vihars as a symbol of their new identity and newly accepted faith. These Viharas are used for religious and socio-cultural purposes. They perform Buddhists Vandana for their each socio-cultural, religious function and life ceremonies. Elites as well as masses follow all the rites and rituals of the Buddhism which contribute to the sense of belonging to the Buddhism and help them in acquiring sense of unity among them.

The most Buddhist under study says that they maintain their identity because new identity has provided them a number of advantages. They have gained sense of self-respect, esteem, dignity, pride, confidence, new values and approaches, humanity, equality and a new nomenclature. This has created self-awareness, revolutionary and political consciousness among them. Their level of education, occupation and income has increased. Their socio-economic status has risen. They become firm about their ideas. They also have learned to think scientifically, logically and rationally. And they got freedom from the cumulative domination of the inhuman practice of Hinduism such as political disfranchisement, economic exploitation, cultural alienation, religion exclusion, and psychological depression. Maintaining new identity implies conceptual change, a change in one's outlook, and was brought about by the rejection of caste. Neo-Buddhist seems to be empowered. They feel that they are on a par with an upper-caste. Buddhists identity has also played a role in reducing the social distance between the Buddhist and the upper caste. There are some transformations such as participation in each other social, cultural and religious functions, trend of having friends inter dinning inter caste marriages taking place in the relationship between the Buddhists and the upper caste men.

Education

Earlier Mahar community was not allowed to take education. They were not allowed to go to school. However conversion to Buddhism has brought a change, they have become conscious and are taking education seriously. Mostly all have taken education in Marathi medium schools. Most elders are educated up to 10th and 12th but there are cases that are Graduates and hold good job in public sector. In case of younger generation they are taking education in English Medium School. Most of them are taking higher education and working in private sector. They have become aware that only education can change their life. However in case of girl child still there is discrimination. Girls are not usually given higher education. We find very few girls who have completed their higher education and Graduation. Most of the converts have taken Ambedkars views on education seriously. Ambedkar has told the masses that only education can change their life. However in our research we found that number of people taking higher education is very few. We observed that very few are taking medical and engineering courses. And in our interview we found that children of uneducated parents are mostly school dropouts or they take up education only up to 10th or 12th. Those who take higher education mostly study social science i.e. subject like history, political science, and Marathi.

Food Habits

If food habit is considered most of them eat both vegetarian and non-vegetarian food. However in non-vegetarian they only eat fish, egg, mutton and chicken. They have totally given up eating beef and all other non-vegetarian food. However, most of them are open to other kinds of food. Very few of them prepare new kinds of food at home, they prefer to eat outside. Their normal food consists of dal, vegetables and roti. They eat non-vegetarian once or twice a week especially on Sunday's. Today, they have changed their food-habits. There is not much difference in food-habits with other communities.

Vihars

When questioned why there they visit to vihars. Most of them stated that they do not visit to vihars regularly they visit to vihars mostly once or twice a year. They mostly visit vihars on 6th December on. However, those who come from native places definitely visit Chaitya Bhoomi, which is situated in Shivaji Park, Dadar. They consider Chaitya Bhoomi as a very important place. Some of them stated that whenever they get time they visit Chiatya Bhoomi. However, very few of them go to Vihars. Few of them visit the temple. In case of younger generation they often visit the temples and also fast. But there is contradiction there are people who are very rigid and do not go to temples at all. But visit vihars regularly, but number of such people is very less.

No doubt conversion gave confidence to Mahars socially and politically, and they became more mobile. Educate, organize and Agitate brought great transformation among the Mahars, rather than other castes when Mahar meet Mahar they wish each other "Jai Bhim", to prove they are different. Even the use of blue color they will relate with Jai Bhim and say that this is Jai Bhim colour and refuse to wear or use it. According to the President of the Buddhist activist, Yeshwant Kamble in 1967 the activities of the Buddhist society of India were manifold. It published a weekly paper and books, it arranged large scale diksha ceremony and provided financial support for the follow-up work after such conversion. The society lobbied for legislation beneficial to the Buddhist. It provided education in family planning, and training Bhikkus (monks) and lay leaders, sometimes called baudhachariyas. In most areas such lay leaders officiated at life-cycle rites including the naming ceremony held for young children, weddings, funerals and diksha or conversion ceremonies while every branch of the society did not perform all of these functions, the most effective work of the organization was performed at the local level.

One has to follow certain rules when they visit Vihar:-

1. Every Sunday from five to seven p.m all children, ladies and men should assemble.

2. They should first wash, and wear no chappals (leather sandals) in the mandir.

3. They may not smoke, drink, chew betel in the mandir.

4. They should first bow three times to the image of the Buddha, then to the presiding monk.

5. All must keep silent

6. Men sit on the right, ladies on the left.

7. Anyone who wishes to smoke, etc., must go at least ten feet away from the temple.

8. No one must damage the temple.

9. Parents must keep their children from disturbing the ceremonies

10. No one can sleep in the temple, nor fight nor abuse one another there.

11. Parents must send their children from five to ten years of age regularly to the temple for instructions.

12. All must help those who are "socially weak" according to the orders of the committed.

13. He who disobeys this will not count as a Buddhist and the others should have no relation with him.

Disease and its Cure

The Mahars generally had rather vague ideas about the human body and about diseases and their causes. As for the reasons of diseases, many Mahars believed to a large extent in supernatural causes. A goddess who had been displeased by not getting a promised sacrifice, many take revenge by making family members severely sick. They also believed that evil eye can also cause diseases. Cure accordingly consisted sometimes in pacifying an offended goddess or in exercising a supernatural being that caused the disease

But things have changed, after conversion most of them visit doctors for cure of disease, and they no more believe in supernatural cause of diseases. They do not pacify god or goddess for cure of disease. Also they do not visit malarias, Bhatt's, or do not rely on magic for cure of diseases.

However, there are very few people who still believe in supernatural cause of diseases. They visit Bhatt's, maul avis sadhus and of diseases. However the figure is very few.

Dress Pattern

In case of dress pattern, they have changed totally. Earlier it was that we could recognize a Mahar from his dress-pattern. But after conversion to Buddhism they have changed their dress-pattern. Man wears pant, shirt like other do and women wear saris and salwar-kurta. It is very difficult to recognize Buddhist from his dress-pattern. However, they do not wear blue colour as they connect this colour with their religion and respect this colour

Marriages

According to the respondent earlier marriages were performed at the age of 16 or 17, but nowadays it is performed at the latter age of about 24 or 25 both in the case of boys and girls.

Marriages are either conducted in Vihar or marriage hall. However, even if marriages are conducted in a hall, photos of Dr. Ambedkar and Buddha are placed. After finishing the marriage ceremony Bride and Bridegroom visit a vihar. They wear white cloth when they visit a vihar. In villages, marriage is performed in front of the house.

If we observe, marriage rituals closely we can see mixture of both Hindu rituals and Buddhist rituals. However, all marriage ceremony right from engagement is performed in white clothes.

In Neo-Buddhist we can observe hypogamy i.e. usually boys get married to the upper caste girls, but girls are not married to upper caste boys. The reason behind this is that when the boy marries the girls of upper caste and brings her home, they think they have improved their status and feel proud that upper caste girl is married to their boy. But they do not allow their girls to marry to upper caste boy, because they do not trust them and they feel that they may cause trouble to their girl.

Mandap

Mandap is prepared ten days or about a month before the marriage. But now-a-days it is built only five days before the marriage.

Sakharpuda (Engagement)

Engagement ceremony takes place two days before marriage or about a month before marriage or at least fifteen days before marriage. Engagement ceremony is performed like Hindu Mahars but some difference is noticed during the time of engagement. Close relatives of bride's and bridegroom's family are present. Then they wear white dress. On a stage a big photo of Dr. Ambedkar and statute of Gautam Buddha is kept. Buddhist monk, who is called Bhantiji he says some mantra (gatha) of Buddha religion. He introduces boy and girl for some time and gives information about their name, education, occupation, etc. Then some mantra (gatha) is said and then later on they put ring to each other. After that pannut is given to the people. Clothes are given to the bridegroom. Blouse piece are given to ladies. Sari and anklet is given to girls. Sometime earrings or whatever she wants is given to bride, from the bridegroom family.

Economic Condition

The economic condition of the non-Buddhist in big cities can be said fairly better. They live in slum pockets and those who are government employees live a fairly comfortable life. They usually have a color T.V., fridge; very few of them have washing machine and computers. They no more follow their traditional occupations. They have got a sense of confidence due to conversion. However most of the youth are employed in private sector, but they desire jobs in public sector as they feel jobs in public sector are more secured and also that they have a right to get jobs in public sector. Elderly people mostly are employed in public sector or hold a good job. Youth however are finding it difficult to get secured jobs and worried about the future. Even parents are worried about their children's future.

Festivals

The Buddhist sacred days are different from those of the Hindus. The sacred days are Dr. Ambedkar Jayanti, Dr. Ambedkar Punyatithi, Dhamma Charka Pavartan Din and Buddha Jayanti. The celebration is Unlike Hindus; there is no astrological time, sacred moment, no sacred place, no need for religious figure to an auspicious presence, blessings. More value is given to teachings of Dr. Ambedkar and Buddha.

During our interview, we found that the most important Buddhist festivals are the birth, the conversion and the death of Ambedkar. The anniversaries of the members of his family, like that of his father Ramji Sakpal and his first wife Ramabai are also commemorated. But these occasions cannot be compared to those festivals celebrated in Ambedkar's honour.

The importance and splendor of Ambedkar' birth anniversary on 14 April, distinguishes this event from any other. The Sanskrit Marathi term "jayanti", generally used to designate this occasion, indicates the enormous amount of respect for the person as well as its religious value Ambedkar's anniversary is an official holiday in Maharashtra. It is for this celebration that the innumerable local Buddhist organizations become active and organize lectures, dance performances, and other events. Some people perform a puja at home to Ambedkar. People clean their houses and decorate it. Kitchens are filled with the aroma of sweet dishes. They wear new clothes and go to town to offer procession garlands to the statue of Babasaheb.

Vijayadashami

The Buddhists celebrate the day when Ambedkar converted to Buddhism in Nagpur as Dhammacakravartan Dina. It is evident that Nagpur, sacred site for pilgrimage, is the place for this celebration. Well-known Buddhists give lectures; people convert to Buddhism. It is also a festive occasion when one can enjoy and meet friends.

Generally, these celebrations take place on the day of Vijayadashami, which is on the full moon day in the month of Ashvina. Why not on the actual day that is 14 October? How can this coincidence of festive traditions be explained? Full moon days are considered auspicious and hence festivals as well as the anniversaries of gods, saints and important personalities are celebrated on a full moon day (purnima). On the other hand Ambedkar's birth and death anniversaries are celebrated according to the secular calendar. Vijayadashami involves a conscious decision to make claims over the Hindu symbolic space.

Ambedkar seems to have decided to convert himself on the occasion of Vijadashami since it was on this very day that Ashoka had renounced violence and converted to Buddhism, having conquered Kalinga after a terrible war, and regretted the carnage. Thus celebrating the conversion of Ambedkar on the occasion of Vijayadashami signifies the rediscovery of the Buddhist past; the Mahars believe that they are the legitimate successors of the ancient Buddhists.

Mahaparinirvana Day

Ambedkar died on 6th December 1956. He was cremated the next day in Mumbai. The 6th of December is commented as the Mahaparinirvana Dina, which indicates that Ambedkar attained nirvana. Commemoration site is in Dadar near Shivaji Park and is called "Caityabhumi". Thousands of Buddhists from Mumbai and from different places visit this place. They arrange various meetings and other presentations. There is a long queue at Shivaji Park throughout the day where thousands of people wish to have Babasaheb's darshan. They light candles and bow in front of the statute. On this occasion prayers are offered.

The Anniversary of the Buddha

The full moon day in the month of Vaishakha (generally in the month of May) is the day when the Buddha was born in Lumbins. This festival is celebrated in many Buddhist countries; Buddha Jayanti is now-a-days celebrated individually in the home. Sweet dishes are prepared. In the evening people go to vihar and nandana gitas are collectively recited, reunions are held and songs on babasaheb and Buddhism are sung. It is however evident that the Buddhists consider the Buddha's anniversary less important that of Ambedkar.

Rites of Passage

According to Hindus an individual's life is structured by samskaras, these are birth, name giving (namakarana), initiation, marriage, and death. Today, these practices have acquired a new meaning and a new Buddhist reference.

Birth

After the birth of a child, the namakaran rite, a (name giving) ceremony where name is given to the child is organized. This ceremony is considered as the first sanskaras in the life of a Buddhist. This ceremony is generally organized within the first five weeks after the baby's birth. The house has to be cleaned and parents wear white clothes and pictures and statues of Buddha and Ambedkar is set up often, the baby's parents invite a bhikshes, a Dhammachar or Bauddhacarya or bantiji.

Some celebrate the first hair cut of a baby. (Jayavala Kapane or Kesha Kapane) Some others celebrate the kana tochane ceremony, when baby's ears are pierced.

The Last Rites

The cremation ceremony (antyasanskara) is the last and a very important sanskara in a man's life. This ritual constitutes homage to the deceased, putting an end to the mourning period. The Mahars tradition buried their dead. According to Daya Pawar (1996:158), the Mahars discarded the old custom and started cremating the deceased, which is custom that belongs to higher classes, only after Ambedkar's dead. The choice of burial or creation depends on the financial conditions of the deceased family (Danda and Samanta 1993:277) obviously, cremation, costs more than burial using cakes of dry cow dung makes the ceremony less expensive and simple, but cremation using wood costs much more.

There are some examples of people trying to hide the fact that they worshipped their family gods or some other gods in their kitchens. When this practice was discovered, it led to furious discussions and awkward reactions.

Images

Ambedkar's personality is a visually impressive one. His intelligence, his leadership qualities, and his political achievements conjure up a symbolic entity that answers the expectations of the Buddhists and allows them to appreciate him, know him and recognize him. These pictures are omnipresent and are the normative decorative for every Buddhist ritual and ceremony. These images are found on the walls, in the houses of Buddhists, and at their work places.

The pictures of Ambedkar are standard ones where he always wears the same clothes a blue coat, a white shirt and, a pen in the coat pocket.

In every Buddhist house we find the images of Buddha and Dr. Ambedkar. Along with this in some families we also found the images of Hindu god and goddess especially Laxmi and even Ganpati. When we asked one of our respondent why she has kept the image of Laxmi when she knows that their religion does not permit worshipping Hindu deities she said that she knows that worshipping Hindu deities is wrong she said she finds it difficult to throw away the image of Laxmi as she is worshipping her since long time and fears that something wrong would happen to her family if she throws the image of Laxmi.

The image of Ambedkar as it is so often depicted in the homes of the Buddhists and in statues in the railway towns of Maharashtra is almost always as a westernized man, complete with a coat, shirt, tie shoes, fountain pen and usually a book [representing the Constitution]. The portrait or statue shows a man serious, determined and proud.

Flag

Buddhist flag is blue in color with a white dharmacakra. Its origin probably dates back to the Scheduled Castes Federation in 1942. They state that their flag gives them a sense of strength and hope.

Inter-Caste Marriages

If we want to get rid of the caste system we should encourage inter-caste marriages. This is not true of the social reality where marriages are still organized among Mahar Buddhists. According to Benei (1996) and K. S. Singh 1993:835), the most preferred match is as with most Maharashtrian – that of a boy with the daughter of his maternal uncle (mamachi mulgi). Most striking are the matrimonial advertisements in the Indian dailies where it is some times written that a Buddhist partner (Mahar) is wanted.

However, there are more and more inter-caste marriages. It is well known that Ambedkar had himself married Savita Kabir, a Saraswat Brahman, as his second wife on 15th April, 1948. But many of his followers immediately criticized this decision and Savita Kabir still has a stigma attached to her name today. Others consider this act Ambedkar, as victory over the Saraswat Brahmans orthodoxy, and urge all Buddhists to follow his example (Guru 1997b:26-7). In fact, one thing seems particularly interesting to me: in the inter-caste marriages that I have known, the husband is generally a Buddhist and the wife is from an upper caste, a Brahman or a Maratha. It must be noted that these inter-caste marriages take place only in urban settings. It is in this environment that the future partners enjoy some freedom and dare to marry out of their castes, without seeking their parent's opinion.

The Buddha

For Ambedkar, the Buddha was not a god or a prophet. This is one of the major differences that distinguish Buddhism from any other religion. The Buddha never claimed divine status. He never claimed to have supernatural powers. He was a historical character concerned with showing mankind the path to salvation. The description of the Buddha is the same religious and devotional language as the English versions of the ancient Sanskrit and Pali texts. Yet the content has changed; the Buddha represents the ideal-humanist, wisdom, tolerant and compassionate leader, who is committed to the cause of the ill and the marginalized. He detested all florins of inequality and poverty. In the case of Maharashtra, 59 castes are listed as SC, i.e. about 9 million people. Unfortunately it is impossible to give the exact figure of the Mahar population because the current census does not make a distinction based on castes.

Between 1951 and 1961 the Buddhist population of Maharashtra went up from 0.01 to 7 percent, of the total population. According to the 1991 Census, there are around 5 million Buddhists.

According to Ambedkar Buddhism is not a religion but a Jivanmarg a way of life. What appeared sometimes were contradiction between what Buddhist said and did. The most important example is of inter-caste marriages. Ambedkar promoted inter-caste marriage but Buddhist usually marry within there own community.

Buddhist living in Maharashtra is more or less marginalized and misery poverty has become their fate. Only in big cities, fairly a small middle class of government employees live in some what comfortable situation.

Conversion to Buddhism

The Buddhist, when they are asked about their conversion they do not respond properly. Mostly, all of them state that they are happy that they got converted to Buddhism and got rid of Hinduism and caste-system. They tell how they were discriminated in Hindu religion. They state that conversion to Buddhism brought a change in the status. They no longer consider themselves untouchables and have got rid of the inferiority complex.

All spheres of life are characterized by specific rituals. However all Buddhists do not practice the same rituals. Nor they perform rituals in similar manner. The enlightened Buddhists claim that they do not practice religious and superficial rituals and assert that they do not believe in supreme powers.

The progress of the Buddhist conversion movement is difficult to access. It has now been almost fifty years since Babasaheb Ambedkar took diksha at Nagpur, and others think it is fair to say that many serious Buddhists are converted, that there still is not a bhikhu in every locality or that Buddhism has not developed the kind of festivals that make Hinduism such a participatory religion. But the outside observer does see change, there are more and more viharas complete with images of the Buddha and

Babasaheb Ambedkar, many of them in slum areas. There are now perhaps dozens of Buddhist nuns as well as several dozen Marathi speaking bhikhus. Literally hundreds of Maharashtrian Buddhists go to the vipassana meditation retreats of fined by the growing movement of Geenka, who now has a permanent center at Igatpuri. The Trailokya Bauddha mahasangha sahayaka gana begun by the Venerable Sangarakshita as the Indian bench of the friends of the Western Buddhist ordains is steadily adding new centers and new dhormacharis - dhormachari rather than bhikhu since the order stresses lay leadership rather than a sangha of monks. At later count, the TBMSG maintained hostels and dhamma work at ten towns in Maharashtra as well as in Goa, Ahmedabad, Agra and Hastinapur. There is a beautiful center of extensive work at Dapodi near Pune and a retreat center in Nagpur, and across from the two thousand year old. Buddhist caves at Karla are retreat centers for today's Buddhists *(From Untouchables to Dalits-Essays on the Ambedkar Movement-Eleanor Zelliot)*.

Narrations and Quotations

When Buddhists were interviewed and asked why they worship Hindu god and goddess one of the interviewer responded who requested her name not to be quoted:" We *live in society and now do not discriminate us so why should we reveal our real caste by not participating in their festivals also we have to live along with them so why should we maintain distance by not participating in their festivals also we find these festivals more colourful than our Buddhist festivals."*

When we asked the youth they were quite rigid about following their religion. One of our respondents Nitin Kedhare says: *"Our religion is free from all superstitions and unnecessary rituals so it is the best religion in the world."*

Our respondent Satish Kasare says: *"Buddhism is not a dharma but a dhamma and only religion which teach equality and good behavior."*

One of our respondents Shweta Puralkar said: "We not even celebrate Diwali we just prepare some sweets so that children do not have to go to other peoples place and children ask why we do not prepare sweets, so to just fulfill their desire we only prepare sweets but do not celebrate the festival."

Many of our respondents have not told anything about their past identity to their children. When we asked why have they not told anything about their past identity to their children one of them said "We don't feel the need to tell them about our past and how we were treated in the past, their lives are lot better than *ours, they have never faced untouchability, what will they understand. Also we don't want to bring any inferiority complex among them.*"

Conclusion

It is now fifty years since Ambedkar led millions of Dalits to Buddhism. Conversion has a profound social implication in India. It has come to mean an entire change of cultural-ethnic affiliation. The large number of intellectuals from Dalit-Bahujan background who pioneered the anti-caste movement from Jotirao Phule and Iyothee Thass through Acchutananada, Mangoo Ram, Pandita Ramabai and others to Periyar and finally Ambedkar all these protested against Hindu caste system. Even after fifty years of conversion since Babasaheb Ambedkar took diksha at Nagpur, many serious Buddhists are concerned that there is still not a Bhiju in every locality or that some who got converted to Buddhism still follow Hindu practices, or that Buddhism has not yet developed the kind of festivals like Hinduism has which make Hinduism such a participatory religion. Conversions of the Mahars to Buddhism have been interpreted as a collective effort on the part of motivated and well organized Mahars to bring about a social change. This conversion is linked to a social movement that finds its origin in colonial India. The Mahars joined the British army, migrated to cities, abandoned their traditional occupations, and formed numerous political associations. The conversion that took place in the year 1956 marks the peak of this quest for emancipation.

The conversion to Buddhism was an attempt to find another way than special privileges to raise Untouchables to a level of equality. It has been effective in building self-respect and in loosening the hold of feeling of inferiority, although it has not essentially changed the status of the Mahar/Buddhist in the caste Hindu mind. The conversion has, however, brought a dilemma to Buddhists. All special privileges under the administration of the central government, and all special privileges in states, except in Kerala and Maharashtra, are closed to those who claim to be Buddhists. While a few Buddhists welcome this lack of "compensatory discrimination". The majority considers the special privileges their right on grounds of past suffering and present economic restrictions, and do not list their children as Buddhists until they have made their way through the educational system and into government jobs. Buddhist leaders claim that the loss of deserved special privileges hinders the conversion movement, and that many would become Buddhists if it did not cut off their educational and economic opportunities. Petitions to government to extend special privileges to Buddhists from Scheduled Caste Communities on a national level have not met with success.

Although a few Maharashtrian Buddhists have become Bhikkus, there are no well known leaders solely within the religious sphere. The spread of the movement, however, indicates its penetration to the masses. And if the discouragement of magic and ritual sacrifice can be counted as modern, the conversion fits into the rubric of modernization. Even the presence of the picture of Dr. Ambedkar in every vihara, although it seems to be in some ways a cult object, recalls the things he most often preached; education, moral (middle-class) living standards rationalism unity, self-respect none of them part of the traditional mode of life for the Mahar (*Dr. Babasaheb Ambedkar and the Untouchables Movement- Eleanor Zelliot*).

HINDU MAHARS

Migration has traditionally been one of the means through which families and groups have left their original moorings in search of better economic opportunities. But in case of Mahars, this is not the case as the Mahars did not have any specific occupation in the village. So they were the first to migrate when Britishers came to India.

As described by Zelliot for the Mahars, these quite extensive service duties included:-

1.   Acting as village watchmen, tracking thieves,

2.   Arbitrating boundary disputes example over lands claimed by different peasant families.

3.   Serving as guides and messengers for government officials, escorting the government treasury.

4.   Calling landowners to pay revenue.

5.   Sweeping village roads, repairing the caudi (village square) and village well

6.   Removing dead cattle

7.   Carrying messages to other villages or houses (especially regarding deaths). *(Dalits and the Democratic Revolution – Gail Omvedt)*

Mahars did not have specific tasks, a Mahar had no specialized work of his own, but he had a number of different duties to perform. However, because of his low caste his work involved no direct contact with houses or people who he would have defiled by his mere touch.

Some jobs of the Mahars were rather low whereas others required skill and high intelligence. Mahars were most useful to the village. Every village has twelve balutedaras consisting of carpenter, blacksmith, goldsmith, potter, the artisans, barber, washerman, priest and the untouchables, mangs and Mahars.

Whereas the other balutedars had very specific tasks, a Mahar had no specialized work, but as a balutedat he has a number of duties to perform.

A theory held by some scholars and writers is that the Mahars are the original inhabitants of Maharashtra. One of the old names used for them, *dharnice* put (sons of the soil) as well as some of their traditional village duties—the arbitration of boundary disputes and the care of the village goddess Mariai—suggest that they may at one time have owned the land. The Mahar also had fixed duties in religious matters, including the kindling of the first Holi festival fire from which other fires were lit and guarding the shrine of goddess Mariai which was in the *Maharwada*. Recompense given by the village for these duties included not only grain and the skins of the dead cattle, but a small amount of land known as watan and a host of other perquisites legendarily numbering fifty-two. The Mahars not required for balutedar work (in recent decades at least, they have worked in turn did agricultural labour, their own watan lands begin insufficient to support them (**From Untouchable to Dalit – ELEANOR ZELLIOT pg. 87 to 88**).

Marriage

Marriage among Mahars as among other communities is the concern not only of the boy and the girl who are getting married, but rather of their families, villages, and the caste. Marriage is essential for the procreation of children who, for most people still, are the only security for a comfortable old age; it is believed that a person who dies unmarried will turn into a malignant spirit. It is therefore the main concern of every father to get his children married before he dies.

The marriage is arranged by the father of a boy or girl whereas the mother does not interfere in the selection of a suitable marriage partner. Practically it is often the mother who selects the marriage partner for her son or daughter.

Of late, among the more educated people, the boy and girl are given a chance to meet each other before marriage, and sometimes the boy has an option not to consent to the marriage if he does not like the girl.

Formerly the Mahars imitating the high caste arranged marriages at a very early age. Nowadays, the age of marriage depends mostly on the level of education. But many girls still do not receive any higher education and are married off at fifteen or sixteen.

In finding a bride for a son certain criteria are important. The boy and the girl have to belong to the same sub-caste. They must have a different surname that is they must belong to different kula (clan). After marriage the girl gives up her father's, surname and belongs to her husband's clan. Boy and Girl must not be parallel cousins; neither must the maternal or paternal grandmothers be sister, nor their grandfather brothers.

Engagement (Sakharapuda, Kunku or Mangani)

Usually the official engagement takes place within a short time after the preliminary engagement. The boy who is to be engaged does not take part in the ceremony, nor does the woman of the boy's and the girl's houses. Like the wedding the engagement is also not performed on Saturdays and days of the full moon (pornima) or the new moon (amavasya).

The Wedding

After the horoscopes of both the boy and the girl have been matched and auspicious date fixed, the wedding can take place. Usually the wedding takes place a short time after the engagement, with a maximum period of six to twelve months. As among the other castes, among the Mahars also weddings are undertakings of several days and require lot of preparation.

Application of Haldi

A few days before the wedding, the mother of the boy and girl, each in their respective villages, go along with some married woman to the temple of maruti. In a brass plate, which is covered with a pink cloth, they carry turmeric roots and Kunku to the temple of Maruti (the monkey-faced God) who guards the border of the maharavada. The first application of haladi takes place two days before the wedding in the village of both the bride and the bridegroom successively.

Third Day of the Wedding
In the Mandapa no marriage can take place without constructing a canopy (mandapa) out side the girl's house.

Arrival of the Bridegroom's Party
On the day of the actual wedding ceremony, that is the third day after the beginning of the wedding rites the bridegroom and many members of his family start in the morning for the village of the bride.

Intra-Caste Relationships
At a first glance the cohesion between members of the Mahar caste seems to be strong. In every village the Mahars live closely together in the Maharavada. They are as a group despised by the higher castes who quite often and without further explanation call them "the worst caste possible". The earlier quoted proverb, "There is a Maharavada in every village," has therefore to be understood accordingly as having the meaning, "There is a black sheep in every flock" Because of the closeness of the caste members to each other most social interactions apart from working relations within the caste itself. In one's own village everybody knows how and where to find another person of the caste almost at any time of the day. Even Mahars who come from other villages have no difficulty in finding their way in places where they have not been before and where they do not know anybody. At first, they have a look at Mahar caved, the social meeting place of the caste members-a stone house in which the front wall has been substituted by a row of pillars, and it is situated in the Maharavada. All social functions which concern the whole caste, take place here. Mahar visitors who come from a different village, may stay in the caved until their business is over, and are looked after by their caste fellows. For Mahars of different villages the market at a 'Bazar-village' – a village where a weekly market is held of fears an opportunity to meet caste fellows. Often people attend to the market just to meet friends and relatives who have come from outside, even if they themselves have no intention of selling or purchasing anything. Mahars who manage to lift themselves up above their

caste-fellows, who get a better education and manage to get a better job than the others want to have as little relations as possible with their caste members. Generally, the feeling of responsibility for each other is not strong among the Mahars even though the theoretical idea of 'belonging together' certainly exists.

Social Relationships within the Sub-Caste

The same that has been said about the caste more or less holds true also for the sub-caste. It very often happens that there is only one sub-caste in a village. In such a case, caste and sub-caste become practically identical for the people around.

The big difference between caste and sub-caste is that marriages are permitted only within the sub-caste. Even today Mahars are very strict about the marriage regulation. They arrange the marriages of their own children according to the caste rules, and will not accept marriage partners from outside the sub-caste. At caste dinners most sub-castes may eat together sitting in mixed rows. If members of the smasanjagi sub-caste happen to be present, they may partake in the meal but have to sit apart. The same is said to hold true also for members of the Domya sub-caste, but nobody was sure about it as no one had ever met a Domya personally.

Extra-Caste Relationships

Among the many Harijan castes the Nahars hold a comparatively high position though they are, never the less, treated as very inferior by all the higher Hindu castes. Mahars were engaged in menial occupations, receiving the leftovers of food in answer to their begging or as their perquisites, as being persecuted by those who were in authority in the temples as being kept at a distance by all and as defiling food by their touch. It seems that the disabilities of the Mahars were most severe during the time of the Brahmin pesavas who, in the eighteenth century were for a few decades the actual rulers of the Maratha country. Then the Mahars had to carry earthen pots hanging from their necks to collect their spittle, and also to drag thorny branches trailing behind them so as to wipe out their footprints from the ground on which they trod.

Even their shadow was considered as defiling "and in some outlying villages, the Mahar as he passes the village well may be seen crouching so that his shadow may not fall on the water drawers" (Bombay Gazetteer, xvii:440).

Like other untouchables, the Mahars two were prohibited from entering temples. It is said that in earlier times a Mahar, venturing close to a temple to hear the sacred texts being recited and was caught, molten metal was poured into his ears.

The situation has changed a lot in the last few decades. Untouchability (asprustha) has been abolished by law. But still the Mahars and other Harijans suffer discrimination by people who belong to higher castes, in smaller and remote villages untouchability is still practiced to a certain extent. Until recently Mahars could not draw water from the wells of the caste-Hindus. They cannot enter the kitchens or go near the house-hold shines (the corner of the house, where the family deities are kept) of many higher caste families some thirty year ago, Mahars who ventured to walk through the village streets of the Maratha quarters wearing shoes were beaten up by the Marathas.

Now in the bigger villages a Maratha may eat at the house of a Mahar or Mahar may be invited to the house of a Maratha. Tolerance of this kind of social intercourse is no more than two decades old. In villages sarpanchas of higher castes may be seen moving freely in the Maharavada, entering the houses and accepting drinking water from the Mahars.

Mahar doctor in Shevgaon was permitted maratha until he constructed his own house However, the Maharavada still exists everywhere nevertheless, and the situation has improved. During the last twenty-five years the nares (barbers) have started serving the Mahars. For his service he is given a meal which he nowadays accepts. Formerly and in some are as all agedly even today, the navi refused to touch a Mahar and the Mahar men had to shave each other as there was no special Mahar navi. It is also said that today the simpi (washerman) is prepared to wash the clothes of the Mahars. However, this could not be verified as in all house holds which were surveyed the clothes were washed by the women of the house.

Of all castes the Mahars have the closest relations with the Marathas. The Mahars said that till ten to fifteen years back in smaller villages many of them were treated like 'slaves' by the Marathas. The latter ordered the Mahars any type of work, and beat them up if they refused to do it. They said that if a man was sick, they even dragged him by force to the fields to make him work. After striking a Mahar, the Marathas did not take both any more to get rid of the ritual pollution that had occurred to them by touching an untouchable. In former times, they first beat up the Mahar but after words took a bath as well to regain the ritual state of purity.

Food Regulations

It should be added that the Mahars are more reluctant to accept food from those castes which eat pork, namely mang and Kolhati for a Mahar eating pork is unimaginable he may not even utter the word pig (dukkar) while he is eating.

Eating Habits

Mahars who can afford it have three meals a day. For the preparation of each meal the women need about an hour or an hour and a half. This is about four to five hours of cooking every day. There are many Mahars who cannot still afford three meals a day, but eat only a morsel and a cup of tea in the morning, lunch at about eleven o'clock, and dinner at about eight o'clock in the evening.

The women who prepare the meals have to wait until the men have finished eating before they themselves can begin their meals.

Mahars have completely given up eating beef. Their food consists of both veg and non-veg. However non-veg food which Mahars eat consists of egg, fish, chicken and mutton. Also they do not eat non-veg on all week days. They mostly eat non-veg on Sundays or twice or thrice a week.

Settlement Pattern

The living quarrels of a caste are called vada in Marathi. A village has a Maharavada, Mangavada, Bahngivada, and so on, which are almost invariably situated in the east of the village. In Shevgaon huts of Mahars can also be found in an area of the village which does not belong to the Maharavada. This has the following reason. The area of the whole village is called pandhari, and every caste owns a certain part of it. The Mahar communities are proprietors of the Maharavada which is distributed among the Mahar clans. When people became more numerous and had less space for each, the clans fought for the prinlege to live in the Maharavada. Tax is charged according to the size of the house. It is calculated per khana, one khana being three feet sometimes, during famine years, when the income of the people is less than normal the grampanchayata may decide to collect no house tax. Afterwards they have to pay more to make up for the years when they paid no tax. In general the Mahars do not live in joint families. As married sons live in separate huts near the parent's house, it sometimes happens that a number of houses are standing close together. But usually there are also parts with ample space between the houses; sometimes a house may even have a garden or courtyard.

Some of the Mahar houses are rather big, and show that their proprietors are quite well off. Anyhow, most houses are mere huts, not spacious, but solid enough, and mostly quite neat and clean, which is contrary to the belief that a typical Mahar's house had to be mean and untidy.

Resolving Disputes

If dispute arises among Mahars concerning the division of property, the eldest brother calls the close relative who lives in the same village and some old respectable Mahar men to the cavadi then oldest man at first explains the reason for the gathering.

If the villagers themselves do not manage to settle the problem in a way acceptable to all of them, until some five to ten years ago the mehetre from the taluka place had to be called in and asked to pass their judgement. Now usually a court of law is approached.

Politics

According to the Mahars, there had been little political exploitation by the Maratha landlords even earlier. The landlord sometimes tried to convince his labourers to vote for party in which he himself was interested, but the Mahar could not be forced to vote for any special party, as voting was secret and the landlord had no opportunity to find out to whom his men had given their votes. Educated Mahars point out that earlier most of the people did not understand at all what the whole talk of voting was about, and that they were quite easily influenced by their landlords. Now the Mahars are politically much better informed. Before the Maharashtra state elections in 1990, heated discussions took place even in the villages, and SC knew very well which political parties had promised to defend the rights of the Harijans. They however do not favor a single political party. 25 percent people support Rastriwadi Party, 15 percent Congress, 10 percent Shiv-Sena, 25 percent B.S.P, 25 percent R.P.I (above 50 years of age).

Food

Like members of other Indian castes, the Mahars also make a differentiation between so-called 'hot food' and 'cold food'. The former which is supposed to warm the body is therefore eaten if somebody has a cold, and generally preferred by everybody during the cold season of the year. 'Cold food' on the other hand, which is supposed to cool the body, is given to people who have fever, and is eaten by everybody with relish during the hot season.

Disease and its Cure

The Mahars generally have rather vague ideas about the human body and about diseases and their causes. As for the reasons of diseases many Mahars still believe to a large extent in supernatural causes. A goddess who had been displeased by not getting a promised sacrifice, may take revenge by making family members severely sick, The evil eye, especially of married childless women, may cause disease in adults, but more likely in small children. Babies are prone to fall sick with sobani. As the causes of diseases are often seen to be supernatural, the cure accordingly consists sometime in pacifying an offended goddess or in exorcising a supernatural being that caused the disease. As stated above Mahars often hold the view that diseases are caused by supernatural causes. In such cases cure is performed in similar fashion. They perform Angara. Angara literally means the ashes of incense-sticks or of cowdung.

Festivals

The festivals followed by Mahars in Maharashtra are also celebrated by other Hindu castes. Also we have noted that there are Mahars who along with their Hindu festivals also celebrate Buddhist festivals.

Gudi Padwa

Gudi Padwa is the Marathi New Year. It falls in the month of Caitra (March-April). A simple ceremony is performed; a piece of cloth is tied to a long bamboo pole and some lemon leaves and garland made of small coconut pieces and a sugar are fixed to it. On the top of the pole, brass vessel is kept. A little haldi and kunkum are sprinkled on the pole, then the decorated bamboo pole is planted in a hole which has been dug in front of the house, or it is tied to a window frame in such a manner that it becomes higher than the house. And after that neem leaves and gud is disturbed. Neem leaves are chewed and spit. It is believed that all the bitterness and hardship of the past year should be over for good, the sweet taste of the gula which is swallowed symbolizes the sweetness which is expected of the New Year. For lunch sweet dish is prepared. The gudhi remains tied to the house for the whole day, and is removed in the evening when the sun touches the horizon.

Vata Purnima

The festival is celebrated by married women in the month of Jeshtha (June). She prays for her husband and for the same husband for seven lives. Married women bring a mango, a lemon and a cucumber from the market. They keep the fruits along with haldi, kunkum, rice and a bundle of threads in a thali and go with the plate to a vata-tree. There they tie the threads seven times round the tree, apply haladi and kunku to it.

Nag Panchami

Naga means snake and panchmi means fifth. Nag Panchami is a festival of married women (suvasina) who on this occasion return from their husband's house to their villages. This festival falls in the month of Shravana (August-September).

Paksa Pitara

The days from full moon to new moon of the month of Bhadrapada (September-October) are called pitarapata that is ancestor period. At this time special dishes have to be prepared and fed to the crows and five or more guests have to be invited for a meal given in memory of the dead.

Dasara

At the last day of Pitra Pata, a period of nine days start, which is called Navaratra. During Navaratra, Goddess Durga is worshipped by installing 'ghatas'. However, only few Mahars install the ghata. Many Mahars fast on all the nine days and few of them on the first and the last day.

The day after Navaratra is called Dasara. It has a special importance and celebrated in a special manner. They worship all the tools and weapons. After worshipping the tools and weapons they give sona leaves to each other. If giver and receiver are of the same age they embrace each other and if one of them is older the younger one touches the feet of the elder ones.

Diwali

Diwali means row of lights. On this day they worship the goddess Laksmi, she is considered goddess of wealth. They celebrate this festival by eating lot of sweets and playing with crackers.

Bhaubij

This is the festival of brother and sister. A small ceremony is performed. The brother sits on a pata. The sister comes with a thali containing a lamp, red kunkum paste, rice grains, a gold ornament, karduda, five or more pana-supari, five pieces of cardamom, and five cloves. The sister makes kunku mark on her brother's forehead and sticks a few rice grains to the same spot. Then she touches his forehead with gold ornament which is supposed to bring him glory. She performs aarati by swinging the plate with the lamp in front of his head and then gives him all the things which had been in the thali. The brother in return presents the sister with a sari, some cloth, ornament or money.

Dress-Pattern

Nowadays men wear shirts and pants of western style. Also difference in dress between Mahar and other caste has disappeared. Women wear saree which is six yards while older women wear nine yards saree.

Education

Most of the Mahars are not educated. Those who are educated are not much educated. However there are some Mahars who are educated quite well. Majority of them wanted their children to take formal education. When asked what they would like their children to become when they grow up most of them have not thought of any special occupation, however they would like to see their sons to work in offices, especially government offices, doctors, teachers, engineers are other few.

However, attitude towards girl's education has not changed. Education of girl child is not taken seriously. This is the reason why we do not find much educated girls among Mahars.

Part 3 :

Conclusion

9
Understanding Religious Conversion from Dalit Perspective

Introduction

For the last few years the word 'conversion' always remained in the news. It is one of the most important issues on which people of non-indic religions specially Christians are targeted. Almost every day there is some news item in the Indian Newspapers on the above subject.[1]

---

[1] "Rashtriya Swayamsevek Sangh think-tank recruits couples as missionaries of Ram Rajya to stop conversions", by Davinder Kumar, *The Indian Express*, 25-6-2000, p.9; "VHP, Christians slug it out over status of reconverts", by Kamal Gopinath, *The Indian Express*, 21-6-2000, p.6; "Puri seer urges Sonia to recognise that conversion is unethical", by Tilak Sharma, *Times of India* (Mumbai), 16-6-2000, p.12; "VHP opens branch in Durban to stop conversion of Hindus", *Asian Age*, 14-6-2000, p.8; "VHP backs Puri seer in debate on reconverts", by Kamal Gopinath & Himanshu Sahoo, *The Indian Express*, 8-6-2000, p.7; "Christian groups carrying out conversions in state: Munde", by Dilip Chaware, Times of India, 15-5-2000, p.8; "Forced conversion probed in Assam", by Manoji Anand, The Asian Age, 15-5-2000, p.1; "Reform Hindu Society to stop conversion", by Vasant Sathe, *Times of India*, 22-1-1999, p.10; "Conversions basic, Fundamental Right: D.M.K. Chief, *The Pioneer*, 22-1-99, p.6; "The non-issue of conversions", Garimella Subramaniam, *The Hindu*, 22-9-1999; "Advani creating conversion nexus", *The Asian Age*, 20-1-1999, p.2; "The Conversion Controversy", by Asghar Ali Engineer, *The Hindu,* 20-1-1999, p.10; More on this, see. Human Rights Violations of Minorities, Dalits and Tribals, Part I, II, III, A Documentation compiled by Valiamangalam, J., Gujarat Vidya Deep, Premal Jyoti, Ahmedabad, 1999; The Pope in India, November 1999, A Documentation compiled by J. Valiamangalam, S.J. Gujarat Vidyadeep, Ahmedabad, January 2000.

A number of statements have been made by different Hindutva organizations. For example the 8th Dharma Sansad of the Vishwa Hindu Parishad (VHP) in February 1999 in Ahmedabad, demands strict anti-conversion laws and a white paper by the Central Government on the 'foreign conspiracy', behind conversions. The Prime Minister, Atal Behari Vajpayee, demanded a 'national debate on conversion' implying that attacks on Christians are due to their conversion activities. Mr. Vajpayee said, "If Christian missionaries continued religious conversions, the government cannot stop reconversions". VHP's Ashok Singhal argued that Professor Amartya Sen's Nobel Prize is a Christian conspiracy to open more missionary-run educational institutions to convert the poor. It was alleged that missionaries use force, fraud and allurements to convert people to Christianity. Funds obtained for welfare activities are used for conversion. All the same conversion from Christianity to Hinduism is encouraged and supported by the Sangh Parivar as "Ghar Wapasi" or homecoming.

Many of these pronouncements by various Hindutva oriented journalists, politicians and religious leaders call for a scientific study on conversion.

Sanskritic Hindus, the Biggest Converters in India

We need to analyze the issue of conversion without prejudice. History teaches us that social change is an inevitable process. Inventions, discoveries, invasions, diffusions and assimilation have been affecting the lives of people all over the world throughout centuries. The anthropological and sociological process of conversions has to be seen in this wide perspective of social change. Usually, when conversion is discussed in India, it is done in the context of conversion to Islam and Christianity alone. In reality, however, conversion has been going on all through the history of India (see Michael, 1998). There have been many cultural and religious encounters and interactions over the ages. India is a sub-continent with a vast population and diverse levels of culture. The cultural inputs and influences coming from the ancient tribes of India, the urban centred Indus valley people, and the whole galaxy of new arrivals – Aryans, Greeks, Scythians, Parthians, Shakas and Huns before the eighth century, as well as Arabs, Persians, Turks, Afghans and Mongols between the eighth and twelfth centuries – was part of a vital and living process of the many migrations into India since time immemorial. Among the different migrants in ancient India, it was the Aryans who vigorously imposed a hierarchical social order the *Varnashrama-dharma* on the heterogeneous population of India. The homogenization process of the multi-cultural, multi-lingual, multi-religious and multi-racial population of India along the lines of a Brahmanic or Sanskritic social order began.

What we today call and designate "Hinduism" was not known till the medieval period. The term "Hindu" originally derived from the name Indus and was used successively by the Achaemenids, the Greeks and the Muslims to denote the population living beyond that river. Anthropological studies on India show that through a process of absorption, assimilation and conquest, Sanskritization took place in ancient India. This process continues even today with much political support. Adivasis or Tribals and other indigenous people are often drawn into the orbit of a Sanskritic world-view.

When Aryan immigrants entered the country they called the original inhabitants *Dasyus.* The word *Dasyu* was used to denote people different from themselves. In the early history of India, Aryan invaders began to exercise their superiority over the other racial people in India. This led non-Aryan tribals to either compromise with the Aryan social order or to run away to the deep forest (Sharma and Sharma, 1998:100). All through the centuries, Sanskritic Hindu dominance influenced and assimilated non-Aryans into different gradations of caste even to the level of untouchability in the Aryan social structure of Varna. The observations of Bradley Birt, Baine (1891:118), Risley (1901:98), O'Malley (1911:235), Shoobert (1931:403), Elwin (1952:35), etc., also testify to the absorption of tribals into the Sanskritic Hindu culture.

During the long Sanskritic period of Indian history when Brahmins and other upper caste people had so much influence over the lower castes, untouchables and tribals, the culture and life style of many of these underprivileged groups submerged into that of Brahmanic Hinduism. Jayant Lele illuminates the process: "The Brahmanic worldview had succeeded on several occasions in the past in capturing the diversity of cults, deities, sects and ideas (by making many compromises) under the rubric of *sanatana dharma*. It had thus stabilized existing practices and subjected them to the supervision and patronage of a *Brahmin* dominated economic and political order. Many of the tribal, low caste deities to which Brahmanism had to adapt ended up as consorts or local incarnations of the pan-Indian patriarchal gods, thus investing these pan-Indian symbols with unprecedented power and potency for popular mobilization" (Lele, 1995:xviii). The history of the lower strata of Indian society cannot be traced exactly and here only Historical Anthropology which includes popular beliefs, legends, myths, tales, short history of local traditions etc., can help us know about their past (Sharma and Sharma, 1998:101).

N.K. Bose also observes that "even in ancient times, Hindu law-makers were clearly conscious of the fact that various *jatis* were coming within their organization and it was necessary to teach them Brahminical morals and Brahminical religious ceremonies in order to bring them closer to the rest of the population" (1967:211). According to Bose, "Hindus hardly left any economic freedom to the *jatis*, but they left intact the original social and religious culture of the tribes in so far as that was possible. Their policy was not to eradicate the old beliefs and practices where they were not inconsistent with Brahminical moral ideas. But it was nevertheless necessary to do something in order to bring the tribal cultures in line with Brahminism, as we have seen in the quotation from the Mahabharata. So they made a rule that each caste, on becoming a part of Hindu society, was to be served by Brahmin priests during marriage, birth initiation and funeral ceremonies. A close and living connection was thus established between the priestly class and the new recruits, and a means of direct infiltration of culture was thus successfully organised. The Brahmins modified the old culture where it went against the grain of their own ideas and left the rest intact. They added to tribal ceremonies certain items of their own, which were to be performed by Brahmin priests on behalf of their new clients" (Bose, 1967:212).

In explaining this process of Brahmanic incorporation, reinterpretation, appropriation and assimilation of tribal and other cultures Bose says: "Once a tribe came under the influence of the Brahminical people and was converted into a caste enjoying monopoly in a particular occupation, a strong tendency was set up within it to remodel its culture more and more closely in conformity with Brahminical way of life" (Bose, 1967:214).

Jayant Lele traces the origins of Brahminism as a hegemonic project (1995: 51-80). He brings to light the struggles of some of the victims against that project and the resistance shown by diverse, self-conscious communities against its attempts to homogenize, reinterpret and control their diverse origins and identities. According to him: "Popular memories of tribal, egalitarian communities and of aspirations for an enriched and expanded life of thriving inter-dependence, kindled during the early years of the Mauryan empire, were subsequently subjugated, reinterpreted and employed to justify a new hierarchical social order" (1995:ix). He also studied the resilience of Brahminism, during centuries of challenges and counter movements through the dual strategies of appropriation and exclusion (Lele, 1995: 81-103). This is done by the Brahmins through a process of reinterpretation of tribal and other communities' histories, distortion of their folktales and disembodiment and rearrangement of their rituals and symbols. According to Lele, "An important step in ensuring the viability of this sort of exercise is to monopolise the institutional mechanisms through which information comes to life as knowledge and is validated as officially acceptable and true" (1995:x).

Jaiswal has thrown light on two processes that have contributed to the resilience of Brahminism: a) the incorporation of immanent critical impulses through their hegemonic reinterpretation and b) marginalization of counter-cultural threats through their designation as permissible but quarantined deviance (*vama marga*). These processes seem to repeat themselves in subsequent periods (Jaiswal, 1981).

A few instances of Hinduization of tribals will confirm the state of affairs. In middle India, the Nagbansi Raja of Chotanagpur, who was the head of the Oranons and the Mundas, seeing the pomp and show of the Hindu Rajas of northern India changed his surname of Rai into Shah or Shahi (around 1628 A.D.). He assumed the title of Maharaja and he began to imitate the ideal of royalty of Hindu Rajas. A suitable palace was constructed. And Shahi Maharaja soon gathered Brahmin priests, Rajput courtiers and *amlahs* and palace-hunters. The Oraons and the Mundas resisted this and, as a consequence, more and more outsiders were called in by the successive Maharajas and the heavy cost had to be borne by the villagers. This period is also remarkable as the period of erection of a number of temples like Jagannath Mandir, Ram-Sita Mandir, etc. The Bhils of Western India also came into direct conflict with the local rulers and Maratha invaders (see Sharma and Sharma, 1998:106-110).

Even today, many of these tribal groups have been Hinduvised through organizing festivals, and using other Sanskritic symbols and rituals. This has been explained by Nirmal Kumar Bose as "The Hindu Method of Tribal Absorption" (Bose, 1967; also see Valiamangalam, 1996: 129-146). After giving several examples for the Hindu method of tribal absorption, N.K. Bose observes: "But besides all these it is absolutely certain that some *jatis* are undoubtedly of tribal origin; and this has been the result of a conscious plan of Hindu society to dominate over and absorb tribal groups within its economic and social framework. It may be recalled in this connection that some of the untouchable castes have cultural traits which clearly show their original affiliation and indicate their tribal origin" (Bose, 1967:208).

In spite of these efforts, because of the geographical isolation enjoyed by the tribals, some of them were still able to preserve to a great extent their socio-religious identity, faith and practices. But when the British introduced roads, postal system and civil government, easier transport and communication were made possible within the tribal areas. This attracted traders and moneylenders. They were followed by Hindu missionaries. This led to the subsequent hinduisation of the Tribals. Before that the Tribals had kept up the purity of their blood because they did not intermarry with non-tribals. Since they did not practice untouchability among them, they were saved from the loss of self-image.

The sacred traditions of the tribals were too far removed from the Vedic dharma of Hinduism. But the Hindu traders, money lenders, and landlords who became resident in the tribal area were able to introduce elements of Hinduism into tribal religion, paving the way for their assimilation into Hinduism (Bose, 1975).

Another way of assimilation of tribals into Hinduism is through close contact with lower caste Hindus, since they intermingle with tribals easily and pass on Hindu religious beliefs and practices (Bhuriya, 1992:17). The dominant Brahmanical religion during its evolution through past centuries subjugated and absorbed many tribal groups with their gods, religious rituals and customs (Bose, 1975). Priests and poets of the brahmanical traditions succeeded in associating tribal gods with one of the deities in the Hindu pantheon. For example, the tribal god of Orissa, Lord Jaganath became identified with Vishnu; and Murugan of Adi-Dravidians became identified with Skanda of the North Indian Hindu traditions. However, the biggest number of conversions was affected through the Hindu census enumerators. They were persuaded to enter tribals as Hindus in the census papers. G.S. Ghurye, an eminent sociologist addressed tribals as "Backward Hindus" (1963:19). He promoted the idea that the tribals of India must refer themselves as part of Hindu society and should not claim an autonomous culture of their own. According to him, "the only proper description of these people is that they are the imperfectly integrated classes of Hindu society" (1963:19).

As tribals were absorbed by Hinduism, the non-Aryan i.e. the *Sudras* and *Ati-Sudras* were also incorporated and Sanskritized into Hinduism. The upper-castes of a particular area exercised such a powerful influence and attraction on the lower castes and outcastes that they also wanted to be integrated into the caste hierarchy by adopting the values and practices of the upper castes. This process is described as 'Sanskritization' by the eminent anthropologist M.N. Srinivas (1989:56). He defines sanskritization as the process by which a 'low' caste or tribe or other group takes over the customs, ritual, beliefs, ideology and style of life of a high and, in particular, a 'twice-born' (dwija) caste". Orthodox Hindus frequently assert that dalit Buddhists are really Hindus because the Buddha is a reincarnation of Lord Vishnu. Just as putting a snake over the head of the Buddha transforms him into an icon of Lord Vishnu, so too clothing statues of the Buddha's five first companions in the Mahabodhi temple compound turns them into the five Pandavas, Hindu heroes of the great epic, the Mahabharata (Lynch, 1998:11).

Distortion of History to Make Believe Indigenous Origin of Aryans

Since the above facts of the social emergence of Hinduism in India go against the very interest of the Sanskritic Hindus, today, there are attempts to deny the Aryan migration (or invasion) into the Indian soil. The Hindutvavadis are beginning to assertively propagate the idea that the Aryans are the indigenous inhabitants of this land. They founded the rich urban Indus Valley civilization. This claim is very important for Hindutva-oriented historians because it helps them to demonstrate that the present-day Hindus are the lineal descendants of the Aryans and the rightful inheritors of the land from time immemorial.

Since 1920 archeological excavations at Harappa have documented that the rich urban civilization of the Indus Valley is much older than Aryan culture in the Indian subcontinent. This left the Hindu nationalists with no recourse but to seek to incorporate the Harappan civilization into the Vedic literary tradition. In this enterprise, the antiquity of the Vedas had to be pushed back several centuries and the Vedic river Sarasvati had to be assigned a greater priority than the Indus as a cradle of ancient civilization.

But the numerous well-established linkages between the Rigveda and the Avesta firmly rule out the Indian origin of the Aryans. Dr. Stephen Fuchs' study on the "Vedic Horse Sacrifice in its Culture-Historical Relations" (1996) also shows that the Aryans have been migrating from inner Asia to India and Europe and thus giving birth to the Indo-European language groups which include most European languages and many languages of western Asia including Sanskrit and Hindi. "Equally definitively, it is simply inconceivable that the Harappan civilization could have been Aryan. A number of arguments are advanced in support of this assertion, one among them being the absence in known Harappan sites of any well-testified remnants of the horse, a crucial animal in Vedic lore" (Muralidhran, 2000:75; also see Mahadevan 1977 and 2000; Thapar, 2000).

But recently the Hindutvavadis have claimed that the Indus script has been deciphered and that the language of Harappa was 'late Vedic Sanskrit' (see Rajaram and Jha 2000; Rajaram and Frawley, 1997; Rajaram, 1999; Rajaram 2000). They have also been claiming that the Harappan civilization gives religious significance to the horse and thus should have been an integral part of Aryan civilization.

The above claim of RSS historians has been clearly refuted by international scholarship. Recently in a cover story article titled, "Horseplay in Harappa – The Indus Valley Decipherement Hoax", in the Frontline Magazine dated October 13, 2000, Michael Witzel, a Harvard University Indologist and Steve Farmer, a comparative Historian, debunked the claims of N.S. Rajaram and N. Jha in their co-authored book, "The Deciphered Indus Script". The book establishes a connection between the Rig-Veda and the Harappa civilization on the basis of inter alia a fabricated horse seal.

International scholarship has in this question been supported by the reputed Indian historian Romila Thapar and Iravatham Mahadevan the leading Indian expert on the Indus Valley script and one of the world's foremost scholars in the field (see Frontline October 13, October 27, November 24, 2000). The international scholars Michael Witzel & Steve Farmer have challenged to offer $ 1,000 to any Harappan researcher who is willing to defend Rajaram's claims. "Not one has taken us up on our offer. So far as the scholarly world goes, nothing is left of Rajaram's Hindutva 'revisions' of history than an as *'va-s' ava* – in plain English, a dead horse" (Witzel and Farmer, 2000:129).

These attempts of the Sangh Parivar to 'rewrite history' has come under great criticism by other eminent scholars and by the public (see The Times of India News Service, January 3, 2001:6; United News of India, January 1, 2001:4; Chattopadhyay, 2001).

With the above clarifications on the latest attempts to distort history, let us once more turn to our main subject of religious conversion in India.

Conversion for Empowerment and Upward Social Mobility

When we turn to conversion movements to Buddhism, Sikhism, Islam and Christianity by the backward and untouchable castes in India, we begin to understand the efforts of the underprivileged for social mobility and social transformation.

With regard to group conversion to Islam and Christianity, several Hindu fundamentalists complain that there have been forceful conversions during the last several hundred years. Firstly, we have to assess different historical periods and different political regimes and the accounts are not the same for each. Further, the idea that missionaries came with the sword to convert, i.e. they always had the backing of the colonial state and the power to use military force to enforce conversions is seriously challenged by the historical data. When we study the significant conversion movements in Indian Christian mission history, we have to take into consideration a multitude of significant factors. Conversion is never an isolated event.

Conversion has been a powerful religio-meaning system to protest and resist caste struggle even in pre-modern times. The existence of such a large number of Muslims in the country can have no other explanation. This has been accepted by even religious leaders like Swami Vivekanand. He says, "Why amongst the poor of India, so many are Mohammedans? It is nonsense to say that was converted by the sword, it was to gain liberty from Zamindars (Feudal lords) and priests" (collected works, Vol.VIII, page 330). With the advent of the Europeans, however, different forms of Christianity presented themselves as a major opportunity to equality and equal social treatment. The message of Christianity is that God is the Father of all, that all humans are children of God. Despite differences, we are all brothers and sisters in Christ. This had obvious strong pull with the disinherited castes of India, often treated inhuman by the dominant castes. The missionary efforts in spreading literacy and their assistance in times of material crises added the necessary existential and practical dimension. Mass conversions started in different parts and among widely separated communities of the country: the Mangs and Mahars of Bombay, the Chuhras and Mazahabis of Punjab, the Doms of Benares, Kumaon and Garwal Hills, the Dhusiya Chamars of Shahabad (Bihar) and Ballia (U.P.), the hill tribes of the North East, the Karta Bhojas of Bengal, the Bhils of central India, the Mallas and Madigas of Andhra, the Sambavars, the Shanars and Parayars of Tamil Nadu.

Studies on mass conversion to Christianity by Aloysius (1998) and Chatterjee (1994) and others "clearly indicate that these emerging communities did not 'accept' Christianity in 'cow-like' obedience, as the upper caste nationalists claim, but indeed consciously and deliberately moved away from one set of religious symbolism, now perceived as sectarian and unjust, to another, again perceived as universal and egalitarian and hence suitable for the situation" (Aloysius, 1998:19).

While Hindu fundamentalist organizations through their assimilation policy claim that tribals and dalits are Hindus, the tribals and the dalits on the other hand reject this superimposed new identity. The upper caste Hindus while trying to get the services of the dalits and tribals paid little attention to alleviate their deprived conditions. They are addressed as "Backward Hindus" (Ghurye, 1963:19). Rejecting this identity, tribals and dalits have found their own ways to move up the social ladder of Indian society. The conversion movements among Dalits and tribals have shown the potential of social change in religion.

The Dalits who tried to adapt first to the Hindu social structure of India, later experienced the burden of untouchability, unseeability and other oppressions of Hindu society. They gradually realized that they would never be able to attain their humanity in the Hindu Dharma. Hence, they also began to search for an alternative identity. Their search took the form of two types of cultural movements aimed at freedom from oppression (Shah 1985:175). The first is reformative, that is, change within the Hindu system. It included the bhakti movement, sanskritization, and the non-vedantic dalit movements, in Maharashtra, Tamilnadu, and elsewhere. The initiative in a few of these movements came from the upper castes, but it was a response to pressure from below (see Fernandes, 1996:15).

The second type of movement includes alternatives from outside the Hindu fold. In some cases these took the form of conversion to Christianity, Islam, Sikhism, and other religions that preached equality (Sharma 1976: 219). Pickett sees one of the motives, and a quite legitimate one, in Dalit conversion, as the desire for social liberation (1933). Webster argues that conversion to Islam and Christianity represented a rejection of a hierarchy, which kept Dalits down (1992). Untouchable converts are often accused of being "rice Christians," persons who embraced Christianity "for a plate of rice," that is, material incentives. But is it so simple? It is true that in many cases the missionary offered material help out of humanitarian considerations. However, Forrester (1980:74) and Fernandes (1996:17) point out that a deeper analysis of the conversion movements, made not from the missionary or upper-caste point of view but from that of the convert, shows that to the untouchables change of religion was not primarily a mode of economic and social improvement. It was, more than anything else, an effort to change social status, a search for freedom from caste oppression. Oddie asks, "If the desire for material advantage and protection was the only consideration, how does one explain the tenacity and perseverance of some converts who, in spite of material losses and persecution, still adhered to the mission?" (Oddie, 1977:19). Julian Saldanha has summarized the different studies on Christian conversion movements in India. He concludes saying, "A sincere analysis of these conversion movements reveal that they were not the result of material inducements, nor were they exclusively religious events. They might better be described as socio-religious movements" (1996:79).

Further studies on conversion movements show that mass conversion of tribals to Christianity is related to the tremendous socio-economic and cultural changes brought about by westernization and modernization (Natarajan, 1977). Snaitang, a Khasi, studying *Christianity and Social Change in North East India* finds that Christianity provided a means through which the tribals could accommodate themselves to the changes that were imposed through British administration and the process of modernization it brought with it. In a situation where radical changes were taking place Christianity provided institutions, a new life style and ideology which protected the tribal society from the danger of detribalization and loss of identity. A new sense of tribal solidarity that transcended the traditional fragmented order was created. This was founded over the maintenance of the traditional kinship code, which was the only feature common to the tribals prior to the coming of the British (Snaitang, 1993). Forrester comments on motives, "The search for material improvement or enhancement of status is seldom if ever the sole or even the dominant motive in a mass movement. Dignity, self-respect, patrons who will treat one as an equal, and the ability to choose one's own destiny – all these are powerful incentives to conversion" (1980:75).

On the positive side, these movements represented an effort on the part of the dalits to gain dignity self-respect and the ability to choose their own destiny for themselves and their social group. There was a growing restlessness among them to have a fuller life of dignity for themselves and their children. John Webster (1992:71-76) observes that "the mass-movements constituted the first stage in the modern Dalit movement"; they were initiated and led by them, and sustained by their heroism in the face of persecution. These were group decisions to belong to a new community which not only had a religious tradition comparable to that of the caste Hindus, but which also began to distinguish itself from the traditional caste community. On the negative side, they were a revolt against a socio-religious system which failed to provide a meaningful response to their needs and aspirations (Boel, 1975).

Two Opposing Views on Conversion

Sociologically, conversion is a process of change from one religion to another. The motive for a change of religion may be due to economic, social or religious reasons. Conversion could be seen as a way to gain protection, education and status. It was something that could be used by the individual to move forward in society, above all through education, and by a group to free themselves from inherited shackles, to better themselves and their children. These shackles might be those of caste, of illiteracy, of economic slavery, of psychological apathy, of disease, or of a religion of fears and taboos. (See Wingate, 1997). But all these factors are always inter-linked and no one of them should be considered in isolation (Michael, 1983:40-52). Forceful conversion should be condemned. All the same, is it wrong if a group of people change their religion when they realize that their poverty and social degradation are due to the legitimized religious values and the structures of the majority society? The prospect of radical change can only seem subversive to those who are committed to the status quo. It is understandable that the beneficiaries of the status quo resent radical changes. But to the oppressed and downtrodden, change is the lever of hope.

Some critiques that are opposed to Christian conversions take recourse to Gandhi's attitude to conversions. It is true that Gandhi was a great opponent and a critique of Christian conversions. All the same one is surprised to learn, with all due respect to the greatness attributed to Gandhi, that he equates the cow with untouchables and considers cows to be holier than the untouchables. We need to examine his attitudes on conversions. The controversy between Gandhi and Ambedkar brings out the two different approaches to religious conversions in India.

Gandhi's conversation with Dr. Mott on the conversion issue brings out the prejudiced mind of Gandhi on untouchables and on Christian conversion. For the benefit of reading the original conversation of Gandhi with Dr. Mott, I reproduce the dialogue:

"Dr. Mott: I agree that we ought to serve them whether they become Christians or not. Christ offered no inducements. He offered service and sacrifice.

Gandhiji: If Christians want to associate themselves with this reform movement, they should do so without any idea of conversion.

Dr. Mott: Apart from this unseemly competition, should they not preach the Gospel with reference to its acceptance?

Gandhiji: Would you, Dr. Mott, preach the Gospel to a cow? Well some of the untouchables are worse than cows in understanding. I mean they can no more distinguish between the relative merits of Islam and Hinduism and Christianity than can a cow" (Gandhi, 1941:240-241).

When some missionary friends of Gandhi took exception to this comparison, he was unrepentant and did not relent, but confirmed that he had no remorse about this analogy (Gandhi, 1941: 98-101).

The issue of conversion remains incomplete and unresolved when looked at from the one-sided and biased position of Gandhi. The views of the untouchables themselves and those of Ambedkar on this issue are very necessary and relevant. Ambedkar's stand on conversion stands in sharp contrast to that of Gandhi.

Dr. Ambedkar tried his best to have a place in the Hindu social order. All the same, Ambedkar was clear that "we do not wish to live as *shudras* in the four-fold *varna* structure." In this direction he led the Chavdar Talav movement in order to have access to public drinking water, and he led the Kalaram temple agitation in order to gain entry into Hindu temples. The violent reaction of the upper caste Hindus to these agitations made him to look towards other religions for the social empowerment of the untouchables. In 1929 Ambedkar advised the untouchables to embrace any other religion that would regard them as human beings, that would give them an opportunity to break off from oppressive structures and that would enable them to act, eat, walk, and live like men (see Wilkinson and Thomas, 1972: 33). Following this a group of untouchables from a village near Nasik decided to embrace Islam (Matthew, 1982:1031). In 1935 at a conference attended by 10,000 untouchables at Yeola, Ambedkar declared: "I solemnly assure you that I will not die a Hindu." He found in Hinduism the cause of his people's wretched condition because, he argued, it was Hinduism's sacred texts that defined untouchables as lowest of the low and polluting. In addition, it was Hinduism's sacred texts that mandated the degrading, humiliating, and unjust treatment from which his people had suffered for centuries.

Ambedkar rejected Gandhi's views on Hinduism and conversion. Gandhi said, "I must say in all humility that Hinduism as I know it, entirely satisfies my soul, fills my whole being, and I find solace in the Bhagavad Gita and Upanishads that I miss even in the Sermon on the Mount" (quoted by Clifford Manshardt). In the perception of Gandhi the ancient Hindus had already achieved an ideal social system with *varnavyavastha*. So according to Gandhi, "The law of varna means that everyone will follow as a matter of dharma or duty the hereditary calling of his forefathers ...he will earn his livelihood by following that calling" (Zelliot, 1992:154) Ambedkar believed that an ideal society had yet to be achieved in India. For him, the priority was not in making

"Hinduism" or Hindu society "shine forth" but building a new, equal, free, open, non-hierarchical, modern India. His own words best explain the sort of society he envisaged: "An ideal society should be mobile, should be full of channels for conveying a change taking place in one part to other parts. In an ideal society there should be many interests consciously communicated and shared. ... This is fraternity, which is only another name for democracy. Democracy is not merely a form of government. It is primarily a mode of associated living of conjoint communicated experience. It is essentially an attitude of respect and reverence towards fellow men" (as quoted by Shashi, 1992:130). Hence, Ambedkar realized that without destroying the *varnavyavastha* an equalitarian society couldn't be built in India.

Keeping with the Hindu belief Gandhi had honoured cows more than the untouchables. Gandhi viewed the conversion attempts of the untouchables to equalitarian religions with disgust. Ambedkar, on the other hand, rejected Gandhi's views and critiqued Gandhi for his attitude towards conversions to equalitarian religions. According to Ambedkar Mr. Gandhi's arguments against Christian Missions "are just clever. There is nothing profound about them. They are the desperate arguments of a man who is driven to wall" (Moon, 1989:449). Ambedkar continues, "All these arguments of Gandhi are brought forth to prevent Christian Missionaries from converting the Untouchables" (Moon, 1989:450).

Ambedkar was convinced that in Hinduism the untouchables would not find their human dignity. Hence, he rejected Hinduism and took a positive step to convert himself and his followers to an equalitarian religion. Ambedkar took his *diksha* on the 14th October 1956 at Nagpur at 9.30 a.m. Assembled were about five lakh Mahars, all of whom converted to Buddhism on that day. His embracing Buddhism was a strong protest against Hinduism and its oppressive worldview (Gore, 1993:144).

Even now the attitude of the upper castes and priests towards untouchables has not changed much. For example, the recent earthquake of January 26, 2001 has killed thousands and made thousands homeless in Gujarat. But, even at this disastrous situation, the caste barriers have hardly changed. Tents have been set up to help the victims to protect themselves from the chill of the nights. But, unfortunately, the lower castes and dalits were not allowed to use these tents because of the caste prejudices (see Ghatwai &Vasavada, 2001:1).

With the rise of Hindutva politics for the last few decades, there are great attempts to convert non-Hindu untouchables from other religions to Hinduism. Even here the reconversion programme of the Hindus to their religion does not recognize the equality of the lower castes. For example, the Shankaracharya of Govardhan Peeth in Puri Jagat-guru Nischalananda Saraswati converted 72 tribal Christians in Orissa in June 2000. Instead of accepting them as equals, he promised to build "low-cost" temples, "as prescribed in Hindu texts". The Puri Shankaracharya's proposal to build separate Swastik temples of Lord Ganesha for the reconverts to Hinduism was strongly supported by the Vishwa Hindu Parishad. Priests[2] at the famous Jagannath temple declared, "The lower caste people, mainly from the Pana community, who had been converted into Christianity are known as Mlechha (untouchables) and they eat the flesh of cows. We cannot allow Mlechha people to enter the Lord Jagannath temple at Puri, whether they are Hindus or Christians" (See Dash, 2000:7).

Conversion movements are not only towards Christianity but also to other religions such as Islam, Buddhism and Sikhism. Sikhism, which drew heavily from Islam as well as Hinduism, attracted low caste untouchables in a big number. Many of them converted to Sikhism in the early part of twentieth century, despite stiff opposition from the Arya Samaj and other elite Hindu streams.

---

[2] "VHP backs Puri seer in debate on reconverts" by Kamal Gopinath & Himanshu Sahoo, *The Indian Express*, 8-6-2000, p.7; see also "Letting the cat out of the bag: Low cost for low caste" by A.J. Philip, *The Indian Express*, 9-6-2000, p.6. "Reconverts should be allowed into Puri temple", by Jatindra Dash, *The Asian Age,* 20 June, 2000, p.3.

Hence, conversion issue should be studied in a holistic perspective, and not from the perspective of Christianity alone.

In constitutional negotiations, Indian Christians gave up the request for separate electorates, and came under the general voters' roll; this helped to ensure they were seen as Indians first and foremost, in a political sense, and not just as Christians. The critical part of the Constitution, adopted in 1949, was Article 25, under 'Fundamental Rights'. This said 'Subject to public order, morality and health and to the other provisions of the Part, all persons are equally entitled to freedom of conscience and the right freely to profess, practice and propagate religion.'

Within this Constitution, there have been repeated attempts to regulate conversions. Prime Minister Nehru announced, "There should be no regulations of Religious Conversions. Such curbs will only lead to other evils." (Lok Sabha Address, 3.12.55). He goes on to say that votaries of every religion can overstep the mark. But it is Christian members of the house who should regulate Christian missionaries, not private-members' bills. He ended resoundingly, "Christianity is as old in India as Christianity itself. Christianity found its roots in India before it went to countries like England, Portugal and Spain. Christianity is as much a religion of the Indian soil as any other religion of India".

Misinformation on Conversion and Distorted Identity of India
There is so much of misunderstanding, misinformation and rumors with regard to conversion. Interested parties with a view to malign minority communities spread stories of proselytisation. It is also highly politicized. Some of the fundamentalist organizations spread rumors and exaggerate things related to one or the other conversion events. Behind this politicization there is a big agenda of Hinduization of India. Some of the Hindu fundamentalists do not recognise the pluralistic nature of Indian society. India and Hindu are often equated when defining Indian culture (see Ludden, 1996; Dalmia and Stietencron, 1995; Basu and others 1993; Andersen and Damle, 1987). Here, the conception of tradition is brahminical and textual, seeking to invent

homogeneous traditions applicable to all Hindus. This process has been well explained by K.N. Panikkar. According to him, "the brahminical-textual view of tradition overlooked the existence of multiple traditions even among followers of Hinduism. A majority of the Hindus were outside 'the great tradition' which in essence was the ideology of the upper-caste domination. The construction of scripture-based Hinduism by upper-caste reformers during the colonial period was in effect an attempt to universalize the brahminical tradition" (Panikkar, 1995: 113). Hindu nationalism defines the Indian nation in a mono cultural fashion as a Hindu Rashtra and seeks to displace and remove alternative, pluralistic definitions. In its efforts to unify India, Hindu nationalists give top priority to their opposition to Islam and Christianity. The Article 25 of the Constitution grants every citizen the right to 'practise, preach and propagate' his faith. Let it not be forgotten that it was Sardar Patel (no mean Hindu or patriot) who insisted on including the right to 'propagate' in Article 25. It is a pointer to the dynamic vision underlying our Constitution, a vision that we have begun to resent!

The glorification of ancient India by nationalist historians meant the glorification of Hindu India. According to the well-known historian Jha this historiography is based on James Mill's three volumes *History of British India*, first published in 1817. Mill divided Indian history into three periods, viz Hindu, Muslim and British. Jha points out that the seeds of communal bias in Indian historiography were thus sown (see Jha, 1997: xv-xviii). To quote Jha, "Mill's periodisation which is based on the wrong premise that ancient Indian kings from 1000 B.C. to AD 1200 subscribed to the Hindu religion were wrongly portrayed as Hindu kings. Some of the major ruling dynasties like the Indo-Greeks, Shakas and Kushans who were not Hindu were ignored. For that matter not even the Mauryans were Hindu. In fact the ancient Indians never described themselves as Hindu. First used by the Arabs and later by others, the term Hindu stood for the inhabitants of Hind (India). The term is foreign to early Indian literature and passed into Indian nomenclature much later" (Jha, 1997:xvii).

In reality, Buddhism and Jainism were widespread in India, but today they are reduced to small minority religions because of the missionary activities of Brahmanic Hinduism. Hence, a deeper study will show that the idea of conversion is part and parcel of the Indian tradition. The Arya Samaj and other Hindu organizations like the Vishva Hindu Parishad promote conversion and reconversion in their programmes not only in India but all over the world (see Jorden, 1977). The *Ghar Vapsi* (Home coming) movement of conversion of Christian tribals and dalits to Hinduism initiated by Dilip Singh Judev, a B.J.P. Member of Parliament from Jashpur targeting Chotanagpur plateau in Madhya Pradesh (now in Chhatisgarh) and portions of Bihar, Orissa and West Bengal is well known (see The Asian Age, 1997:4). The Sikhs and Buddhists believe in a process of conversion towards human dignity and emancipation. In this context, the Hindu fundamentalists recognize as valid only one kind of conversion, namely reconversion to the Hindu fold. This attitude is out of tune with Indian tradition and contradicts the fundamental rights of the people of India.

Religious Freedom and Conversion - Human Right Issues

India is a sovereign nation. It has a written Constitution, the solemn pledges of our founding fathers; it is a document especially treasured for broadness of vision and egalitarian values. This Constitution is drawn and promulgated in the context of the debate on the pluralistic nature of Indian society. The founding fathers of the Indian nation were well aware of the multi-cultural, multi-religious, multi-lingual and multi-ethnic nature of Indian society. Hence, it is very important to affirm the pluralistic nature of Indian society and its traditions; and that no religious group can lay claim to India as their exclusive property.

Conversion has been taking place all through Indian history. Anthropological studies on India show that through a process of absorption and assimilation and conquest tribals and other indigenous communities have been drawn into the orbit of Sanskritic Hinduism. Even today this process of Hinduization is going on with political support by the State and the Central

Governments. Moreover, conversion is not only to Christianity but also to other religions. There is so much misinformation, rumors and political overtones with regard to Christian conversions. Hindu fundamentalists do not recognise the pluralistic nature of Indian society. Hence, they politicize even the very idea of conversion to Christianity. Therefore, the sweeping statements and vicious accusations often made against Christians on conversion require to be met with the real facts of history and an unprejudiced mind.

Conclusion

In opposition to the prevalent view, which conceives of society in terms of "functional coordination, integration, and consensus", Ralf Dahrendorf has called for a reorientation of Sociology toward "problems of change, conflict, and coercion in social structures" (see Collins, 1997 and Zeitlin, 1996). The conflict approach to social change analyzes social process in terms of the actors pursuing their interests.

The conflict approach assumes that conflict is the dominant process in society, that social arrangements represent the dominance of a powerful establishment over the masses and that once the masses become aware of their plight, they will overthrow the prevailing order and establish a more just world. Charismatic leadership is very significant in this process.

Dharendorf viewed societies as co-ordinated systems. Authority structures are an integral part of every social organization, which leads to the formation of interest groups with potential source of conflict. Various positions in society have different amounts of authority. There is differential distribution of authority, of positions of domination and subjection. Those in positions of authority have legitimate rights to exercise control over others. Authority structures consist of relations of super ordination and subordination. It defines rights and obligations as well as sanctions to ensure conformity.

These positions hold interests that are "contradictory in substance and direction". Such distribution of authority leads to the formation of conflict groups with possibilities of conflict arising out of opposing interests. Those in dominant position seek to maintain the status quo while those in subordinate position desire change.

In the traditional Indian society, the dominance of the upper caste Hindus was legitimate. The lower castes permitted the upper castes to control them. When conflicts arose between the two groups they were quickly resolved without disturbing the authority structures. Society returned to normalcy by maintaining the status quo, and the superordinate element retaining their dominance.

The impact of Christian mission, the process of industrialization, urbanization and the British rule in India began to bring changes in the power structure of traditional Hindu society. In the changed circumstances the values of equality, fraternity and social justice began to influence the traditional Hindu social order. The pervasiveness of this ideology began to be a reality through the new structures of education and socio-cultural empowerment through social service. The law courts and parliamentary democracy also expedited the process of social change in India. This affected and questioned the traditional authority structures in India. The Christian world-view of equality and fraternity had obviously a strong pull with the underprivileged sections of Indian society. The lower castes indeed took the opportunity to move away from one set of religious symbolism, now perceived as oppressive and unjust, to another, perceived as universal and egalitarian.

Actually conversion has been a powerful religio-meaning system to prevent and resist caste struggle even in pre-modern times. As pointed out earlier, the persistence of such a large number of Muslims in the country can have no other explanation. Hence, the issue of conversion is very complex and it requires complex analysis in terms of the marginalized and the underprivileged seeking for empowerment and social transformation.

References and Bibliography

Aloysius, G., 1998, *Religion as Emancipatory Identity. A Buddhist Movement among the Tamils under Colonialism*, New Delhi: New Age International Publishers.

Andersen, W.K. and Damle, S.D., 1987, *The Brotherhood in Saffron: The Rashtriya Swayamsevak Sangh and Hindu Revivalism*. New Delhi: Vistaar Publications.

Asian Age, 1997, "VHP Plans Ghar Vapsi to Reconvert Christian Tribals", *The Asian Age*, 25th October, p.4, Calcutta edition.

Baine, Sir A., 1891, *Census of India, 1891*, Report.

Banerjee, B.N., 1983, "A Hindu Attitude to conversions", *International Review of Missions*, No.287, pp.393-397.

Basu, Tapan and Others, 1993, *Khaki Shorts Saffron Flags*. New Delhi: Orient and Longman.

Bhuriya, Mahipal, 1992, "Reconversion of Tribal Christians to Hinduism in Madhya Pradesh," *The New Leader*, June 16-30.

Boel, J., 1975, *Christian Mission in India: A Sociological Analysis*, Amsterdam.

Bose, Nirmal Kumar, 1967, *Culture and Society in India*. Bombay: Asia Publishing House.

1975, *The Structure of Hindu society*. New Delhi: Orient Longman.

Bose, Sugata and Jalal, Ayesha, 1998, *Modern south Asia: History, Culture, Political Economy*. Delhi: Oxford Publications

Chatterjee, Partha, 1994, *Nation and Its Fragments*. Delhi: Oxford University Press.

Chattopadhyay, Dhiman, 2001, "ASI projecting Vedic Civilisation the RSS way", *The Times of India*, Feb.24, p.9.

Collins, Randall, 1997, *Theoretical Sociology*. New Delhi: Rawat Publications.

Dalmia, Vasudha and Stietencron, H. von (eds.)

1995, *Representing Hinduism: The Construction of Religious Traditions and National Identity*. New Delhi: Sage Publications.

Dash, Jatindra, 2000, "Priests say no to converts at Orissa temple", *Deccan Chronicle*, June 18, 2000, p.7.

Elwin, Verrier, 1952, *The Loss of the Nerves: A Comparative Study of the Contact of People in the* Aboriginal Areas of Bastar State, Central Province of India.

The Examiner, 1999, "The Other Cheek" by Prof. Ram Puniyani, May 20, p.8.

"The Endangered Species – I", May 20, p.5-7.

2000, "Update: Attacks on Christians", September 16, p.6-7.

Fernandes, Walter, Geeta Menon, and Philip Viegas

1988   *Forests, Environment and Tribal Economy: Deforestation, Impoverishment and Marinalisation in Orissa.* New Delhi: Indian Social Institute.

Fernandes, Walter, 1988a, "The Draft Forest Policy 1987; The National Water Policy 1987", *Social Action* 38.

Frontline, 2000, "Horseplay in Harappa. In the `Piltdown horse' hoax, Hindutva propagandists make a little Sanskrit go a long way," *Frontline*, Oct. 13, 2000.

2000, "Horseplay in Harappa", *Frontline*, Oct. 27, 2000.

2000, "New Evidence on the 'Piltdown Horse' Hoax", *Frontline*, November 24, 2000.

Forrester, D.B., 1980, *Caste and Christianity: Attitudes and Policies on Caste of Anglo Saxon Protestant Mission in India.* London: Centre for South Asian Studies, University of London.

Fuchs, Stephen, 1979, *Anthropology for the Missions.* Allahabad: St. Paul's Publications.

1996, *The Vedic Horse Sacrifice in its Culture-Historical Relations.* Delhi: Inter-India Publications.

Gandhi, M.K., 1941, *Christian Missions.* Ahmedabad: Navjivan Publishing House., (1960: 2nd ed.)

Ghatwai, Milind & Vasavada, Jignesh, 2001, "You thought death was the great leveller? Ask these Dalits", *Indian Express*, February 10, 2001, p.1, Mumbai Edition.

Ghurye, G.S., 1963, *The Scheduled Tribes.* Bombay: Popular Prakashan.

Gladstone, J.W., 1976, "19th Century Mass Movement in South Travancore - A Result of Social Liberation", *Indian Church History Review*, No.1, pp.53-66.

1986, "Christian Missionary work and socio-Religious Movements in Kerala: 1850-1910" *Ibid.*, No.1 pp.30-42.

Gore, M.S., 1993, The Social Context of an Ideology. Ambedkar's Political and Social Thought. Delhi: Sage Publications.

Grafe, H., 1990, *The History of Christianity in Tamilnadu in the 19th and 20th Centuries.* Vol. 4, part 2 of the Church History Association of India. History of the Indian Church, Bangalore, CHAI.

Hardgrave, Robert L.Jr., 1969, *The Nadars of Tamil Nadu.* Bombay.

Jaiswal, Suvira, 1981, *The Origins and Development of Vaisnavism,* Delhi: Munshiram Manoharlal.

Jha, D.N., 1997, *Ancient India. An Introductory Outline*. New Delhi: Manohar.

Jordens, J.T.F., 1977, "Reconversion to Hinduism, the Shuddhi of the Arya Samaj", *Religion in South Asia*. G.A. Oddie (ed.), New Delhi: Manohar, pp.145-161.

Legrand, Lucien, 1996, "Conversion in the Bible: A Dialogical Process", *Mission and Conversion: A Reappraisal*. (ed.) Joseph Mattam and Sebastian Kim, Mumbai: St. Paul's Publications.

Lele, Jayant, 1995, Hindutva: The Emergence of the Right. Madras: Earthworm Books.

Ludden, David (ed.), 1996, *Making India Hindu*. New Delhi: Oxford University Press.

Lynch, Owen M., 1998, "Dalit Buddhism: The Liberate Bodh Gaya Movement", *Dalit International Newsletter*, Vol.3, No.1 February, 1998.

Mahadevan, Iravatham, 1977, *The Indus Valley Script: Texts, Concordances and Tables*. New Delhi: Memoirs of the Archaeological Survey of India.

2000, "One sees what one wants to", *Frontline*, November 24, p.125.

Matthew, G., 1982, "Politicization of Religion: Conversions to Islam in Tamil Nadu", *Economic and Political Weekly*, No.25, pp.1027-1034; No.26, pp. 1068-1072.

Michael, S.M., 1980, *The Cultural Context of Evangelization in India*. Indore: Satprakashan.

1983, "Sociological Perspectives of conversion in India", *Indian Missiological Review*, January, Vol.5, No.1, pp.40-52.

1996 "The Cultural Context of the Rise of Hindutva and Dalit forces", *Vidyajyoti: Journal of Theological Reflection*, May, Vol.60, No.5, pp.294-310.

1998, *Anthropology of Conversion*. IIC Occasional Papers, Mumbai: Institute of Indian Culture.

2000, "Real Issues Behind the Violence", *Mission Today*, Jan-Mar 2000, Vol. II, No.1, pp.9-22.

Moon, Vasant, 1989, *Dr. Babasaheb Ambedkar Writings and Speeches*. Vol.5, Bombay: Education Department, Government of Maharashtra.

Muralidharan, Sukumar

2000, "Questions about the Aryan identity", *Frontline*, December 22, 2000, pp.73-75.

Natarajan, Nalini, 1977, *Missionary Among the Khasis*. New Delhi: Sterling Publishers.

Oddie, G.A. (ed.), 1977, *Religion in South Asia*. New Delhi: Manohar Book Service.

O'Malley, L.S., 1911, *Census of India*, Report.

Panikkar, K.N., 1995, *Culture, Ideology, Hegemony. Intellectuals and Social Consciousness in Colonial India*. New Delhi: Tulika Publishers.

Parpola, Asko, 2000, "Of Rajaram's `Horses', 'decipherment', and civilisational issues", *Frontline*, November 24, pp.124-125.

Picket, J.W., 1933, *Christian Mass Movements in India. Lucknow*: Lucknow Publishing House (2nd Indian Edition)

Rajaram, N.S. and N. Jha, 2000, *The Deciphered Indus Script: Methodology, readings, interpretations*. New Delhi: Aditya Prakashan.

1999, *From Sarasvati River to the Indus Script*. Bangalore: Mitra Madhyama.

Rajaram, N.S. and David Frawley, 1997, *Vedic Aryans and the Origins of Civilization*. New Delhi: Voice of India.

Risley, H.H., 1901, *Census of India*, India Report.

Saldanha, Julian, 1996, "Patterns of Conversion in Indian Mission History", *Mission and Conversion: A Reappraisal* (eds.), Joseph Mattam and Sebastian Kim, Mumbai: St. Paul's Publications.

Shah, Gyansham, 1985, "Anti-Untouchability Movements", *Caste, Caste Conflict and Reservation*, I.P. Desai, et. al. (ed.) Delhi: Ajanta Publications.

Sharma, S.P. and J.B. Sharma, 1998, Vol.1 New Delhi: Radha Publications.

Sharma, Ursula, 1976, "Status-Striving and Striving to Abolish Status: The Arya Samaj and the Low Castes", *Social Action* 26.

Shashi, S.S. (ed.), 1992, *Ambedkar and Social Justice*. New Delhi: Government of India.

Shoobert, 1931, *Census of India 1931*. C.P. and Berar Report.

Snaitang, O.L., 1993, *Christianity and Social Change in North East India*. Shillong: Vendrame Institute.

Srinivas, M.N., 1989, *The Cohesive Role of Sanskritization and Other Essays*. New Delhi: Oxford University Press.

Thapar, Romila, 2000, "Hindutva and History", *Frontline*, October 13, pp.15-16.

The Times of India News Service, 2001, "Amartya hits out at Sangh Parivar for trying to 'rewrite history', *Times of India*, January 3, 2001, p.6, Mumbai.

United News of India, 2001, "RSS Attempts Rewrite History", *The Indian Express*, January 1, 2001, p.4, Mumbai.

Valiamangalam, Joseph, 1996, "Conversion in Indian Religions", *Mission and Conversion: A Reappraisal*. (eds.) Joseph Mattam and Sebastian Kim, Mumbai: St. Paul's Publications.

Vidyarti, L.P. and Rai, B.K., 1977, *Tribal Culture of India*. Delhi: Concept Publishing Co. Webster, John C.B.

1992, *Dalit Christians: A History*. Delhi: ISPCK Wingate, Andrew

1997, *The Church and Conversion. A Study of Recent Conversions to and from Christianity in the Tamil Area of South India*. Delhi: ISPCK.

Wilkinson, T. and Thomas, M.M. (eds.), 1972, *Ambedkar and the Neo-Buddhist Movement*. Madras: CLS.

Witzel, Michael and Steve Farmer, 2000, "Horseplay in Harappa: The Indus Valley Decipherment Hoax", *Frontline*, October 13, pp.4-14.

2000, "New Evidence on the `Piltdown Horse' Hoax", Frontline, November 24, pp.126-129.

Zeitlin, Irving, 1996, *Rethinking Sociology: A Critique of Contemporary Theory*. New Delhi: Rawat (Reprinted)

Zelliot, Eleanor, 1992, *From Untouchable to Dalit: Essays on the Ambedkar Movement*. Delhi: Manohar.

10
Cultural Diversity and Inculturation from Dalit Perspective in India

Introduction

India is an ancient civilization composed of various strands of cultural complexes. It has given rise to several religions, which are active and alive, and co-exist with each other, and influence the life patterns of people, not only in India, but also in different continents of the world. India, at the same time, is a place of contradictions. The disparity between the rich and poor is scandalizing. The conflicts and violence in the name of religions, languages, ethnicity and cultures inflict pain on the civilization which is God fearing, hospitable and pluralistic in its essence. Hence, India has both the roles of enriching humanity with its vast experience of living with diversity of cultures as well as of learning from other cultures of their richness and of their experiences. All these offer opportunities and challenges for the evangelization of cultures and inculturation of Christian faith in India.

This chapter tries to understand the diversities of Indian cultures and their implication for inculturation, evangelization of cultures and intercultural dialogue. Since these are an important area of the life of the Church in India, we need more scientific research in the cultures of India as well as the interaction between the Gospel and cultures.

India: A Land of Diversity of Cultures

a. *Ancient Heritage*

India is a land not only with a rich and ancient heritage but also with an ancient history, comparable with that of China, going back to 3000 B.C. or earlier. The Harappan civilization, the first known civilization of India, stood alongside the Egyptian and Mesopotamian civilizations as the early, advanced civilizations of humankind. They belonged to the Neolithic and Chalcolithic periods. Although historically later than the civilizations of the Nile and the Twin Rivers (Euphrates and Tigris), the Indus civilization was spread over a wider area of one thousand square miles and maintained links with Mesopotamia, both by land and by sea (for details see D'Souza, 2007:1-55).

India also has the distinction of being one of the few countries of the world, along with China, to have a continuous tradition from ancient periods. This tradition, however, does not represent one culture and one people. It is more a reflection of the diverse cultures that have co-existed and then synthesized over a period of time, with different strands, sometimes meeting, sometimes conflicting, sometimes merging, but continuously co-existing (*ibid*).

b. *Cultural Diversity*

India is a subcontinent with a vast population of the most diverse levels of culture. Anthropological knowledge of the people of India reveals that almost all known racial groups have migrated to India at different times in the past with their own language, religion and culture. The cultural inputs and influences from the ancient tribes of India, the urban centred Indus valley people, and the whole galaxy of subsequent arrivals – Sanskrit speaking people, the so called Aryans (pastoral nomadic, horse-riding) laid the foundation for the cultures of India. Since there was plenty of space, the migrating cultural and racial groups could pass on and penetrate further into the interior without much opposition. Thus, the various cultural groups did not destroy each other, but continued to live on and consolidate into the main components of the present-day population (see Jha, 1997). The caste system also helped to keep the diverse racial, social and cultural groups apart, for it prevented them effectively from mixing with one another. There were other later cultural influences in India from the Greeks, Scythians, Parthians, Shakas and Huns before the eighth century, as well as Arabs, Persians, Turks, Afghans and Mongols between the eighth and twelfth centuries – was part of vital and living process of the many migrations into India since time immemorial.

Thus, the population of India is very heterogeneous. Variety and diversity permeates the whole subcontinent, every state and district, every town and village. Thus, Indian civilization is the outcome of a confluence of various cultural, religious, linguistic and ethnic traditions. Over the years of mutual fecundation, synthesis and challenge, Indian civilization has come to be characterized by diversity of cultures, religions, languages, races and caste groups. According to Kothari, "in the absence of a centralized political authority it was `the Indian civilizational enterprise' which `over the centuries achieved a remarkable degree of cohesion and held together different sub-systems in a continental-size society'" (1988:2223). So, the unifying force of Indian civilization was the acceptance of multicultuality and linguistic diversity rather than a political ideology of regimentation.

A Diversity of Cultures in Co-Existence

This unity in diversity in terms of cultures, religions, languages and ethnicity in India need to be valued highly. While there is so much violence in the world more particularly in India's neighborhood, India's ability to co-exist with many cultures, religions, languages and ethnic groups need to be highly appreciated.

Researches on the reasons for the variations in cultures and civilizations in different parts of the world point out that ecological background and history of a people influence their cultures (see Michael, 1989). Hence, the diversity of Indian cultures is rooted in its history and the differing ecological background. Geographically India is very diverse and the historical background of different ethnic communities varies. These and other differences between ethnic communities have helped for the existence of diverse cultures in India. Natural geographical boundaries and a sense of tolerance and mutual co-existence helped to maintain the specific cultural identity of different ethnic communities in India.

Sudhir Kakar, a well known psychologist in India is of the opinion that Indians have an ego which is relatively less differentiated than its western counterpart, thus indicating that Indians are less individualistic. Hinduism is strongly influenced by the thought that the human soul (*atma*) is but a part of the universal soul (*parmatma*/ God). In this capacity the human being always remains trivial and inconsequential before the larger, omnipotent universal self. The consciousness of being a mortal, a sheer grain of sand in the vast cosmos, tends to take the wind out of egocentric sails. Thus, India is a country where diverse languages, races, ethnic groups, religions, subcultures, times, climates and attitudes coexist. This enormous plurality thrives upon paradoxes. Any assertion about India has to be qualified with the equally opposite characteristic. For example, India is both deeply religious and secular. Indians enjoy a great deal of freedom, but are at the same time very much bound by the family, the community or social norms (see Wandel, 2004).

The West focuses more upon individualism, specialization in jobs, dividing life up into private and public spheres, workplace and home, work and vacation. Indian cultures do not seem to be so focused, less individualistic and the boundaries between various spheres of life are not so well drawn. God or the divine mystery is not the 'you' outside of 'me'. He is not the object as opposed to the subject. In the Indian understanding the divine mystery is intimately connected with the person or subject who seeks God (see Wandel, 2004).

Hence, the richness of India lies with its deep spirituality as well as its ability to deal with diversity.

Diversity under Challenge

a. Misconception of India as Monolithic Culture

Having said that India has something beautiful to offer to the world, especially of its long experience of living with diversity, we need also to look at today's situation with caution. Although India stands out among the comity of nations in the world as a model of unity in diversity, nevertheless it is a unity which is very much threatened by economic disparities, religious fundamentalism and ethnic conflicts. There are cultural movements which try to depict India as a mono-cultural entity. These ideological groups have been depicting Christians, Muslims, Parsis and some others as foreigners in their own native land. There has been communal violence in the name of culture, religion and ethnicity. Today, the interesting debate in India is of its cultural identity (see Michael, 2003:78-107).

According to Hindu nationalists the Hindu religion and culture form the basis of the political identity of India. They identify India with a monolithic Sanskritic culture. They name their movement as Cultural Nationalism. Anybody who does not subscribe to this vision is considered an enemy of the nation. This idea of Hindutva implies that to be Indian is to be Hindu, to be an Indian, according to them is defined by one's religion. Analysis on the attacks on Christians in India would show that one of the reasons for it is related to the above ideology of Hindutva on Indian nation (Michael, 2000a: 9-22).

Dayananda Saraswati (1824-1883), urged a regeneration of Hindus through adherence to a purified "Vedic faith." He founded Arya Samaj in 1875. Its favourite mottoes being "Back to the Vedas" and "Aryavarta for the Aryans". This view simply equated Indian culture with Brahmanic Hinduism and Sanskritic culture; all non-Hindu aspects were regarded as contaminating influences. The Vedic Aryans are described by Dayandanda as a primordial and elect people to whom the Veda has been revealed and whose language - Sanskrit - is said to be the "Mother of all languages". They would have migrated in the beginning of the world from Tibet - the first land to emerge from the Oceans - towards the

Aryavarta. This territory, homeland of the Vedic civilization, covered the Punjab, Doab and Ganges basin. From this position, the Aryans would have dominated the whole world till the war of the Mahabharata, a watershed opening a phase of decadence. The national renaissance implied precisely, for Dayananda, a coming back to the Vedic Golden Age.

The Arya Samaj is probably the first movement in India defining nationalism in terms of ethnicity. These views of Dayananda Saraswati are said to be the basis from which the later-Hindu movements and organizations such as the Hindu Mahasaba, R.S.S., Siva Sena, V.H.P., Bajrang Dal and BJP are formed. The leaders of the Hindu nationalist movement based on a revival of Hindu culture openly acknowledged their identification of nationalism with Sanskritic or Upper Caste Hinduism (Michael, 2003: 78-107).

b. *Indological and Orientalists Foundational Misunderstanding of India*

There are several approaches to the understanding of Indian society. Whatever approach one chooses will influence his/her missiological methodology to the Christian mission in India. Today, there is a debate on what constitutes 'Indian Culture' and 'Indian Identity'. Anthropological writing on India over more than 50 years has provided some of the key reference points for these debates (Ganesh, 2005).

The 19th and 20th century Indological approach to the understanding of Indian society as developed by the Orientalists and Colonial Administrators perceived the Sanskritic culture as the mainline culture of India. That gave the identity to the Indianness. But today with the increasing anthropological knowledge of India, there are several movements challenging the idea of homogenous Indianness. Despite the power and influence of Indology, with its reliance on classical texts and high culture, the bulk of the work of anthropologists and sociologists after independence has been towards empirical documentation of the enormous diversities in society and culture of India.

There are two major axes along which issues of cultural identity are currently manifesting in India. One is an idealized homogenized notion of Indian culture. The other is contrasting notion of composite culture which conceptualizes Indian culture as plural. These two axes and their ramifications are at the heart of debates on culture and identity in India today (see Robinson 2003).

Traditionally the missiological approach to inculturation and mission in India has been largely from an Indological perspective. With the increasing anthropological knowledge on the pluralistic nature of Indian identity, the tribals and Dalits are asserting their cultural identity in the emerging India of 21st century. This has a lot of missiological implications for the Church in India.

c.   *Current Anthropological Understanding of India*

Earlier ideas of the origin of India in the Aryan-speaking people now stand corrected. These ideas were initially put forward by the leading Indologist Max Muller, who had spoken of (i) the Aryan origin of India, and (ii) the Aryan people as a racial group. It was largely due to the scholarly position of Muller that these ideas got easily accepted and popularized today as a reality, though later scientific findings have denied this as fact (see D'Souza, 2007: 2).

Orientalism, as Inden (1990), Trautmann (1997) and Thapar (1997) point out, includes both the knowledge produced by European scholars and the European representation of the Orient. The work of an entire body of Indological scholars and administrators came together in the construction of the racial understanding of Indian civilization that was established with the Aryan theory. The idea also being put forth and popularly accepted today, is that the cultural and religious identity of India can be traced back solely to an Aryan origin. These scholars included William Jones, H.H. Wilson, Henry Colebrooke, Charles Grant, James Mill, Max Mueller and others. These scholars interweave to form certain kinds of patterns. One of the dominant and best known paradigms that such Orientalist knowledge generated was the Aryan theory. As Thapar (1997:xiii) elucidates, even the discovery of the pre-Vedic Indus Valley Civilization did little to dislodge the Aryan theory. Rather, various elaborate efforts were made to contain the Indus Valley Civilization within the confines of the myth of the Aryan race. The people of the Indus Valley Civilization were sometimes treated as non-Aryans who were conquered (as were the Dravidians) by the Aryans. Otherwise, attempts were made to redefine the Indus Valley Civilization as an Aryan civilization.

It appears to me possible to argue that the search for the mythical Hindu Arya has had widespread ramifications for the understanding of the cultures of India, its identity and religio-political history. One of the ramifications of the orientalist understanding of India is the definition of India as "Hindu" India and the understanding that a central position has to be accorded to caste as the most important social and cultural marker of India. Concomitantly, one might also trace the marginalization of the study of other communities and their cultures (Robinson, 2003).

This Orientalist and Indologist understanding of India is shown to be fallacious today, based on the recent scientific findings of several sciences of paleontology, archeology and linguistics. Today, Archeological evidences, supported by Linguistic Paleontology and other modern sciences, point out the multi-cultural history of India.

Indian Diversity and Its Implications for the Church in India

a.   Importance of Scientific Research in Inculturation and Evangelization of Cultures

For the last several decades the Indian Church is actively involved in the process of Inculturation of its Church. Immediately after Vatican II, there were several vigorous attempts in the form of research, seminars, publications, and practical workshops towards inculturation of the Church in India. But this enthusiasm seems to be weakening day by day and there is not much progress towards inculturation in the Indian Church.

Historically, we know that many missionary movements have originated not from theories but from the missionaries' struggles and their search for authentic Christian life. When we examine the reasons for this lack of interest in inculturation we propose the following could be one of the possible causes. The Indian Church is made up of a large number of tribals, dalits and people from non-Brahmanic castes. But the earlier attempts of inculturation have been mainly from the upper caste (Sanskritic) perspective. This approach to inculturation was a result of the understanding of India mainly from Indological perspective. This is a direct follow up from the colonial understanding of India from Indological and Oriental perspectives. Today, anthropological field researches have shown that the field reality of India is very different from the text oriented Indological and Orientalist approaches (Michael, 2006:40-50).

Moreover, there is a power shift in the self understanding of the cultural reality of India. For the last three thousand years, the Brahmins and other upper castes have been defining the identity of the culture of India. With the coming of democracy and each individual having a vote to elect their representatives, the power is slowly shifting to middle, lower, dalit castes and tribals. All these affect the very self-understanding of the culture and identity of India (see Dahiwale, 2005).

Hence, any attempt towards inculturation in India must take into account the field reality of India and the changing self perceptions of the different segments of the Indian population. This requires a scientific research.

b. *Inculturation – Call for a Prophetic Role*

Through the process of inculturation, the Church inserts itself in the culture of a people. It integrates the Christian life and its message into a given culture. This implies that the Church involves itself in the life-realities of people by participating and struggling in their historical search for meaning and emancipation. This process of inculturation is very important for the local Church to play a creative role in the midst of constant change. The emerging culture in India is greatly influenced by globalization, mass media and internet, and they are providing opportunities as well as challenges to traditional Indian cultures and values. Growing secularization and materialism are silently undermining the values and principles of traditional Indian cultures. By the process of inculturation, local Christians play a vital role in giving direction to culture change through their selective assimilation and cultural continuity. In the process of inculturation the symbol-creativity of a people and their search for meaning are manifested in the changing cultural scenario without alienating themselves from their cultural roots (Michael, 1990: 6-18).

The inherent nature of inculturation has two important dimensions. One is the celebration of cultures of its life giving values and the second is the transformation of (challenge) of values which are life negating (Michael 2000:167-173).

As pointed out above, India is a pluralistic country with many religions, cultures, languages and racial groups. But, today, this notion of Indian reality is under great threat. The Cultural Nationalists forces are increasingly seeking to homogenize the cultures of India towards an upper caste, Sanskritic, Brahmanic culture. Anything outside of this cultural orbit is denied legitimate existence in Indian society. The Hindu fundamentalist organizations claim the tribals and untouchables (Dalits) to be backward Hindus. But the tribals and Dalits reject this super imposed identity. They are struggling for their survival, human dignity and cultural identity. The visionaries from the suppressed masses like Jotirao Phule, E.V.R. Periyar and Dr. Ambedkar battled for a true humanism and for the equal of dignity of all by vigorous critique of Brahmanic culture to the perpetuation of caste-based discrimination (Michael 2007:108-131).

Conversion movements have been one of the means by which they have been moving up in the social ladder of Indian society. A large number of Dalits and tribals have converted themselves to Buddhism, Sikhism, Islam and Christianity (Michael, 2007a). More than seventy percent of Indian Christians today are from these lower layers of Indian society.

The above socio-cultural and political reality has to be also taken seriously in the process of inculturation. While the mystical and interiority traditions of Hinduism are very important in inculturation, at the same time, Christians need to view them critically and assimilate them selectively (Michael, 1990:6-18). This is because the credibility of contemplative values of Buddhism, Jainism and especially Hinduism need to be tested in the light of the Indian social reality of grinding poverty and its vast system of legitimized social oppression. The Hindu religious world view is not able to give the minimum of human dignity to the vast majority of its people. Millions of people do not have even the minimal resources for their survival. At the same time, there are people who enjoy all the privileges and comforts of life. The tribals, untouchables (Dalits) and other Backward Caste communities are struggling to get bare necessities, because for a long time they have been treated with contempt and oppression. Thus, the impression of India as a paradise of religion is deceptive in the context of its grinding poverty and its vast system of legitimized social oppression. Hence, the process of inculturation also implies a prophetic role by challenging (transforming) the oppressive cultural values in Hindu traditions. The relevance of Jesus lies precisely in the context of social concern and the reconstruction of modern India.

The Christian commitment to equality, fraternity and dignity by abolishing of poverty, ignorance, injustice, and other forms of deprivation calls for a deeper and varying methods of inculturation. Recognition and empowerment of tribal and Dalit and other ethnic communities' cultures are also very important in inculturation. Inculturation must pay attention to this pluralistic cultural reality of India. For example, the values of the world views of indigenous peoples (tribals) are particularly significant. Their sense of community, solidarity, rejection of greed, and eco-friendliness, embody a humanism that is holistic and life giving. Christians can treasure such humanism as precious gift from God, and integrate it with the good news of salvation.

c.   *Dynamic Nature of Culture and Inculturation*

The process of inculturation must take the dynamic nature of culture. Culture is never a finished product. All cultures are dynamic, adapting themselves to ever-new situations. Today we are living in a global village where each culture is influencing the other. In this context, India cannot isolate itself. In modern times, the world has been transformed by information technologies into what we just called the global village. In essence, globalization is an ever-growing, fine meshed network of interconnections and inter-dependencies that characterize modern life (Tomlinson, 1999:2).

Thus, in today's world we see two important cultural processes taking place simultaneously. On the one hand, due to the increase of communication systems, cultures are exposed to one another, and there is a kind of universal culture in the making. On the other hand, increasing nationalistic tendencies seize all opportunities to mobilize their people in their unique and specific cultural identities and heritage.

Inculturation has to be in this context of universal and particular cultural realities. Since Christianity is universally present with specific cultural identities, the inculturation process must have certain universal Christian symbols and rituals to express its universal faith, morals and celebrations, as well as particular cultural expressions in terms of theologically acceptable symbols, rituals and celebrations. Hence, inculturation is both universal and particular. That is why the interaction between Gospel and culture is a process of Inter-culturation.

d.   *Inculturation and Inter-culturation*

It is also very important to understand that inculturation is a process of interculturation. It is because the Gospel itself comes to a culture with its own cultural moorings. Hence, inculturation is a process of mutual fecundation between Gospel and cultures, i.e. the dynamic relationship between the Christian faith and cultures that is the meeting of two cultures which is interculturation. This implies inculturation is more than Hinduization; it is the Gospel interacting with Indian cultures. As a result, the Indian cultures get enriched and the Gospel finds better expression of its values within Indian cultures.

The cultures of India are not extrinsic to Indian Christians. Indian Christians are insiders to and inheritors of their cultures. Christians bring the treasures of their cultures to their faith and become believers rooted in their soil. In Indian religions and cultures, there is an emphasis on respect for all life, compassion, and hospitality. The universal solidarity of all peoples as in **Vasudhaiva kutumbakam** ("the whole earth as a family) is a tradition that is being retrieved by people's movements and dialogue initiatives of India (Editorial, Vidhyajyoti, 2008:241-244). Such humanism needs to be reaffirmed in the context of narrow cultural nationalism, regionalism and communalism.

The Gospel culture interaction should shine forth as a light within us. Evangelization of culture is a continuous process. To be evangelized and to evangelize go together. In our zeal to evangelize others, we need to be ready to be evangelized by others. The humanism of the Gospel should be at the heart of evangelization. It celebrates and challenges cultures for conversion (transformation). It helps to detect its presence in cultures and religions, and opens the way to dialogue and collaboration to build a just, humane and peaceful society. Thus, inculturation is also inter-cultural dialogue.

Conclusion

India is an ancient country, whose history goes back at least five thousand years. Historically it has never been a closed territory, but more of an open vista. It has to co-exist with different migrant populations with their cultures. The Indian experience of living with diversity has an important lesson for the world and for the Indian Church.

Inculturation, Evangelization of cultures and inter-cultural dialogue in India must take this cultural diversity very seriously. With the past experience, we now understand that Inculturation is a complex and constant process of implanting the Christian faith in the cultural creativity of Indian people. This could be done through:[1]

1. A deep spirituality of mysticism and interiority. Indian cultures have been marked by a deep sense of the spiritual where God occupies a central place. With globalization, secularizing tendencies are creeping into our cultures, we must make sure that globalization does not deny God nor exclude Him, the Creator who is the source and fount of everything. Indian Christians must incorporate, value and live the Indian values such as love of silence and contemplation, simplicity, harmony, detachment, non-violence, discipline, respect for elders, hospitality, compassion, a sense of community. Appropriate institutions like Christian Ashrams, community centres should be created to imbibe the above Indian cultural values. The three *margas*, i.e. ***Jnana Magra***, ***Karma Marga*** and ***Bhakti Marga*** should form the part of Christian spirituality. Attempts should be made to explain the Christian mystery in the Indian Philosophical traditions in the manner St. Thomas Aquinas did with Greek philosophical wisdom.

2. Social involvement in the reconstruction of modern India in the values of equality, fraternity and social justice. As citizens Christians should actively participate in politics and peoples' movements which are promoting human dignity and promotion of life.

3. Since language is the embodiment of culture, creating good and valuable Christian literature in regional and national languages and dialects of India is a must. Indian Christians must be rooted in their mother tongue, and they should be creative and competent in their languages.

4. The Indian Church must recognize, appreciate, value and empower the cultures of India and encourage cultural creativity of tribals, Dalits and other ethnic communities. In

---

[1] Here are a few practical suggestions that could indicate the process of inculturation which is not an exhaustive or comprehensive list.

short, it means that the recognition of the diverse cultures of India should be the basis of inculturation in India. In negative terms, it means that inculturation should not be limited to Hinduization or Sanskritization of Christian life.

5. There should be mutual interaction and respect between the Local Church and the Universal Church in terms of expressing Christian meaning and life in symbols and rituals in liturgy and life. For example, in the context of India, the Hindu *Om* cannot replace the Christian *Cross*, because the theological foundations and the world view of these are very different in terms of their meaning, content and moral implications. Even when inculturation took place in the context of Hellenistic culture the Greek letters *Alpha* and *Omega* were used not exclusively but with the *Cross*, as for example in Easter Vigil Service. As the Greek letters *Alpha* and *Omega* do not fully express the mystery of the *Cross*, similarly the Sanskritic *Om* is inadequate to signify the meaning of the *Cross*. There are variegated and contradictory meanings of the term *"Om"* in Hindu traditions. If theologically acceptable and agreeable consensus of the term *"Om"* is arrived at among theologians and the Indian Christian community, then *"Om"* could be used together with *"Cross"* in an esthetically appropriate manner. But this requires much research, deep reflection and pastoral prudence.

Similarly, the use of *saffron shawl* in Latin liturgy requires re-examination. The Universal Church has developed a well thought out colour symbols to mark the different liturgical seasons of the year. Violet or purple to mark Advent and Lent as preparations; white for Christmas and Easter seasons; green for Ordinary times; red for the martyrs; white for virgins; and gold for solemnity, etc. This is a very meaningful symbol in the Universal Church. Using saffron shawl on Christmas Day, Good Friday, Easter and Pentecost does not bring out the emotional and esthetic aspects of the Christian celebration. Moreover, today, the saffron colour is getting highly politicized to mark the political power of the Cultural Nationalists of the Hindutva ideological organizations.

If the use of a shawl is very meaningful in liturgy, and a mark of inculturation in India, then why not use a shawl of different colours, like white, green, red, purple, golden etc. according to different liturgical seasons and occasions? This will bring unity (universality) and uniqueness (particularity) between the Universal Church and the Local Church. We need to be more creative in our inculturation rather than merely sanskritizing Christian liturgy.

6. Indian Christians must become more creative in incorporating the appropriate symbols, arts, rituals, music, dance and other aspects of culture which are truly Indian as well as truly Christian.

7. The Christian community in India should actively celebrate regional and national feast and festivals which are compatible with the Christian vision of life and promote peace and harmony among cultures and ethnic communities.

8. The most important events in a culture are the rites of passage. Christian meaning of life can be well articulated without alienation from the Indian context if Christians in a culture adopt their rites of passage with Christian interpretation and meaning (for more details see Michael 1990a:76-90).

9. Christians in India must live and actively promote our cultural values of family, community, and respect for elders, modesty, hospitality and other life giving values.

10. We humans are both rational and emotional. The cultures we create have these contents. Hence, Christian faith should be expressed both rationally and emotionally. The intellectual articulation of Christian faith in theology must be expressed emotionally in the Indian cultures through well thought out and theologically sound popular devotions, pilgrimages, observance of fast, processions, parish feasts, bhajan singing (chanting), story telling, passion plays etc. (These ten points have been already suggested by me some time ago, see

Michael, 2000:166-172).

To conclude we reiterate that India is known for its diversity of cultures and they co-exist with mutual respect and recognition in spite of recent efforts for homogenization. As Christians we need to learn our lessons from this experience of cultural diversity. Though the roots of Christianity in India are very ancient and deep, yet its cultural integration still remains at large. In this context, inculturation and evangelization of cultures are urgent.

The Christian Cultural Centres in India need to engage themselves actively in doing research for a deeper understanding of the cultural forces at work, and offer their services for an effective, relevant and meaningful inculturation in India.

References and Bibliography

Dahiwale, S.M. (ed.) 2005, *Understanding Indian Society. The Non-Brahmanic Perspective*. New Delhi: Rawat Publications.

D'Souza, Leela 2007, Cultural *History of Ancient India. Diversity, Syncretism, Synthesis*. Delhi: Rawat Publications.

Ganesh, Kamala 2005, *Culture and the Making of Identity in Contemporary India*. New Delhi: Sage Publications.

Inden, R. 1990, *Imagining India*. Oxford: Basil Blackwell.

Jha, D.N. 1997, *Ancient India. An Introductory Outline*. New Delhi: Manohar.

Kothari, Rajini 1988, "Integration and Exclusion in Indian Politics", *Economic and Political Weekly*, October 22, 1988.

Michael, S.M. 1989, *Culture and Urbanization*. Delhi: Inter India Publication.

__________, 1990, "Beyond Inculturation", **Vidya Jyoti: Journal of Theological Reflection**. No.54, 1990, pp.6-18.

__________, 1990a, "Cultural Performance as Christian Celebration", *Indian Missiological Review*, April 1990, Vol.12, No.1, pp.76-90.

__________, 2000, "Inculturation in the Context of India", *In His Foot Steps. Together Towards the New Millennium. Divine Word Missionaries 1875-2000*. ed. Clarence Srampical and others. Indore: Divine Word Missionaries.

__________, 2000a "Real Issues Behind the Violence", *Mission Today*, Vol.II, No.1. pp. 9-22.

__________, 2003, "Culture, Nationalism and Globalization: Politics of Identity in India", *Globalization and Social Movements. Struggle for a Humane Society*. Eds. P.G. Jogdand and S.M. Michael, Delhi: Rawat Publications, pp.78-107.

__________, 2006, 'From Indology to Anthropology: A Paradigm for Christian Mission", *In the Service of Mission. Studies in Honour of Archbishop Thomas Menamparampil*. Eds. Thomas Manjaly, Kuriakose P., and Peter Haokip. Shillong: Oriens Publications., pp. 40-50.

__________, 2007, "Dalit Vision of a Just Society in India", *Dalits in Modern India: Vision and Values*. (ed.) S.M. Michael (2nd Edition), New Delhi: Sage Publications.

__________, 2007a, *Conversion, Social Mobility and Empowerment – View from Below*. Mumbai University: Department of Sociology. Occasional Paper Series: No.4.

Robinson, Rowena 2003, *Christians of India*. Delhi: Sage Publications.

Thapar, R. 1997, Forward, in T. Trautmann, *Aryans and British India*. New Delhi: Vistaar Publications.

Tomlinson, John 1999, *Globalization and Culture*. Cambridge: Polity Press.

Trautmann, T. 1997, *Aryans and British India*. New Delhi: Vistaar Publications.

Wandel, Reinhold 2004, *India: Unity in Diversity*. Berlin: CornelsenVerlag.

Vidyayajoti (Editorial) 2008, "Editorial – Integral Humanism Our Precious Resource", *Vidyajyoti Journal of Theological Reflection*. Volume 72, N0.4, April 2008. pp.241-244.